A TECHNOLOGY OF READING AND WRITING

Volume 2

Criterion-Referenced Tests for
Reading and Writing

A TECHNOLOGY OF
READING AND WRITING
VOLUME 2
Criterion-Referenced Tests
for Reading and Writing

Criterion-Referenced Tests for Reading a
Writing is both a complete testing system fo.
grades K-6 and a source book for test-makers.
Its criterion tests are based upon the stimuli of
language instruction (letters, words, etc.) rather
than upon grade level curricula or inferred
mental processes. The book presents some 350
subtests of skills in the domains of letters,
words, sentences, paragraphs, and discourse,
based on a taxonomy of language described in
Volume 1, organized hierarchically, and gra-
dated using try-out data. Every subskill area
contains a sufficient number of items to allow
the generation of new items and the development or selection of prescriptive teaching materials. The book gives methods for room, school,
and systemwide application of these tests, as
well as a method for evaluating instructional
material and examples of its use. It also includes a discussion of theoretical issues, a rationale for each subtest series, and an administration manual.

Researchers in language learning and in special
education will find this volume of the series
particularly interesting.

EDUCATIONAL PSYCHOLOGY

Allen J. Edwards, Series Editor
Department of Psychology
Southwest Missouri State University
Springfield, Missouri

Phillip S. Strain, Thomas P. Cooke, and Tony Apolloni. Teaching Exceptional Children: Assessing and Modifying Social Behavior

Donald E. P. Smith and others. A Technology of Reading and Writing (in four volumes).

Vol. 1. *Learning to Read and Write: A Task Analysis (by Donald E. P. Smith)*

Vol. 2. *Criterion-Referenced Tests for Reading and Writing (by Judith M. Smith, Donald E. P. Smith, and James R. Brink)*

Joel R. Levin and Vernon L. Allen (eds.). Cognitive Learning in Children: Theories and Strategies

Vernon L. Allen (ed.). Children as Teachers: Theory and Research on Tutoring

Gilbert R. Austin. Early Childhood Education: An International Perspective

António Simões (ed.). The Bilingual Child: Research and Analysis of Existing Educational Themes

Erness Bright Brody and Nathan Brody. Intelligence: Nature, Determinants, and Consequences

In preparation:

Donald E. P. Smith and others. A Technology of Reading and Writing (in four volumes).

Vol. 3. *The Adaptive Classroom (by Donald E. P. Smith)*
Vol. 4. *Preparing Instructional Tasks (by Judith M. Smith)*

Herbert J. Klausmeier, Richard A. Rossmiller, and Mary Saily (eds.). Individually Guided Elementary Education: Concepts and Practices

Samuel Ball (ed.). Motivation in Education

J. Nina Lieberman. Playfulness: Its Relationship to Imagination and Creativity

Harry Hom, Jr. (ed.). Psychological Processes in Early Education

Harvey Lesser. Television and the Preschool Child: A Psychological Theory of Instruction and Curriculum Development

Donald J. Treffinger, J. Kent Davis, and Richard E. Ripple (eds.). Handbook on Teaching Educational Psychology

A TECHNOLOGY OF READING AND WRITING

Volume 2

Criterion-Referenced Tests for Reading and Writing

Judith M. Smith

School of Education
The University of Michigan
Ann Arbor, Michigan

Donald E. P. Smith

School of Education
The University of Michigan
Ann Arbor, Michigan

James R. Brink

Ann Arbor Public Schools
Ann Arbor, Michigan

ACADEMIC PRESS   New York San Francisco London 1977

A Subsidiary of Harcourt Brace Jovanovich, Publishers

ACADEMIC PRESS, INC.
111 Fifth Avenue, New York, New York 10003

United Kingdom Edition published by
ACADEMIC PRESS, INC. (LONDON) LTD.
24/28 Oval Road. London NW1

Library of Congress Cataloging in Publication Data

Smith, Judith M
    Criterion-referenced tests for reading and writing.

    (A Technology of reading and writing ; v. 2)
(Educational psychology)
    Includes index.
    1.   Reading–Ability testing.   2.   English language–
Composition and exercises.   I.   Smith, Donald E.P.,
joint author.   II.   Brink, James Ralph,   (date)   joint
author.   III.   Title.   IV.   Series: Smith, Donald E. P.
A technology of reading and writing ; v. 2.
LB1050.S572   vol. 2   [LB1050.46]   372.6'044s
ISBN 0–12–651702–9   [372.6'044]   76-56744

PRINTED IN THE UNITED STATES OF AMERICA

CONTENTS

PREFACE

One of the defining characteristics of a science is the quantification or measurement of its subject matter. Certainly no technology is possible without some measurement system. Attempts to develop a scientific base for the teaching of reading and writing have been fettered by lack of a widely accepted measure of literacy.

In 1970, the Secretary's (U.S. Department of Health, Education and Welfare) National Advisory Committee on Dyslexia and Related Reading Disorders, a group of distinguished language specialists and laymen, made the measurement of literate behavior the first order of business for the correction of reading deficits. Its recommendations apparently went unheeded, however, as the attention of funding agencies turned to theoretical models of the reading acquisition process (Davis, 1971).

In 1972, we committed ourselves to the task of constructing a measurement system of criterion-referenced tests basic enough and broad enough to guide the development of instructional materials for the elementary grades.

Initial funding and tryout populations were provided by the Chelsea, Michigan public schools. Ed-Ventures, Inc., a development group, provided resources to ooo the effort to its completion in 1975 with financial support provided by sale of early editions (Tri-Level Educational Materials of Ferndale, Michigan).

This book is the end result of that effort. It presents *STARS* (Standard Achievement Recording System), a set of criterion tests for reading and writing, with its rationale and administration procedures.

* * * * *

This volume is almost completely the formulation of Judith M. Smith. She has constructed virtually all of the tests, using as necessary the linguistic contributions of Kenneth Pike; the taxonomy of language appearing in Volume 1; suggestions given by teachers; the word-frequency data of E. B. Coleman and of J. Carroll, P. Davies, and B. Richman; and feedback data from school tryouts. She has also described the rationale for each test series.

James M. Brink has provided statements on the theory of criterion testing, most of the psychometric data, and a section on test administration.

ON CRITERION-REFERENCED TESTS

I. How Much Does Johnny Know?

Teachers and administrators are often asked the question, "How much does Johnny know?" How they answer depends on the measure they use. If they use a standardized test, they can look at his "obtained" or "raw" score, refer to a table of norms, and say, "Johnny stands at the 40th percentile for second graders" or "Johnny scores at Grade 2.3—3 months into the second grade."

"I see. But **how much** does Johnny know?" Well, he knows as much as the second grader who ranks 40th from the bottom among 100 second graders. Or, he knows as much as the average child in the third month of Grade 2. These statements are not meant to be evasive. They are simply the best answer possible based on standardized tests.

Standardized tests, or norm-referenced tests (NRT), refer to or get their meaning from a ranking or norm. They do not tell us what or how much Johnny knows. They tell us where he ranks. Standardized tests tell us how Johnny is doing with reference to **other children.** But we want to know more. Never mind the other children; how is he doing with reference to the **number of skills** he must learn? Does he know 50% of them, or 90%, or 100%? What does he know—and what must he still learn? There were no measures we could use to answer these questions until criterion-referenced tests were developed.

1

Criterion-referenced tests (CRT) are designed to measure a specified set of skills called **criterion behaviors.** These tests refer to or get their meaning from a pool of criterion behaviors; hence the name, criterion-referenced.

The CRT score can be expressed as a ratio, the total number of skills learned divided by the total number of skills required:

$$\frac{\text{Number of skills learned}}{\text{Number of skills required}} = \text{Score in } \%$$

For example, if Johnny has mastered 190 words out of a total of 200 words on a spelling test, his score would be 190/200, or 95%.

II. Methods of Test Construction

As the purposes of NRTs and CRTs differ, so do the methods used in their construction. (See Table 1.1.)

Both NRTs and CRTs include subtests. CRT subtests tend to be more comprehensive in their coverage. However, the only dependable way to identify a CRT is by the kind of score it yields. NRTs yield a ranking (e.g., percentile) score or a grade level score; they do not yield a ratio score. CRTs yield all three scores.

(1) a ratio score (90% of the spelling words learned);
(2) a ranking (80% percentile); or
(3) a grade level score (Grade 4.2).

Method of test construction also influences the validity of the test.

Table 1.1
Methods of Test Construction

Norm-referenced tests	Criterion-referenced tests
1. Identify groups of individuals, one group superior in the skills, one group inferior.	1. Identify all the skills that must be learned.
2. Generate items that appear to sample the skill.	2. Generate items that measure all the critical subskills (or most of them).
3. Try out items on both groups. Discard items on which both groups do well or poorly. Keep items on which the superior group surpasses the inferior group. (Items need not represent the curriculum. They merely separate the two groups reliably.)	3. Arrange items by difficulty or by order of acquisition. (Items must represent the curriculum.)

III. The Validation Problem

When we question the validity of a test, we are asking whether the test measures what it purports to measure. What the answer is depends, at least in part, on the role of the person asked.

I[1] am a test user—not a statistician or a psychometrist, but an evaluator in a Title I project. Faced with a set of very practical problems in the management of instructional services, I recognized in early drafts of *STARS* certain characteristics that might contribute to the solution of those problems. The problems relate to the precision and flexibility with which instructional services are delivered to students. Even more, they relate to the struggle of every teacher and administrator who attempts to achieve a balance between the forces of analysis and synthesis—the tendency to divide things up and to put them together; to separate and to integrate; to build and to break down. *STARS,* like any assessment tool, is in its nature analytical, separating the process of learning to read and write into its components. If it is a good system, it does so with a respect for the nature of the process observed and with as perfect a balance of parsimony and exhaustiveness as can be mustered.

But, as with any tool or advance of technology, there are dangers and temptations to be faced. A friend of mine recently removed her daughter from a first grade class because the teacher, having recently discovered behavioral objectives, and having been encouraged to set objectives unilaterally and uniformly for all students, was applying the technology with such ferocity that the children were becoming ill. Educational technologists have a stereotype of the warm, motherly teacher who speaks of the "whole child," uses the "language experience" approach, and considers all testing an instrument of the devil. I would much rather attempt to persuade such a teacher of the joys of gentle analysis and humane accountability than unload the system on an eager teacher or principal ("I want objectives for all your kids for the year in my office by half-past four on Friday") and worry that it might be used as a weapon.

So that we may introduce this possibly wondrous and potentially dangerous tool with proper care both for it and for its potential users and beneficiaries, we must include a few remarks about its properties as a measurement device, and we must give some advice on how to use it. We shall begin with a brief discussion of *STARS* as an instrument of measurement technology or psychometry. Following that, we shall present some preliminary field test data as the first steps in a necessarily extended effort to provide evidence for the quality of the system. Finally, guidelines for teachers, principals, and project managers will be offered in order to suggest appropriate uses for the system and to anticipate any problems of implementation that may arise.

[1] James Brink.

IV. Measurement Properties of *STARS*

Although the term *criterion-referenced* has been with us for over a decade now (Glaser, 1963), the concept of measurement based on units of learning rather than on comparisons among learners has been around somewhat longer. In 1931, Dr. Henry Morrison (1931) discussed valid methods of "appraising the pupil's educational development [p. 72]." He said that "the problem before us is to **identify the presence [or absence] of learning as a quality**, and not to **measure performance as a magnitude** [p. 72]." Anticipating the CRT movement, Dr. Morrison concluded, "Any appropriate method of appraising pupil progress must then rest on a **count of the true learning products** which the pupil has attained and in which his mastery has been verified by the best evidential means at our command [p. 73]."

One could easily maintain that this is what good teachers have always done. However, only recently have attempts been made to publish substantial assessment packages that meet the "criterion-based" specification. These attempts have all been plagued by the lack of consensus about standards of quality for such instruments. An astonishing number of schools and school systems have required their teachers to generate "criterion-referenced" tests, usually in elementary reading and math, arguing (with some logic) that if items no longer have to be selected "scientifically" (statistically) then their committee of test-generating teachers is probably as good as anyone else's.

Thus, publishers have been unable to use task analytic or statistical evidence to justify their tests. In order to take advantage of the CRT boom, they have been reduced to selling their systems on the basis of management conveniences such as self-administered tests, elaborate cross-referring from test items to prescriptive materials, machine scoring and reporting systems, and services such as "Give us your objectives and we'll make the test."

The serious attempts to solve the problem of standards have ranged from a variety of suggested alternatives for defining and measuring reliability (Brennan, 1974) to a variety of alternative strategies for systematically or objectively generating test items (Guttman, 1969; Hively, in press; Millman, 1974; Popham & Husek, 1969). One might expect these writers to focus on test construction. But it is now evident that the selection of items and item formats, the grouping of items, decisions concerning test length, and the like, all issues of test construction, are also related to the kind of instructional decisions resulting from the use of the instrument.

In classical test theory, the point is sometimes made that estimates of reliability and validity pertain not so much to properties of tests as to properties of **responses** to the tests by people taking them. This is why it matters very much to whom the test is administered and under what conditions. Similarly, the validation of any instrument ought to include the correctness, in terms of consequences, of any decision whatsoever that is made as a function of a person's performance.

We are, it appears, getting beyond the notion that a criterion-referenced item or test can be evaluated merely in terms of its correspondence to an instructional objective or a collection of objectives. Indeed, it may be that the popular production of instructional objectives may itself be an exercise in unnecessary abstraction. In the case of *STARS,* the tests stand or fall as independent objectifications of the critical components of the process of learning to read and write. They may be judged with reference to the usefulness of the pass/no pass information in deciding whether or not some unit of instruction is appropriate, and for their contribution to **defining** the unit of instruction. In turn, the usefulness of such a decision about appropriateness rests upon (*1*) the availability of instructional resources designed to take care of the competency deficit or pattern of deficits revealed by the test; (*2*) upon the tendency of the student to interact with the resource; and (*3*) upon the actual validity (consequence) of the instructional resource with reference to the student's subsequent performance.

In a sense, then, the instrument is not separate from the student, the teacher, the instructional materials, and, perhaps, the custodian. It is part of a system, or it is nothing. We could declare it valid, but its validity could only be asserted **in context,** in an environment, in an educational ecosystem in which it plays some part. This is simply to put the issue of validation into some perspective, not to diminish its importance. Paradoxically, since we are proposing that the tests actually be used, it is obvious that their quality, one at a time and as a collection, must continuously be assessed as conditions change.

V. Validity of *STARS*

We propose that the validity of *STARS* be considered in the following three major categories, all relating to different structural properties of the individual tests, and of the system:

(*1*) task analytic properties;
(*2*) psychometric properties; and
(*3*) systemic or functional properties.

Each set of properties will be evaluated at length.

A. Task Analytic Validity

Task analysis refers to specification of the components or parts of a task. In this instance, the task is one faced by every student in elementary school: learning to read and write. The validity of *STARS* in terms of its task analytic properties, has at least the following dimensions:

(*1*) The correspondence between the ways humans characteristically function and first, the general linguistic theory used in the analysis and second, the psychological model of the learning process used in the analysis.

(*2*) The exhaustiveness of the analysis (every critical component covered— nothing left to chance).

(*3*) The aptness (literally, artfulness) with which critical component learnings are isolated and transformed into test formats, items, and groups of items.

(*4*) The specificity of tests and items, that is, control of the **amount of information** contained in each unit of the system.

With all these dimensions to consider, the best way to get at the question of task analytic validity is simply to describe the analysis as clearly and completely as possible. Before beginning the description, we simply note that the selection of items and tests in *STARS* is rather close, in spirit and in effect, to Millman's description of domain-referenced tests (Hively, in press; Millman, 1974). Items on a domain-referenced test are selected either randomly or in a stratified random fashion from some well-defined domain, to the end that an unbiased estimate may be made from the test to the universe of hypothetical items of which the test is a sample. Since a number of the *STARS* tests actually include the universe or population of items, they exceed the domain-referenced-test specification. Other tests in *STARS* stratify the domain by using standard word-count specifications. In these instances the items are samples from a larger population of hypothetical items, although the strict randomness of such samples is not asserted here. In actuality, what *STARS* offers the user is by no means a certification of each item, but rather the **analysis itself,** with tests representing units of the analysis, and items representing further specifications and a sampling illustration of the given unit. The user may, of course, use the illustration given or draw a different sample from the specified domain.

The following section provides a description of the tests and a task analytic rationale for the total system and for its units, individually. (For an outline of all the tests, see the Language Arts Competency Profile, pages 7–11.)

LANGUAGE ARTS COMPETENCY PROFILE: STARS (Standard Achievement Recording System)

NAME _____ SCHOOL _____ Begin ___/___ Complete ___/___
mo. yr. mo. yr.

MASTERY LEVELS COMPLETED	Kindergarten	1st	cum.	2nd	cum.	3rd	cum.	4th	cum.	5th	cum.	6th	cum.
CERTIFIED BY (Teacher)													
Grade-level code													

Directions: Fill in box with appropriate color when ML is passed. Slash in box indicates ML attempted.

PERCEPTUAL ASPECTS

L. 1. *Letter skills:* SHAPES: Given a letter (the model) and an adjoining array of letters, one or two of which are identical to the model, student circles the target letters.

1 ☐ 2 ☐ 3 ☐ 4 ☐ 5 ☐ 6 ☐ 7 ☐ 8 ☐

L. 2. *Letter skills:* MANUSCRIPT FORM: Given model, copy to specified criteria.

1 ☐ 2 ☐ 3 ☐ 4 ☐ 5 ☐ 6 ☐ 7 ☐ 8 ☐ 9 ☐ 10 ☐ 11 ☐ 12 ☐ 13 ☐ 14 ☐

L. 3. *Letter skills:* CURSIVE FORM: Given model, copy to specified criteria.

1 ☐ 2 ☐ 3 ☐ 4 ☐ 5 ☐ 6 ☐ 7 ☐ 8 ☐ 9 ☐ 10 ☐ 11 ☐

EQUIVALENTS

L. 4. *Letter skills:* NAMES: 1-6: Discrimination: Given an array of letters. Circle the one named. | 7-8: Recognition: Name randomly ordered letters.

1 ☐ Cap   2 ☐ L.C.   3 ☐ Cap   4 ☐ L.C.   5 ☐ Cap   6 ☐ L.C. | 7 ☐ Cap   8 ☐ L.C.

L. 5. *Letter skills:* LETTER-SOUND EQUIVALENTS: Given a spoken word and two or three graphemic alternatives consisting of letters or word elements, student circles the (one) corresponding alternative.

1 ☐ 2 ☐ 3 ☐ 4 ☐ 5 ☐ 6 ☐ 7 ☐ 8 ☐ 9 ☐ 10 ☐ 11 ☐ 12 ☐

Initial consonants | Final consonants | Short vowels | Long vowels (silent e) | Vowel combinations | Initial s. blends | Initial Cons.-vowel combinations | Final | Consonant Vowel, Allographs

FUNCTIONS

L. 6. *Letter skills:* FUNCTIONS 1 ☐   2 ☐   3 ☐   4 ☐   5 ☐   6 ☐

Write name | Alphabet: Recite | Order | Write | Alphabetical order

PERCEPTUAL ASPECTS

W. 1. *Word skills:* SHAPES: Given a word or phrase (the model) and several alternatives, one of which is identical to the model (the target), student circles the target word.

1 ☐ 2 ☐ 3 ☐ 4 ☐ 5 ☐

Endings | Similar words | Letter order | Spaces | Interiors

W. 2. *Word skills:* PHONOLOGY

1 ☐ 2 ☐ 3 ☐ 4 ☐ 5 ☐ 6 ☐ 7 ☐

Sentence | Letters | Generate Rhyming / Alliteration words | Matching
Memory

8 ☐ 9 ☐ 10 ☐ 11 ☐ 12 ☐ 13 ☐ 14 ☐ 15 ☐ 16 ☐ 17 ☐ 18 ☐

Hearing words in sentences | Hearing sounds in words | Word junctures | Rhyming discrimination | Initial sound discrimination | Count syllables in words

Designed by James Brink

EQUIVALENTS

W. 3. *Word skills:* WORD RECOGNITION: Given a printed sentence, and one or two spoken words,
                                         student circles named word(s). (Exceptions: ML's 4 and 8.)

MASTERY LEVELS   1   2   3   4   5   6   7   8   9   10   11
                    ☐   ☐   ☐   ☐   ☐   ☐   ☐   ☐   ☐   ☐   ☐
                                   Read   Read
                                   sentence   phrase

W. 4. *Word skills:* SPELLING: Given a word list of specified difficulty, approximately
                                  one third of which are misspelled, student marks the misspelled words.

MASTERY LEVELS   1   2   3   4   5
                    ☐   ☐   ☐   ☐   ☐
                    freq. 1-100   freq. 1-300   freq. 1-300   freq. 301-600 freq. 601-1000
                                   Short words   Long words

GRAMMATICAL MEANING

W. 5. *Word skills:* VOCABULARY: SYNTACTIC FACTOR

	Given sentence, select illustration.				Select words w/ similar meaning			Answer questions				Fill in blank
1	2	3	4	5	6	7	8	9	10	11	12	13
☐	☐	☐	☐	☐	☐	☐	☐	☐	☐	☐	☐	☐
Sing/ Plur	Action Actor Object	Action	Actor	Object	Tense	Actor	Object	Scope	Action	N/V, V/mod NV, N/mod		Infl. cues

W. 6. *Word skills:* VOCABULARY RANGE: (Three range paradigms, 18 mastery levels.)

(A). Given an incomplete sentence and several
      alternatives, student circles all alter-
      natives which fulfill sentence conditions
      ("make sense in the sentence").

            1   2   3   4
            ☐   ☐   ☐   ☐

(B). Given a noun, determine appropriate:

            5   6   7
            ☐   ☐   ☐
         Class name   Action   Modifier

(C). Given incomplete sentences, choose appropriate completion word.

     8   9   10   11   12   13   14   15   16   17   18   19   20
     ☐   ☐   ☐   ☐   ☐   ☐   ☐   ☐   ☐   ☐   ☐   ☐   ☐

REFERENTIAL MEANING

W. 7. *Word skills:* VOCABULARY: SEMANTIC FACTOR
       Given sets of 3 sentences with the same word underlined, student marks the two
       sentences in which the underlined word has the same meaning.

1	2	3	4	5	6	7	8	9
☐	☐	☐	☐	☐	☐	☐	☐	☐
Noun: within class	Noun: between classes		Main verb/ auxiliary verb	Verb within class	Verb: between classes	Modifier: within class	Modifier: between classes	Usage

W. 8. *Word skills:* VOCABULARY: CLASSIFICATION FACTOR: Given a word or a sentence, select another word
                                                          having a specified relationship to the model.

1	2	3	4	5	6	7	8	9	10	11	12
☐	☐	☐	☐	☐	☐	☐	☐	☐	☐	☐	☐
Syn	Syn	Ant	Hom	Syn	Ant	Class	Class	Syn	Syn	Emphasis	Analogies

W. 9. *Word skills:* VOCABULARY FLUENCY

1	2	3	4	5	6	7
☐	☐	☐	☐	☐	☐	☐
Complete partial sentence	Names of things	Can do...	Fill blank	Words that start with... (letter)	Words that end with... (sound)	Words that start w/ (blend).

PERCEPTUAL ASPECTS

S 1. *Sentence skills:* ORAL READING: Read sentences with appropriate intonation.

1	2	3
☐	☐	☐
4-7 Words	8-14 Words/Quotes	15-24 Words/Dramatic

S 2. *Sentence skills:* SPACES BETWEEN WORDS: Recognize and produce spaces between words.

1
☐

S 3. *Sentence skills:* SENTENCE MEMORY: Reproduce sentences of increasing complexity.

1	2
☐	☐
3-5 Words	5-8 Words

S 4. *Sentence skills:* DICTATION: Write dictated sentences.

1	2	3	4	5	6
☐	☐	☐	☐	☐	☐
	Frequencies 1-300			301-600	601-1000

GRAMMATICAL ASPECTS

S 5. *Sentence skills:* CAPITALIZATION: Use capitals correctly.

1	2	3	4	5	6	7	8	9	10
☐	☐	☐	☐	☐	☐	☐	☐	☐	☐
Initial Words Names	Place Names	Titles Initials	Time	Address Organization	Religious	Vehicles Plants Animals	Trade names	Quotes	Titles

S 6. *Sentence skills:* PUNCTUATION: Use punctuation marks correctly.

1	2	3	4	5	6	7
☐	☐	☐	☐	☐	☐	☐
Marks						Direct quotes

8	9	10	11	12	13	14
☐	☐	☐	☐	☐	☐	☐
Compound sentence	Series	Interjections	Appositive	Antithetical	Dates Places	Parenthetical elements

15	16	17	18	19	20	21
☐	☐	☐	☐	☐	☐	
Mistaken junctions	Intro- clauses	Nonrestrictive	Sentence break	Series		Combination

S 7. *Sentence skills:* TRANSFORMATIONS: Rewrite sentences to fulfill grammatical constraints.

1	2	3	4	5	6	7	8
☐	☐	☐	☐	☐	☐	☐	☐
Singular	Plural	Negation	Pronoun	Pronoun	Tense: Present	Tense: Past	Tense: Future

9	10	11	12	13	14	15	16	17
☐	☐	☐	☐	☐	☐	☐	☐	☐
Aux. *have*	Aux. *be*	Aux. *be* + *have*	Passive	Links	Links	Links	Links	Word order

REFERENTIAL ASPECTS

S 8. *Sentence skills:* DIRECTIONS: Follow workbook and test directions.

1	2
☐	☐
Circle Underline Cross out	Draw Make Put

S 9. *Sentence skills:* QUESTIONS: Produce questions controlled by answers.

1	2	3	4	5	6
☐	☐	☐	☐	☐	☐
Who	What	Where	When	Why	How

S 10. *Sentence skills:* SENTENCE MEANING: Choose meanings which conform to particular constraints.

1	2	3
☐	☐	☐
Picture constraint	Internal constraint (sense)	External constraint (paragraph)

S 11. *Sentence skills:* FIGURATIVE LANGUAGE: Recognize idioms and similes.

1	2	3	4
☐	☐	☐	☐
Recognize idioms	Recognize idioms	Recognize idioms	Interpret similes

9

FORM

P 1. *Paragraph skills:* FORM CONVENTION: Recognize and produce indented form.

1	2
☐	☐

P 2. *Paragraph skills:* GRAMMATICAL PATTERNS: Recognize and produce consistent tense, number and structure.

1	2	3	4
☐	☐	☐	☐
Parallel structure		Tense	Number

P 3. *Paragraph skills:* PHONOLOGICAL PATTERNS: Recognize and produce rhyme, alliteration, rhythm (poetry).

1	2	3	4	5
☐	☐	☐	☐	☐
Rhyme	Alliteration	Rhythm	Combined	Produce

CONTENT

P 4. *Paragraph skills:* UNIVERSE OF DISCOURSE: Recognize universe of discourse by vocabulary and style.

1	2
☐	☐
Topic	Genre

P 5. *Paragraph skills:* TOPIC: Identify topic by listening and reading; produce a paragraph orally.

1	2	3	4	5
☐	☐	☐	☐	☐
Oral: Recognize topic	Oral composition	Read: Recognize topic	Part - Whole	Read: Name topic

P 6. *Paragraph skills:* PLOT: Recognize and produce 8 paragraph plots.

1	2	3	4	5	6	7	8
☐	☐	☐	☐	☐	☐	☐	☐
Similar-Different		Example-Reason		Space-Time		Restate-Cause	
Recognize-Produce		Recognize-Produce		Recognize-Produce		Recognize-Produce	

P 7. *Paragraph skills:* REFERENTIAL LINKS: Recognize and produce referential links.

1	2
☐	☐
Referential	
Recognize/Produce	

P 8. *Paragraph skills:* RELATIONAL LINKS: Recognize relational links and rewrite sentences adding links.

1	2	3	4	5	6
☐	☐	☐	☐	☐	☐
Recognize links	Recognize links	Recognize links	Produce links	Recognize links	Produce links

P 9. *Paragraph skills:* INFORMATION: Identify answers to information questions and produce questions.

1	2	3	4	5	6	7	8	9
☐	☐	☐	☐	☐	☐	☐	☐	☐
	Who, What, Where, When, Why			Questions		Questions		Questions
	Recognize			Produce		Recognize-Produce		Recognize-Produce
				I		II		III

EQUIVALENTS

P 10. *Paragraph skills:* SUMMARIZATION: Recognize and produce summary statements outside and within paragraphs.

1	2	3	4	5
☐	☐	☐	☐	☐
Recognize summary-statement		Recognize main idea in paragraph		Produce summary

P 11. *Paragraph skills:* INDUCTION (inference): Recognize and produce valid inductions.

1	2	3	4	5	6
☐	☐	☐	☐	☐	☐
Recognize inference		Recognize and produce an inference		Infer reasons	Produce inference

P 12. *Paragraph skills:* DEDUCTION: Use syllogistic reasoning to draw conclusions.

1	2	3
☐	☐	☐
Solve syllogism	Recognize logical conclusion	Produce logical conclusion

10

P 13. *Paragraph skills:* FOCUS: Identify focus (setting, topic, action, time, motive).

1	2	3	4	5
☐	☐	☐	☐	☐
Select focus	Recognize time & motive	Recognize setting description	Recognize topic description	Recognize action description

P 14. *Paragraph skills:* POINT OF VIEW: Recognize and produce paragraph reflecting point of view.

1	2	3	4
☐	☐	☐	☐
Recognize point of view (who)	Produce paragraph from a point of view	Recognize pro or con point of view	Produce pro or con point of view

P 15. *Paragraph skills:* MOOD: Recognize mood.

1	2	3
☐	☐	☐
Sad Happy	Mysterious Adventurous	Humorous Serious

P 16. *Paragraph skills:* ORAL READING:(dramatic): Read aloud with appropriate intonation.

1	2	3	4
☐	☐	☐	☐
Essay & Drama	Essay & Drama	Story	Poetry

B 1. *Book skills:* FICTION: Recognize and produce fictional works.

1	2	3	4	5	6	7
☐	☐	☐	☐	☐	☐	☐
Reference data	Genre	Book report	Write stories: Character	Write stories: Setting	Write stories: Action	Write stories: Motivation

B 2. *Book skills:* NONFICTION: Recognize and produce nonfictional works.

1	2	3	4	5
☐	☐	☐	☐	☐
Reference data	Genre	Research	Organize report	Produce report

B 3. *Book skills:* TEXTBOOKS: Use a textbook properly.

1	2	3	4	5	6	7
☐	☐	☐	☐	☐	☐	☐
Orientation	Reference data		Skimming	Formulate study questions	Answer study questions	Technical terms

B 4. *Book skills:* REFERENCE WORKS: Use appropriate reference works.

1	2	3	4	5	6	7	8	9
☐	☐	☐	☐	☐	☐	☐	☐	☐
Dictionary		Encyclopedia			Thesaurus	Almanac	Library	

B 5. *Book skills:* PERIODICALS: Find and use books and newspapers.

1	2	3
☐	☐	☐
Newspaper	Newspapers	Magazines

B 6. *Book skills:* LETTERS: Identify letter format; write letters for differing purposes.

1	2	3	4	5	6
☐	☐	☐	☐	☐	☐
Recognize format	Produce format	Recognize format	Produce format	Produce letter of complaint	Respond to a survey

11

RATIONALE

When selecting skills to be measured and measurement formats to be used, I[2] was guided by psychological and linguistic considerations and by current classroom practices. Those considerations are reviewed here and paradigms for the various domains of skills are presented.

The domains. Since it is inconvenient to deal with the extremely complex domain of all language skills, that domain is usually divided in some way. Often skills are divided by grade level. In that case, a survey is made of the typical curriculum for each grade and tests are constructed representing each area of study. But sometimes skills are arranged according to inferred intellectual processes. That method leads to a series of tests of word recognition, comprehension, spelling ability, creative thinking, and so on.

Although each of these methods has advantages, neither leads to a comprehensive analysis of all aspects of language. Both methods are dependent on existing curriculums and instructional materials, and neither method is definitive in its selection and allocation of skills. There is no standard curriculum in the United States. Second grade items in one city may be first or third grade items in another city. Items classified as **inductive thinking** in one skill analysis might logically be called **comprehension** or **drawing conclusions** in another.

To avoid these problems, the *STARS* tests are based on a different analysis. They are based on the stimuli of language instruction (letters, words, sentences, paragraphs, and books), rather than on responses to language, or skills. The basic stimuli are viewed as a hierarchy:

Books
Paragraphs
Sentences
Words
Letters

This is a modified form of the hierarchy found in Volume 1. **Contours,** the lowest level of that hierarchy, is not included because responses to contours are seldom part of the school curriculum except as they relate to differences between letters and words. In those cases, tests are included at the letter or word level. The highest level of the Volume 1 hierarchy is Discourse and is equivalent to the Books level here. It was felt advisable to use the more common descriptor for these tests.

The hierarchical view of language on which the *STARS* tests are based was enunciated by Pike and Pike (1973). They have suggested that language is hierarchical in at least three ways: phonologically, grammatically, and referentially. The three hierarchies are interrelated, but they are not completely correlated. The items in each hierarchy are as follows:

[2] Judith M. Smith.

Phonological Hierarchy	*Grammatical Hierarchy*	*Referential Hierarchy*
Rhetorical Periods	Conversation	Performative Interaction
Pause Groups	Exchange	Story
Rhythm (Stress) Groups	Monolog	Event
Syllable Units	Paragraph	Participant Cluster
	Sentence	Identity
	Clause	
	Phrase	
	Word	
	Morpheme	

Elements from each hierarchy must be learned (recognized and reproduced, we would say) in different contexts in the course of mastering the language. The terms **grammatical** and **referential** will appear frequently in the labels of tests in the *STARS* battery when items from one of the hierarchies appears as a stimulus. In the case of written language, the graphic aspects of letters and words form another hierarchy: the **Graphic Hierarchy**.

> Book
> Paragraph
> Sentence
> Word
> Letter
> Letter Parts (Curves, Lines)

The graphic and phonological hierarchies deal with perceptual aspects of the language. They will frequently be combined under the label **perceptual**.

I used the following procedure for analyzing each level:

(*1*) Determine all aspects of the stimulus at a given level. (By **aspects** I mean characteristics of the stimulus as well as different forms of the stimulus.)

(*2*) Determine all relevant responses to each aspect of the stimulus.

Responses may be classified as either recognitions or reproductions (see Volume 1, Chapter 2). Thus, for each level of the hierarchy, a matrix may be constructed to describe the tests included:

	STIMULUS ASPECTS								
RESPONSES									
Recognition									
Reproduction									

For some stimulus forms, only recognition tests or reproduction tests—not both types—may be appropriate.

It will become clear that the stimulus hierarchy I have described is not a developmental hierarchy. There are tests at each level that are appropriate for kindergarten through second grade and others at the same level appropriate for Grades 3–4 or 5–6. For each stimulus aspect, a series of criterion tests samples increasingly complex skills. Beginning, intermediate, and advanced skill levels are tested where relevant to provide detailed feedback on the progress of students and to suggest the direction of instruction.

Use of the tests. The criterion-referenced tests in this volume may be viewed as a resource. Tests appropriate for the curriculum of a particular class or for desired skill levels may be selected to form an individualized mastery series. The order of the tests in a series has been determined empirically by administering them to classes at different levels. Since any skill is amenable to training, however, the order of tests may be changed to reflect a particular curriculum.

Test directions. The *STARS* tests use the fewest possible directions and formats in order to eliminate those variables in test performance. Wherever possible, the same words are used to instruct students. Page layouts are also standardized. The number of items is controlled in order to avoid stress. In many cases, sample tests provide instruction in the process required for a series of tests. If a teacher suspects that (*1*) directions will be confusing to a student or (*2*) performance on a test does not represent a true picture of skill level, special instruction should be given on the directions for the test(s). If sample tests are not provided, the teacher should prepare a test that uses the same directions, and then administer that test, step by step, until it is clear that the student understands the procedure to be used in responding to test items. If a simple change in test directions will simplify the test for a given group, the teacher should not hesitate to make such a change. Unlike many standardized tests, criterion-referenced tests are not intended to measure one's ability to follow complex directions (unless, of course, that is the criterion skill).

Letters

Letters have three main aspects to which learners must respond: **perceptual aspects** (letter shapes, both manuscript and cursive forms); **equivalents** (letter names and letter sounds); and **functions** (in this case, personal name and alphabet). The recognition and reproduction tests for each aspect are shown in the chart.

| RESPONSES | LETTER ASPECTS | | | | | | |
| | Perceptual | | | Equivalents | | Functions | |
	Letter Shapes	Manuscript Form	Cursive Form	Letter Names	Letter Sounds	Personal Name	Alphabet
Recognition	1–8			1–6	1–12	1	
Reproduction		1–14	1–11	7,8		1	2–6

The relevant aspects of letters were determined empirically in the course of the development of *The Michigan Language Program* (Smith & Smith, 1975). It was found that training in the discrimination of letter shapes was necessary to the development of reading, writing, and spelling skills, and was usually a critical deficiency of poor readers. Manuscript and cursive letter forms were necessary for communication and for the expressive form of reading.[3]

Letter names became relevant to the children only when spelling was introduced. Children could not recall the order of letters in words unless they knew the names of the letters. Without names, they resorted to descriptive terms (*hump letter, chair, circle,* and so on). Letter–sound equivalents were necessary for the development of word-attack skills. Although a few children drew the necessary generalizations by themselves, most did not discover the regularities of the language without specific training. It was also found that letters could not be mastered (i.e., remembered) as abstract units. They had to serve certain functions of importance to the learner. The most common function, of course, is to form elements of words students are learning to read. The elements-of-words function is tested at the word level in the *STARS* battery. Two other functions of letters are of interest to the beginning reader: the letter's use as an element of the reader's own name, and its use as an element of the alphabet. However, a surprising number of children never learn to write the alphabet correctly (almost

[3] Cursive Form and Manuscript Form tests are actually the reproduction tests for Letter Shapes. However, since letter discrimination and penmanship are usually viewed as different parts of the curriculum, they are presented separately in this battery.

50% of seventh graders in one study (Beutler, 1974). This in itself may not be a serious deficiency, but it may prevent them from using the dictionary, encyclopedia, library, phone book, and so forth, in an efficient manner.

Perceptual aspects: Letter shapes

Objective: Given a letter (the model) and an adjoining array of letters, one or two of which are identical to the model, circle the target letters.

Tests 1–6   Letter Matching
Tests 7, 8   Capital–Lowercase Equivalents

Tests 1–6 are tests of visual discrimination of letters. Capital and lowercase letters are included with a **free-choice** format—i.e., the target letter may appear more than once among the wrong choices (or **foils**). The tests increase in difficulty from Test 1 to Test 6: The number of items increases; spacing between items decreases; size of type decreases; perceptual aids (like lines between items) are faded out; and the number of confusable letters is increased.

Tests 7 and 8 require the discrimination of the relationship between the lowercase and capital forms of a letter.

Tests 1–8 are usually completed by children in kindergarten and first grade.

Perceptual aspects: Manuscript form

Objective: Given a model, copy it to specified criteria.

Standards

Test 1   Contiguity or "connectedness"
Test 2   Use of baseline
Test 3   Use of midline: capitals
Test 4   Contiguity of straight and curved lines within a letter
Test 5   Use of topline
Test 6   Use of midline: lowercase
Test 7   Placement of descenders; use of midline
Test 8   Placement of bar on midline and parallel to baseline; curvature of bar on lowercase *r*
Test 9   Use of diagonals (capitals), topline, midline, baseline
Test 10   Use of diagonals, topline, midline, baseline
Test 11   Use of diagonals (lowercase), midline, baseline
Test 12   Use of curved lines (capitals), topline, baseline
Test 13   Words: correct form and spacing of letters
Test 14   Sentences: correct form, spacing of letters, spacing of words

The 14 tests that pace printing skill begin with the drawing of connecting lines and finish with the printing of sentences. Each response is evaluated by applying one, two, or three standards of correctness—e.g., "Be sure your letters touch the baseline [or bottom line, ground line]." Since the child's product is to be evaluated using these standards, he must understand them. Therefore, the teacher is encouraged to instruct as necessary to ensure understanding of the standards, as well as understanding of the directions.

Perceptual aspects: Cursive form

Objective: Given a model, copy to specified criteria.

Standards

Test 1   Letter or connecting strokes meet baseline (lowercase)
Test 2   Base, midline (capitals)
Test 3   Baseline, with descenders (capitals)
Test 4   Baseline, overstrokes (lowercase)
Test 5   Baseline, midline, slant (lowercase)
Test 6   Baseline, height, form (capitals)
Test 7   Baseline, height, form (capitals)
Test 8   Form, slant (lowercase)
Test 9   Baseline, slant, form, height, spacing (words)
Test 10 Baseline, slant, form, height (capitals)
Test 11 Baseline, slant, form, height, spacing (sentences)

Cursive writing skill is paced by 11 tests. The first test measures placement on the baseline with single letters; the last measures baseline, spacing, slant, height, and form with whole sentences. That is, orthographic standards are added, one by one, through the series.

Equivalents: Letter names

Objectives: Given an array of letters, circle the one named. Name randomly
              ordered letters.

Tests 1, 3, 5, 7   Capitals
Tests 2, 4, 6, 8   Lowercase

Knowledge of letter **names** (not sounds) is measured by eight tests: Three tests measure recognition of capitals and three measure recognition of lowercase; two require identification (or **naming**) of all capital and all lowercase letters.

The first tests are appropriate for use in kindergarten. Tests 7 and 8 should be completed by second grade.

Equivalents: Letter–sound equivalence (phonics)

Objective: Given a spoken word and two or three graphemic alternatives consisting of letters or word elements, circle the one corresponding alternative.

> Test 1   Initial Consonants
> Test 2   Initial Consonants
> Test 3   Final Consonants
> Test 4   Short Vowel Sounds
> Test 5   Long Vowel Sounds (Silent *e*)
> Test 6   Advanced Vowel Sounds
> Test 7   Advanced Vowel Sounds
> Test 8   Initial Consonant Blends
> Test 9   Initial Vowel–Consonant Combinations
> Test 10 Word Bases
> Test 11 Allographs[4] (Consonants)
> Test 12 Allographs (Vowels)

The 12 tests in this sequence begin with two tests of initial consonants and end
with two tests that approximate sounding out of words (independent reading).

Letter functions: Personal name, alphabet

Objectives:

Test 1   Recognize letters in personal name. Write name.
Test 2   Say the letters of the alphabet in order.
Test 3   Place cutout letters in order, to form an alphabet.
Test 4   Write the complete lowercase alphabet and the complete capital-letter
alphabet, without regard to printing standards.
Test 5   Place words in alphabetical order, where all initial letters are different.
Test 6   Place words in alphabetical order, where some initial, second, and third
letters are the same.

Tests 1 and 2 are suitable for kindergartners. Test 6 is appropriate for third or
fourth grade.

Words

Words have four main aspects to which learners must respond: **perceptual
aspects,** which include phonological features and graphic features (word shapes);

---

[4] **Allographs** are "other (*allo*) letters (*graphs*)"—other letter groups that signify certain
sounds.

equivalents (word–sound equivalents, the identification of which is termed **word recognition,** and the spelling of words); **grammatical meaning** (the syntactic factor, discussed later); and **referential meaning** (including the range, semantic, and classification factors, to be discussed). The recognition and reproduction tests for each aspect are shown in the chart on page 20. At the word level, a special kind of reproduction test is appropriate, that of **fluency.**

The requirements for learning to read a word (discussed in Volume 1) include (*1*) discrimination of word shape (and sometimes the interior), (*2*) discrimination of the sound of the word, and (*3*) discrimination of the shape–sound composite. Thus, each perceptual aspect and its equivalent are tested in the *STARS* battery. The equivalence of word shape to sound (**word recognition, reading**) and the equivalence of sound to word (**spelling**) are both included as equivalence aspects of words.

The meaning aspect of words is more complex. Knowledge of word meaning is acknowledged to be an important factor in general measures of intelligence (MacDonald, 1971; Osborne & Lindsey, 1965; Singer, 1965; Spearman, 1970) and in tests of reading comprehension and academic achievement (Marshall & Powers, ED064377; Vineyard & Massey, 1957). However, most such tests of vocabulary skill rest on a concept of **meaning as synonym.** These tests are usually limited in that they do not measure the student's facility with words (ability to use words properly in different contexts, to recognize the nuances of meaning, and to choose the right word to achieve a particular focus or emphasis). These aspects of meaning, in addition to synonymy, should be included in the curriculum and in a comprehensive battery such as *STARS.*

In this analysis, a word may be viewed as a **form–meaning composite** (Pike & Pike, 1973). The form aspects (perceptual and equivalents) have been discussed. The meaning aspect includes (*1*) communication impact, i.e., the actual effect on the receiver of the message and (*2*) communication intent, i.e., the desired effect of the sender. When impact and intent are equivalent, communication is clear and specific. When they are not equivalent, meaning is ambiguous.

A word may have numerous potential impact–intents. The particular impact–intent that is communicated is determined by a number of factors acting on the receiver, on the sender, and on both. Personal experience—of the receiver and of the sender—is one potent factor. The meaning of some words will be highly idiosyncratic to a particular individual because of that person's unique experiences. Such idiosyncratic meaning is not transmitted to a receiver who has not had similar experiences. It is not possible to predict the nature of a shift in meaning due to personal experience without knowing the precise nature of the experience involved. Thus, the factor of personal experience, although a potent determinant, will enter into this description only as a factor in performance on

WORD ASPECTS			Recognition	Reproduction	Fluency
Referential Meaning	Classification Factor		1–10		
	Semantic Factor		1–11	1	
	Range		1–20	2,3	
Grammatical Meaning	Syntactic Factor		1–11	4	
Equivalents	Spelling		1–5	Teacher Tests	
	Word-Sound Equivalents		1–11		
Perceptual	Phonological Features		5–18	1–4	5,6,7
	Word Shapes		1–5		

RESPONSES

the Range section, which requires knowledge of the **general** meaning of a large number of words.

The meaning of a word is determined by (*1*) the grammatical context in which it occurs (grammatical meaning) and (*2*) the referent—object, quality, concept— of the word (referential meaning). Grammatical meaning is that conferred by a slot in a sentence (subject, predicate, and so on) and by the word's role (actor, action, object, and so on). Also included is the meaning conferred by inflections and affixes. Such meaning is not specific to the particular word occupying a slot. Thus, in *They brogled in the yard* we know that *brogled* carries the meaning of action and past time.

Referential meaning, on the other hand, is specific to a particular word in a particular meaning context. The referential meaning of a word is expressed by a synonym or paraphrase (same meaning) or by an antonym (opposite meaning). Thus, the meaning of *hot* may be expressed by the terms *scalding, very warm,* or *opposite of cold.* Other facets of referential meaning depend on knowledge of particular features of a referent. Thus, words may be used analogously (the *arm* of the chair), or inclusively (*dog* includes the meanings "mammal" and "animal").

A class of paraphrases that shares a specific impact—intent and occupies the same position in a sentence frame may be called a **hypermeaning** (Pike & Pike, 1973). Members of such a class differ in emphasis, focus, or detail. Thus, *hot* and *scalding,* although they are synonyms, convey differences in degree of heat, and the latter term conveys additional information (liquid).

The word-level tests described next have been designed to sample the relevant facets of word meaning and the perceptual and equivalence aspects of printed and spoken words.

Perceptual aspects: Word shapes

Objective: Given a word or phrase (the model) and several alternatives, one of which is identical to the model (the target), student circles the target word.

> Test 1 Word Endings
> Test 2 Similar Words
> Test 3 Letter Order
> Test 4 Spaces between Words
> Test 5 Word Interiors

This visual-discrimination series can be used at the beginning of first grade or when Letter Shapes, Test 3 is completed. Test 5 (Word Interiors) is a prerequisite for spelling "long words" of highest frequency. Such words appear in Spelling, Test 3.

Perceptual aspects: Phonological features

Objectives:

Repeat sequences:	Test 1	Given sentences aurally, repeat them orally.
	Test 2	Given letters aurally, repeat them orally.
Generate initial and final sounds:	Test 3	Given three words that rhyme, generate a fourth.
	Test 4	Given three words that start the same, generate a fourth.
Discriminate initial, medial, final sounds:	Test 5	Discriminate similar words differing in final sound.
	Test 6	Discriminate similar words differing in initial sound.
	Test 7	Discriminate similar words differing in medial sound.
Discriminate words within sentences:	Test 8	Discriminate name words within sentences.
	Test 9	Discriminate connectives within sentences.
Discriminate sounds within words:	Test 10	Discriminate complex terminal sounds in words.
	Test 11	Discriminate complex initial sounds in words.
Discriminate word junctures:	Test 12	Given sequences of words, count the words.
	Test 13	Given two- to five-word sentences, count the words.
	Test 14	Given less common sentence forms, count the words.
Discriminate complex final and initial sounds:	Test 15	Discriminate similar words differing in final sounds.
	Test 16	Discriminate similar words differing in initial sounds.
Count syllables in words:	Test 17	Given one-, two-, and three-syllable words, count syllables.
	Test 18	Given three-, four-, and five-syllable words, count syllables.

This comprehensive auditory series paces development from the beginning of first grade to the end of third grade. All the early tests are prerequisite for phonics mastery. The last two tests are required for spelling competency.

Equivalents: Word–sound equivalents

Objectives: Given a printed sentence and one or two spoken words, student circles named word(s).

Given printed phrases or sentences, student reads them aloud.

The 11 tests in this series are carefully graded, beginning with basic sight words and ending with infrequent words that may be sounded. Two tests (4 and 8) require oral reading. The first test is appropriate for the first term of first grade; the last test should be passed by the end of fourth grade.

Equivalents: Spelling

Objectives: Given a word list of specified difficulty, approximately one-third of which are misspelled, student marks the misspelled words.

Test 1 Frequency 1–100
Test 2 Frequency 1–300 (short words)
Test 3 Frequency 1–300 (long words)
Test 4 Frequency 301–600
Test 5 Frequency 601–1000

These five tests constitute year-end tests for Grades 1–5. The words are based on the Rinsland–Horn list of 1000 words used most frequently by children in their written work (Coleman, 1970). As described in the directions to the teacher that precede the spelling tests, the *STARS* tests should be supplemented by teacher-make tests reflecting current work in the several subject-matter areas.

Grammatical meaning: Syntactic factor

Objective: Given a word, select a picture illustrating a specific grammatical meaning.

Test 1 Singular/Plural
Test 2 Actor, Action, Undergoer
Test 3 Action
Test 4 Actor
Test 5 Undergoer

Objective: Given a sentence, choose which of several alternatives is the actor, action, undergoer, and scope.

Test 6 Tense
Test 7 Actor
Test 8 Undergoer
Test 9 Scope
Test 10 Action

Objective: Given a word in a sentence, select another word in a sentence with the same grammatical meaning.

Test 11 Noun/Verb, Verb/Modifier Contrast
Test 12 Noun/Verb, Noun/Modifier Contrast

Objective: Given a sentence with a blank, select a nonsense word that demonstrates the appropriate grammatical meaning.

Test 13   Inflection Cues

Referential meaning: Range

Objective: Given incomplete sentences and several correct and incorrect completion words, circle all the correct words.

Test 1 Direct Object, Infinitive
Test 2 Modifier, Preposition
Test 3 Object of Preposition, Predicate Nominative, Direct Object
Test 4 Interrogative, Verb, Auxiliary, Preposition, Direct Object

Objective: Given a noun, determine the appropriate characteristic.

Test 5 Class Name
Test 6 Action
Test 7 Modifier

Objective: Given incomplete sentences, choose the appropriate completion word.

Tests 8–20 Target words of increasing difficulty

Range tests begin in Grade 2 and are completed in Grade 6. Target words are selected on the basis of frequency tables provided by Carroll, Davies, and Richman (1971). Although Tests 1–7 are described in terms of the part of speech of target items, knowledge of grammatical terms is not required (or appropriate) as entry behavior for learners.

Referential meaning: Semantic factor

Objective: Given sets of three sentences with the same word underlined, mark the two sentences in which the word has the same referential meaning.

Tests 1–3 Noun
Test 4   Main Verb/Auxiliary Verb
Tests 5, 6 Modifier

Objective: Given an incomplete sentence, choose appropriate completion
          word(s).

Test 9   Usage

Referential meaning: Classification factor

Objective: Given a word or sentence, select another word having a specified
          relationship to the model.

Tests 1, 2	Synonyms
Test 3	Antonyms
Test 4	Homonyms
Test 5	Synonyms
Test 6	Antonyms
Tests 7, 8	Class Names
Tests 9, 10	Synonyms
Test 11	Emphasis
Test 12	Analogies

Sentences

   The relevant aspects of sentences are **perceptual, grammatical,** and **referential.**
Each aspect is composed of several related factors, as shown in the chart on page
26.

   The three groups of tests correspond to the three hierarchies discussed previously. The special graphic feature of the sentence is the space between words.
Phonological aspects are displayed by oral reading, by sentence memory
(miming), and by writing from dictation. The processes involved are graphic–
aural, oral–aural, and oral–graphic.

   Grammatical tests include tests of capitalization and punctuation. Both of
these require identification of grammatical units and knowledge of conventions.
Transformation tests involve the manipulation of grammatical units, with meaning remaining the same or varying in a systematic way.

   Referential (meaning) tests include responding appropriately to directions,
forming relevant questions, identifying the literal meaning of sentences, and
interpreting figurative language.

Perceptual aspects: Oral reading

Objective: Read sentences with appropriate intonation.

Test 1	Length of 4–7 words
Test 2	Length of 8–14 words, quotes
Test 3	Length of 15–24 words, dramatic reading

SENTENCE ASPECTS			Recognition	Reproduction
Referential	Figurative Language, Idioms		1–4	
	Sentence Meaning		1–3	
	Questions			1–6
	Directions			1,2
Grammatical	Transformations			1–17
	Punctuation		2–21	1,2 3,4 7,21
	Capitalization		1–10	
Perceptual	Dictation			1–6
	Sentence Memory			1,2
	Spaces between Words		1	1
	Oral Reading			1–3
RESPONSES			Recognition	Reproduction

These tests should be treated as dramatic performances, with adequate opportunity for rehearsal.

Perceptual aspects: Spaces between words

Objective: Recognize and reproduce spaces between words.

Test 1   Length of 4–6 words

This discrimination is critical for beginning reading.

Perceptual aspects: Sentence memory

Objective: Reproduce sentences of increasing complexity.

Test 1   Length of 3–5 words
Test 2   Length of 5–8 words

Ability to recall sentences of some length and complexity is necessary for sentence comprehension, especially when reading is slow and labored.

Perceptual aspects: Dictation

Objective: Write dictated sentences.

Tests 1–4   Words of frequencies 1–300
Test 5   Frequencies 301–600
Test 6   Frequencies 601–1000

Dictation tests involve auditory discrimination, sentence memory, and spelling skill. They approach the actual task of writing from auto-dictation.

Grammatical meaning: Capitalization

Objective: Use capitals correctly.

Test 1   Initial Words, Names, Personal Pronouns
Test 2   Place Names
Test 3   Titles, Names, and Initials
Test 4   Time-related Names
Test 5   Buildings, Addresses, Organizations
Test 6   Religious Names
Test 7   Transport Vehicles, Plant Names, Animal Names
Test 8   Trade Names, Astronomical Names
Test 9   Direct Quotations
Test 10 Titles

Conventions for capitalization are from *A Manual of Style* (Chicago: University of Chicago Press, 1969). Teachers may, of course, use other conventions and mark tests accordingly.

Grammatical meaning: Punctuation

Objective: Use punctuation marks correctly.

Test 1	Reproduce Marks
Test 2	Period
Test 3	Period, Question Mark
Test 4	Period, Question Mark, Exclamation Point
Test 5	Quotation Marks
Test 6, 7	Direct Quotations
Test 8	Comma: Compound Sentence
Test 9	Comma: Series, Coordinate Adjectives
Test 10	Comma: Interjections, Transitionals
Test 11	Comma: Appositives
Test 12	Comma: Antithetical Elements
Test 13	Comma: Dates, Places, Titles
Test 14	Comma: Parenthetical Elements
Test 15	Comma: Mistaken Junctions (*that is, namely, for example*)
Test 16	Comma: Introductory Phrases and Clauses
Test 17	Comma: Nonrestrictive Phrases and Clauses
Test 18	Semicolon: Sentence Break
Test 19	Semicolon: Series
Test 20	Colon
Test 21	Multiple Punctuation

Conventions for punctuation are also from *A Manual of Style*. Again, teachers may use other conventions and mark tests accordingly.

Grammatical meaning: Transformations

Objective: Given a sentence, perform the indicated transformation.

Test 1	Singular Subject
Test 2	Plural Subject
Test 3	Negation
Tests 4, 5	Pronouns
Test 6	Present Tense
Test 7	Past Tense
Test 8	Future Tense
Test 9	Auxiliaries (*have*)
Test 10	Auxiliaries (*be*)
Test 11	Auxiliaries (*be + have*)
Test 12	Passive
Tests 13–16	Links
Test 17	Word Order

Ability to perform these transformations indicates facility and flexibility in the use of language, as well as command of the structural constraints of English.

Referential meaning: Directions

Objective: Follow workbook and test directions.

Tests 1, 2   Underline, put an X next to, circle, etc., specified items.

Performing the correct response to a test or exercise can mean the difference between high and low scores, regardless of content knowledge. Students must become sensitive to desired response indicators.

Referential meaning: Questions

Objective: Produce a question that is answered by a given sentence.

Test 1   Who
Test 2   What
Test 3   Where
Test 4   When
Test 5   Why
Test 6   How

Producing questions about particular content material is a valuable exercise for two reasons: First, it is a useful study technique. Second, it demonstrates the interrelationship between questions and their answers, enabling students to direct their answers appropriately to the questions addressed to them.

Referential meaning: Sentence meaning

Objective: Choose which of several sentences conforms to particular meaning constraints.

Test 1   Picture Constraints
Test 2   Internal Constraints (Sensibleness)
Test 3   Paragraph Constraints

The meaning of a sentence, as tested here, can be defined in three ways. The first is the accuracy of its relationship to external events (pictures, in this case). The second is internal consistency, the possibility of the sentence describing **any** real event, given one's knowledge of the real world. Such inconsistency is here signaled by a mismatch of referent and pronoun, animate verbs and inanimate nouns, and so on. The third way is its function in a larger whole (the paragraph, in Test 3). Many paragraphs have the following structure: introduction of topic, discussion, summary. In such a paragraph, it is possible to identify which of these functions a sentence performs.

Referential meaning: Figurative language

Objective: Recognize idioms and similes.

                    Tests 1, 2, 3   Idioms
                    Test 4   Similes

Words have many meanings—some literal and some figurative. Ability to interpret figurative usages is important for reading and for creative writing.

Paragraphs

The relevant aspects of paragraphs are **form**, **content**, **equivalents**, and **impact**. Each aspect is itself composed of several factors, as the chart on page 31 shows.

.For purposes of this analysis, a paragraph is defined as a cluster of related sentences. Although some writers have questioned the existence of structures above the sentence level (Katz & Fodor, 1963), pedagogically there is little question that it is not sufficient to read and write isolated sentences. The aspects listed in the chart are different from those at the sentence level. They have been organized within the general rubrics of format, content, equivalents, and impact.

Format aspects of paragraphs include their graphic form (block form, usually with the first word indented), grammatical patterns (e.g., parallel sentences), and phonological patterns (stress patterns, rhyme, and alliteration). All these aspects are relatively independent of the lexical content of the paragraph, and are thus considered part of the format.

Content aspects of paragraphs are dependent on their referential content. The first and most general is the universe of discourse of which the paragraph is a part. Other aspects are the paragraph topic, plot, links between related sentences, and the literal information contained in the paragraph.

It is assumed in this analysis that there exist paragraphs (or sentences) equivalent to any particular paragraph under consideration. Such equivalents are recognized as such by native speakers and bring about the same behavior on the part of the reader, although they may differ from the original in focus, detail, impact, aesthetic acceptability, and amount of detail. The equivalences tested are summarizations, inductive statements (often called inference), and deductive statements.

In any paragraph, it is usually possible to distinguish a set of features that determine the kind of impact delivered to the reader. These include the focus, or emphasis, of the paragraph; the point of view demonstrated by the paragraph; the mood of the author and that of the reader; and particular phonological aspects when the paragraph is read aloud.

Aspects of impact overlap with aspects of equivalents, content, or format. Certain format features—parallel structures, phonological patterns—may be

PARAGRAPH ASPECTS		Recognition	Reproduction
Impact	Oral Reading		1–4
Impact	Mood	1–3	
Impact	Point of View	1,3	2,4
Impact	Focus	1–5	
Equivalents	Deduction	1,2	3
Equivalents	Induction (Inference)	1,2, 4	3,5, 6
Equivalents	Summarization	1–4	5
Content	Information	1–4, 6,8	5,7, 9
Content	Relational Links	1–3, 5	4,6
Content	Referential Links	1	2
Content	Plot	1,3, 5,7	2,4, 6,8
Content	Topic	1,3, 4	2,5
Content	Universe of Discourse	1,2	
Form	Phonological Patterns	1–4	5
Form	Grammatical Patterns	1–4	1
Form	Form Conventions	1	2
RESPONSES		Recognition	Reproduction

employed to produce a certain mood or focus. The item in focus is probably that which has been identified as the topic. The point of view of the author is related to the universe of discourse. If these are treated as a separate category, however, they achieve a special emphasis.

Form: Form convention

Objective: Recognize and produce indented block form.

> Test 1   Recognition Tasks
> Test 2   Reproduction Task

The most commonly used paragraph form (indented block) is used here.

Form: Grammatical patterns

Objective: Recognize and produce consistent tense, number, and structure.

> Tests 1, 2   Parallel Structures
> Test 3   Consistent Tense
> Test 4   Consistent Number

Teaching of the conventions regarding grammatical patterns is often neglected until problems are encountered in high school or college, but is probably easily incorporated at a lower level.

Form: Phonological patterns

Objective: Recognize and produce rhyme, alliteration, and rhythm (poetry).

> Test 1   Rhyme
> Test 2   Alliteration
> Test 3   Rhythm
> Test 4, 5   Rhyme, Rhythm, Alliteration

Appreciation of poetry is enhanced when students can recognize the phonological features that characterize much of the poetry they will read. It should be noted that alliteration is a factor in much prose, as well as in poetry.

Content: Universe of discourse

Objective: Recognize universe of discourse by vocabulary and style.

> Test 1   Topic
> Test 2   Genre

Any paragraph belongs to some universe of discourse. That larger context determines the meanings of many words and the significance of many statements contained in the paragraph.

Content: Topic

Objective: Identify a paragraph topic by listening and reading. Produce a paragraph orally.

Test 1   Oral—Recognize Topic

Test 2   Oral Composition

Test 3   Recognize Topic

Test 4   Topic Elaboration

Test 5   Name Topic

We have assumed in our definition that sentences of a paragraph must be related in some way. The most obvious relationship is that all sentences deal with a simple or conjoined topic. Such a topic plays a role similar to that of a subject in a sentence.

Content: Plot

Objective: Recognize and produce eight paragraph plots.

Tests 1, 2   A is similar to B; A is different from B.

Tests 3, 4   A is an example of B; A is a reason for B.

Tests 5, 6   A and B exist in spatial array; A and B exist in temporal array.

Tests 7, 8   A is a restatement of B; A is a cause of B.

A plot distinguishes a paragraph from a series of random sentences. Young, Becker, and Pike (1970, pp. 317–318) have shown that sentences in a segment of schizophrenic speech are related to one another (in unusual ways), but lack coherence because of the absence of an overall plot structure. They identify the following generalized plots:

B is an instance of A.	B is a cause of (or reason for) A.
B is a restatement of (or clarification of) A.	B is different from A.
	A and B exist in temporal (or spatial) array.
B is similar to A.	

Content: Referential links

Objective: Recognize and produce referential links.

Test 1   Recognize

Test 2   Reproduce

In order to avoid constant repetition of words in a paragraph, authors employ a variety of links. These include personal, demonstrative, and relative pronouns; the article *the*; adverbs, conjunctions, and synonyms (Horn, 1972).

Content: Relational links

Objective: Recognize and produce relational links.

Tests 1–3	Recognition
Test 4	Reproduction
Test 5	Recognition
Test 6	Reproduction

Links between sentences (such as *therefore, of course,* and *later*) may be viewed as grammatical correlates of the particular relationship (plot) illustrated by the paragraph. Several formats are used in these tests: (*1*) Identify links equivalent in meaning in a given context. (*2*) Identify sentence links. (*3*) Produce links in a given context. (*4*) Rewrite sentences changing their order. The last format is particularly effective in demonstrating the function of sentence links.

Content: Information

Objective: Identify answers to information questions; produce questions.

Tests 1–4   Identify *who, what, where, when, why* questions.
Test 5   Produce *who, what, where* questions.
Tests 6–9   Answer and produce questions of increasing difficulty.

A paragraph, like a sentence, is intended to convey facts or judgments to the reader. Because a paragraph is a complex structure, a great deal of information may be included. These tests deal only with "literal" information.

Equivalents: Summarization

Objective: Recognize and produce summary statements.

Tests 1, 2	Recognize summary statements.
Tests 3, 4	Find summary statements.
Test 5	Produce summary statements.

A paragraph can be summarized in a statement (or two) that carries the same core meaning as the expanded form. The topic sentence may be, but is not necessarily, a summary statement.

Equivalents: Induction (inference)

Objective: Recognize and produce valid inductions.

Tests 1, 2	Recognize inference.
Test 3	Produce inference.
Test 4	Infer similarity and difference.
Test 5	Infer reasons.
Test 6	Produce inference.

If the content of a paragraph allows a reader to reasonably induce a general principle, that inductive statement is deemed equivalent to the paragraph as a whole. This process is often called **inference**.

Equivalents: Deduction

Objective: Use syllogistic reasoning to draw conclusions.

> Test 1   Solve syllogisms.
> Test 2   Recognize logical conclusions.
> Test 3   Produce logical conclusions.

If the content of a paragraph leads logically to a particular deduction, that deductive statement is deemed equivalent to the paragraph as a whole. This process is sometimes called **drawing conclusions**.

Impact: Focus

Object: Identify focus (setting, topic, action, time, motive).

> Test 1   Select Focus
> Test 2   Time, Motive Description
> Test 3   Setting Description
> Test 4   Topic Description
> Test 5   Action Description

In a well-written paragraph, it is usually possible to discover who or what is emphasized by the writer. Other topics or actions mentioned may serve to illustrate or contrast with the item in focus. Failure to discriminate this feature may lead the reader to draw erroneous conclusions and to misinterpret the paragraph in other ways.

Impact: Point of view

Objective: Recognize and produce paragraphs reflecting a particular point of view.

> Tests 1, 2   Author's Bias
> Tests 3, 4   Pro or Con

A paragraph may represent the view of any participant, or of an outside observer. The reader must ask himself these questions: Who is telling the story? What biases are inherent in the narrator's point of view?

Impact: Mood

Objective: Recognize mood

> Test 1   Sad/Happy
> Test 2   Mysterious/Adventurous
> Test 3   Humorous/Serious

This aspect is somewhat difficult to identify—probably because it involves a subjective judgment on the part of the reader. One must identify both the tone of the author and the mood the paragraph evokes in the reader. These may or may not be reciprocal. That is, an author may write indignantly; the reader may respond with anger, or perhaps with condescension.

Books

The relevant forms of books are textbooks, fiction, nonfiction (other than textbooks); reference works (such as dictionaries, encyclopedias and almanacs); and periodicals. The aspects appear in the chart below.

Any multiparagraph stimulus will be included in the Books section of *STARS*. Thus, letters, stories, newspapers, and magazines will appear. For each aspect, learners will be asked to identify features, such as relevant parts (title, table of contents) and genre (where appropriate). They will also be asked to demonstrate the use of the item (research strategies, study techniques, book reports, and so on).

Fiction

Objective: Recognize and produce fictional works.

Test 1   Reference Items
Test 2   Genre
Test 3   Book Report Form

	BOOK ASPECTS					
RESPONSES	Textbooks	Fiction	Nonfiction	Reference Works	Periodicals	Letters
Recognition		2	2			1–3
Reproduction	1–6	1,3–7	1,3–5	1–9	1–3	2,4–6

Test 4   Stories—Character
Test 5   Stories—Setting
Test 6   Stories—Action
Test 7   Stories—Motivation

Learners are tested on their knowledge of reference items (such as title, author, copyright, table of contents, and chapters) and on their knowledge of genre. On the basis of typical titles, they identify a book as a mystery, an adventure story, an animal story, and so on. Also included is a book report form that may be reproduced for as many book reports as are required. This form is consistent with the other tests in the series in the kind of information requested. Learners are also asked to produce samples of the parts of a story—character, setting, action, and motivation.

Nonfiction

Objective: Recognize and produce nonfictional works.

Test 1   Reference Items
Test 2   Genre
Test 3   Research
Tests 4, 5   Reports

Nonfiction books treated here are those other than textbooks and standard reference works such as encyclopedias. As for fiction, learners are asked to identify reference items and genre (in this case, biography, drama, science, and the like). Since a major use of such works is in researching a report, learners are required to demonstrate that they can (*1*) locate relevant sources, (*2*) subdivide a topic into more manageable units, and (*3*) prepare a report using at least two source books other than encyclopedias.

Textbooks

Objective: Use a textbook properly.

Test 1   Orientation
Tests 2, 3   Reference Items
Test 4   Skimming
Tests 5, 6   Study Questions
Test 7   Technical Terms

The textbook series contains the lowest level test of the Book level—Test 1, Orientation. It is appropriate for kindergarten children who are just learning to open a book, look at pictures, etc. Any book may be used for this test, although it must contain pictures. Reference items are again tested. The last four tests deal with study skills—the use of textbooks. The learner must complete the **skim**, or **pre-read** step, in which a general idea of content is obtained. Next, learners formulate and answer study questions. Finally, they define technical terms in the chapter. Learners who complete these steps will have mastered a study technique that will be valuable to them throughout their school experience.

Reference works

Objective: Use reference works appropriately.

> Tests 1, 2   Dictionary
> Tests 3–5   Encyclopedia
> Test 6   Thesaurus
> Test 7   Almanac
> Tests 8, 9   Library

Dictionary skills include decoding a pronunciation key; using index words; finding definitions, part of speech, derivation, and synonym; finding word divisions and accents; determining correct spelling; and identifying appendices. Encyclopedia skills include using index words; finding specific information; identifying related topics; using a study guide; writing a report based on encyclopedia entries; and writing reports based on encyclopedia information. Learners are also asked questions requiring the use of a thesaurus and an almanac. Reference items are identified for each type of reference work. Finally, learners are required to map and use their local library.

Periodicals

Objective: Find and use newspapers and magazines.

> Tests 1, 2   Newspapers
> Test 3   Magazines

Learners must find information in a newspaper and produce a newspaper of their own. They must identify the nature of magazines—their different functions.

Letters

Objective: Identify letter format. Write letters for different purposes.

> Tests 1, 2   Friendly Letters
> Tests 3, 4, 5 Business Letters

Learners must identify the parts of both friendly and business letters. They must write (*1*) a friendly letter, (*2*) a request letter, (*3*) a complaint letter, and (*4*) a response to a survey.

B. Psychometric Validity

Most readers will have noticed our cavalier disregard for the traditional categories of validity, namely, **construct, content, concurrent,** and **predictive** (Cronbach, 1971). The application of psychometric and other technical standards to criterion-based measures is currently a subject of debate in the literature and has not yet settled into anything resembling a consensus.

There are, as we see it, two major areas of uncertainty in the current discussion of standards. One of these is the question of whether "classical" test theory (Guilford, 1954; Nunnally 1967) is applicable, wholly or in part, to criterion-referenced testing. Most discussion of classical test theory has been limited to **measurement error,** and it has led to a number of proposals for new types of reliability coefficients.

A second area of uncertainty pertains to the aforementioned four-part taxonomy of Cronbach, which has traditionally been used in discussing the validity of instruments. This part of the current controversy deals with the degree to which criterion-based measurement calls for particular emphasis on some aspects of validity as contrasted with others (Popham & Husek, 1969), or whether construct validity is a universal requirement and should always be provided for. Recently the taxonomy discussion has taken another turn, with Popham's proposal for an entirely new set of categories (Popham, 1974). The position we wish to take amidst all this uncertainty may be characterized as **conservative radical**: We want to be very careful not to throw the baby away with the bathwater, but our inclination is to be utterly ruthless with the bathwater itself.

For example, let us turn briefly to the issue of reliability, the first of the two major areas of uncertainty cited. Reliability refers to the trustworthiness of an instrument in the sense of its **consistency.** An instrument with low reliability is roughly analogous to a yardstick whose inches are of varying sizes or which tends to expand or contract a great deal in different temperatures, and whose measurements therefore differ unpredictably from those of other yardsticks.

Concerning reliability, then, we are not persuaded that a case has been made against classical test theory as it applies to measurement error, although a few adjustments may be appropriate to take account of the necessity to use only **one person's** score rather than a **distribution** of scores in order to arrive at an estimated "true" score for an individual (Brennan, 1974). And, needless to say, the item-analysis techniques often used to inflate internal-consistency coefficients have little or no place in the development of criterion-based measures.

It is necessary, however, to pay some attention to the sample prior to gathering evidence of reliability. In order to show evidence of consistency, the instrument must have at least the opportunity to show **inconsistency.** Thus, a sample should be selected before, rather than following, training. The sample should preferably be of students for whom the test is moderately difficult. The point, of course, is not to demonstrate high reliability by hook or by crook, but to use whatever information can be gathered in order to improve the instrument or to gain confidence in its use.

It would be entirely appropriate, consequently, to present evidence relating to the *STARS* tests' reliabilities in the three conventional senses in which that term is used: namely, that of equivalence (correlation between parallel forms), stability (test–retest), and internal consistency (correlation among parts). An example of such evidence is provided in Table 1.2, which presents internal-consistency data (Kuder–Richardson Formula 20) and related statistics for the phonology section in the Word level of *STARS,* based on the administration of this section to 132 first grade students in four Ann Arbor, Michigan, public schools (data from Fillyaw, 1975).

These data provide evidence that it is possible to achieve substantial reliabilities with rather short tests, and illustrate the somewhat delicate and tenuous

Table 1.2
Internal Consistency and Related Statistics
for Phonology Tests in First Grade (Spring 1974)[a]

Phonology tests[b]	Number of items	Mean score	Variance (SD^2)	Σpq	KR 20[c]
AM 1	6	5.9	.088	.0489	.53
AM 2	6	5.2	1.010	.6000	.49
RHY 3	5	4.6	.704	.3254	.67
ALL 4	5	4.6	.844	.5325	.46
MAT 5	10	9.5	.995	.4152	.65
MAT 6	10	9.4	1.735	.4591	.82
MAT 7	10	9.6	1.350	.2787	.88
WIS 8	8	7.6	.967	.4106	.66
WIS 9	8	7.4	1.405	.5460	.70
SIW 10	20	16.9	10.100	2.1963	.82
SIW 11	20	16.0	9.550	3.0320	.72
JUNC 12	6	5.8	.396	.1722	.68
JUNC 13	6	5.7	.845	.2915	.79
JUNC 14	6	4.5	1.329	.9122	.38
RHY 15	10	8.6	3.510	1.1825	.74
INS 16	10	8.7	2.854	1.1794	.65
SYL 17	10	8.3	3.582	1.3235	.70
SYL 18	10	7.7	3.126	1.5138	.57

[a]Number of students = 132.
[b]See Profile, Word Level, Phonology, p. 7 for test designations (e.g., AM = auditory memory).
[c]KR 20 = Kuder–Richardson Formula 20.

relationships that exist among the various factors that contribute to internal consistency or the lack thereof: number of items, test variance, difficulty level, and the distribution of item difficulties within a test.

Additional data of this type are needed, as well as evidence of stability, equivalence, and the effects on reliability of the innumerable variations that are possible in clustering and grouping of items and tests.

With regard to reliability, two structural properties of *STARS* should be pointed out. The first, mentioned earlier, is the emphasis **in the analytic process** on confining any particular test to **exactly one** critical element in the learning-to-read-and-write process. This was done for several reasons: to ensure the possibility of an unambiguous instructional specification following from the test; to facilitate creation of sampling variations and alternate forms; and simply to make the analysis itself capable of explication. However, the effect of such a strategy contributes as much to reliability as it does to validity. At the same time, it illustrates their interdependence. Confining a test to one kind of item or issue makes it interpretable and consistent, minimizes the number of items required for a reliable measurement, and permits the constraints of content sampling rather than those of measurement error to dictate the length and relative difficulty of the test.

The second of these structural properties that contribute to reliability pertains to the criterion score. A distinction is sometimes made between criterion-referenced tests and **mastery tests.** The latter is a special case of the former, having the added specification of an absolute level of performance on the test that serves as a cutting score, at or above which a student is regarded as having exhibited mastery.

Thus, when the recommended 100% criterion is applied to a student's perfor-mance on a given *STARS* test, a decision may be arrived at and acted upon as to the student's need for additional instruction. The test is then being used as a mastery test.

When this happens, it is possible to view the issue of test reliability (and other aspects of validity) as applying to the **decision process** itself, rather than simply to the test score. In that sense, a test is reliable and valid to the extent that it avoids random and systematic errors of **misclassification**—viewing a student as having mastered something when she or he really has not (Type I error), or viewing the student as having **not** mastered something when, in fact, it has been mastered (Type II error).

A large part of the teacher's strategy in mastery testing is deciding which of these errors is the more costly one to make. If Type I is seen as more costly, the criterion or cutting score will be set high and any judgment of mastery will be relatively certain. On the other hand, if the Type II error is seen as relatively more costly, the criterion will be set low and the judgment of mastery will often give the student the benefit of the doubt.

But this decision cannot be made in a vacuum, because which of the errors is more costly depends on the instructional environment, particularly what consequence follows evidence of nonmastery. The two critical alternatives here are both examples of an individualized learning environment. In one, which we will call the **programmed prescriptive environment**, evidence of nonmastery is followed by specific instruction engineered to take care of the deficit (Individually Prescribed Instruction, Individually Guided Education, Program for Learning in Accordance with Needs, see *EPIE,* 1974). In the other (the **self-shaping** or **adaptive environment** described in detail in Volume 3), evidence of nonmastery is followed by an opportunity on the part of the student to **select,** from a number of instructional resources, one that provides instruction directed toward the deficit in question. Since the teacher's job in the adaptive environment is simply to make good things available to the student and to provide for relevant feedback, it is obvious that the cost of a Type II error is vastly less than it is in the programmed prescriptive environment. In that kind of classroom, in order to avoid overwhelming the child with useless instruction, the teacher must never make the mistake of underestimating his achievement. In the self-selective or self-shaping environment, in a great leap of faith, the teacher assumes that what he or she is dealing with is a student of vast intelligence, who is perfectly capable of deciding to accept an absurd challenge on one day and muddling through something close to trivial on another. Under these conditions, the Type I error is the one to avoid.

But we were talking about reliability! The higher the criterion-score or cutting score used, the higher the reliability of the test in a decision-theoretic sense, simply because one is using more of the information provided. If the 100% criterion is used, one is using **all** the information provided. Such a high criterion is, of course, rather demanding; but there is no cost to the student who makes an error on a test. It is simply information, a chance to work in the area of that skill some more (if desired) and/or to take the test (or a parallel form) again whenever he or she is ready. Are we arguing from psychometry to open educational environments, respect for the student, and lofty achievement aspirations? It certainly seems that way.

Having mentioned reliability as one aspect of psychometric validity, we must return for a moment to the overall outline of this discussion. We are in the middle of a three-part discussion of validity, the parts of which we have called task analytic, psychometric, and systemic, thereby implying that although classical measurement theory is to be largely retained, the conventional categories of validity are to be jettisoned, at least for purposes of this discussion.

Note, for example, that both content and construct validity are included in what we have chosen to call **task analytic** validity. This is not the place to evaluate arguments that all measurement must be construct-referenced (Cronbach, 1971; Messick, 1975) or even to discuss whether reading, per se, or any of its developmental components can rightly be called constructs.

We assert, simply, that from a validation perspective the important thing is not whether letter discrimination or recognition of relational paragraph links **exists,** or, indeed, how much of "it" the student possesses. Rather, the important thing is whether the analysis leading to these and other instructional particulars is or is not the best available specification of components **with reference to** the capacity of an instructional system using the analysis to produce literacy in its clients. The constraints and rewards, in other words, are those associated with engineering, not science; the thing may be profound and elegant, but it has to work.

The set of categories we are using is also an acknowledgment that the traditional set of categories is incomplete. If the use of an instrument—and therefore its quality—depends on a context, an environment, then that context or use-environment must be to some degree specified also (see under Systemic Validity).

Moreover, grouping into one category (psychometric) all forms of validation that in any way involve data analysis is an acknowledgment of both the limitations and the interdependence of all these formal methods. For example, a very common element of test validations is a report of correlations with other measures of the same variable **(concurrent validation).** Table 1.3 presents a set of correlations between raw scores on the *Wide Range Achievement Test (WRAT),* Reading, Level I, and a number of *STARS* tests used as a diagnostic battery in Grade 1 by paraprofessional teachers. The students were all qualified as educationally needful under ESEA Title I guidelines. This is an example of the use of *STARS* as a composite test of reading and writing competencies, in which the score is simply the number of tests passed at the 100% criterion level. The tests used, in this instance, were all at the Letter and Word levels. The maximum number of tests that any student could have attempted was 55. The average number of tests passed by these students was 33.

Since correlations of .63 and .64 had been attained for similar data in 1974

Table 1.3
Correlations of *STARS* Scores with
Wide Range Achievement Test **Scores in First Grade**
(Spring 1975)

	Correlations		
	School A (*N* = 26)	School B (*N* = 14)	School C (*N* = 19)
Product—moment correlations	.61	.66	.48
Significance level	.001	.005	.018

with somewhat larger groups, these can be regarded as characteristic levels. However, these results appear to say more about the *WRAT* than they do about *STARS,* confirming that variations in *WRAT* scores, even at relatively low scoring levels, can be shown to account for more than 40% of the variance in an extremely varied battery of performance tests such as *STARS.*

The difficulty of providing correlational evidence of validity is clearly complicated here by the fact that *STARS* may represent a more comprehensive analysis of the developmental components of literacy than other measures so far available. Thus, there is always the question of which measure is providing the criterion of literacy. Moreover, although it is very simple and convenient to use the 100% criterion and the number or proportion of tests passed as a score, it is nevertheless evident that what *STARS* produces for the user is a **profile of competencies** far more complex and meaningful than any score, no matter how elegantly normed: and that what requires validation, finally, is not a score but the profile itself.

With regard to the profile, then, it is possible to think of validation in at least two directions; **across** the various performance categories (elements of the task analysis), and **within** the categories. Table 1.4, which is actually a series of 37

Table 1.4
Proportions of Students in Two Field-Test Populations
Who Obtained 100% Mastery Scores on *STARS* Tests[a,b,c]

L. 1. Letter Skills: **Shapes**

Population	Grade	Number of students	1	2	3	4	5	6	7	8
GSP (Fall)	1	50	98	93	81	70	66	36	74	74
	K	101–189	96	79	53	51	–	–	27	17
SPP (Spring)	1	98–103	100	99	98	90	78	51	76	73
	2	57– 58	100	100	96	100	91	81	91	95

L. 2. Letter Skills: **Manuscript Form**

Population	Grade	Number of students	1	2	3	4	5	6	7	8	9	10	11	12	13	14
	K	101–189	64	42	41	–	–	–	–	–	–	–	–	–	–	–
SPP (Spring)	1	90	89	71	54	58	52	48	46	43	40	–	–	–	–	–
	2	47	96	81	87	81	85	70	66	55	53	51	45	43	47	45

[a]Proportions in each cell are based on the number of students who took each test.
[b]GSP: general school population; SPP: special projects population.
[c]– indicates that the test was not administered; 0 indicates that none were correct.

continued

L. 3. Letter Skills: Cursive Form

GSP (Fall)	3	51–55	81	47	40	18	17	45	45	36	13	24	0
	4	58–59	100	64	61	29	36	59	81	64	58	56	14

L. 5. Letter Skills: Names

Population	Grade	Number of students	1	2	3	4	5	6	7	8
GSP (Fall)	1	26–50	91	86	80	27	55	38	58	46
	2	49–50	100	100	98	70	92	86	82	54
SPP (Spring)	K	189	61	43	29	13	–	–	–	–
	1	95	94	92	83	67	80	69	67	48
	2	59	100	100	97	97	97	97	92	90

L. 5. Letter Skills: Letter–Sound Equivalents

Population	Grade	Number of students	1	2	3	4	5	6	7	8	9	10	11	12
GSP (Fall)	2	48–51	92	78	35	48	27	27	50	39	22	22	2	6
	3	52–54	98	91	89	94	94	91	91	68	81	85	42	36
SPP (Spring)	1	95	71	48	42	10	11	3	0	–	–	–	–	–
	2	59	93	83	68	37	37	20	17	24	14	12	–	–

L. 6. Letter Skills: Functions

Population	Grade	Number of students	1	2	3	4	5	6
GSP (Fall)	1	50	–	72	68	24	–	–
SPP (Spring)	K	189	–	35	–	–	–	–
	1	98	–	68	57	34	–	–
	2	58	–	93	90	58	–	–

W. 1. Word Skills: Shapes

Population	Grade	Number of students	1	2	3	4	5
GSP (Fall)	1	30	30	20	17	47	0
	3	13	92	92	92	85	23
	4	16	94	100	88	100	19
SPP (Spring)	1	72	40	42	–	–	–
	2	59	68	46	37	39	10

continued

Table 1.4 (continued)

W. 2. Word Skills: Phonology

Population	Grade	Number of students	1	2	3	4	5	6	7	8	9	10	11	12	13	14	15	16	17	18
GSP (Fall)	1	31	52	74	74	77	77	19	81	74	35	—	—	100	90	52	87	42	16	13
	2	48–50	—	—	—	—	—	—	—	—	—	10	19	—	—	—	—	—	—	—
	3	13	85	92	85	100	100	92	100	85	77	27	79	100	100	85	92	77	85	77
	4	16	88	94	88	94	100	88	94	94	81	—	—	94	94	69	94	94	83	94
SPP (Spring)	K	101–189	85	31	34	32	56	51	—	—	—	—	—	—	—	—	—	—	—	—
	1	91	92	49	63	51	63	67	62	49	36	26	11	—	—	—	—	—	—	—
	2	59	90	69	85	85	90	93	93	90	81	49	36	59	53	20	27	25	—	—
GSP (Spring)	1	144	94	55	78	74	69	70	76	77	69	60	33	88	83	20	66	67	31	13

W. 3. Word Skills: Word Recognition

Population	Grade	Number of students	1	2	3	4	5	6	7	8	9	10	11
GSP (Fall)	1	21–22	57	52	45	—	—	—	—	—	—	—	—
	2	11–15	93	93	87	92	82	82	82	36	82	64	73
	3	14	—	—	—	—	93	100	93	71	79	64	57
SPP (Spring)	1	89	54	29	—	—	—	—	—	—	—	—	—
	2	59	81	73	75	36	39	—	—	—	—	—	—

W. 4. Word Skills: Spelling

Population	Grade	Number of students	1	2	3	4	5
GSP (Fall)	1	20–22	18	0	—	—	—
	2	12	91	58	0	0	0
	3	14	64	50	0	0	0
SPP (Spring)	1	72	42	—	—	—	—
	2	59	73	17	—	—	—

W. 5. Word Skills: Syntactic Factor

Population	Grade	Number of students	1	2	3	4	5	6	7	8	9	10	11	12	13
GSP (Fall)	1	17	—	47	53	76	53	—	—	—	—	—	—	—	—
	2	12	—	92	42	92	100	—	17	0	42	8	58	50	8
	3	8–11	100	91	0	73	100	38	27	0	73	27	64	36	18
SPP (Spring)	1	72	33	44	40	36	—	—	—	—	—	—	—	—	—
	2	59	49	69	53	49	54	—	8	—	—	—	—	—	—

continued

W. 6. Word Skills: Vocabulary Range

Population	Grade	Number of students	1	2	3	4	5	6	7	8	9	10	11	12	13	14	15	16	17	18	19	20
GSP (Fall)	3	6–11	17	17	43	29	73	27	9	55	73	55	55	64	45	18	45	9	36	0	0	9
SPP (Spring)	2	59	34	14	8	10	—	—	—	—	—	—	—	—	—	—	—	—	—	—	—	—

W. 7. Word Skills: Semantic Factor

Population	Grade	Number of students	1	2	3	4	5	6	7	8	9
GSP (Fall)	3	8	38	38	0	0	13	0	0	0	8

W. 8. Word Skills: Classification Factor

Population	Grade	Number of students	1	2–12
SPP (Spring)	1	72	72	—
	2	59	15	—

W. 9. Word Skills: Vocabulary Fluency

Population	Grade	Number of students	1	2	3	4	5	6	7
SPP (Spring)	1	72	40	25	—	—	—	—	—
	2	59	36	22	20	10	5	3	—

S. 1. Sentence Skills: Oral Reading

Population	Grade	Number of students	1	2	3
GSP	3	27	67	37	4

S. 2. Sentence Skills: Spaces between Words

Population	Grade	Number of students	1
GSP	3	27	37

S. 4. Sentence Skills: Dictation

Population	Grade	Number of students	1	2	3	4	5	6
GSP	3	27	4	7	4	4	0	0

continued

Table 1.4 (*continued*)

S. 5. Sentence Skills: **Capitalization**

Population	Grade	Number of students	1	2	3	4	5	6	7	8	9	10
GSP	3	27	11	0	0	0	0	0	0	0	0	0

S. 6. Sentence Skills: **Punctuation**

Population	Grade	Number of students	1	2	3	4	5	6–21
GSP	3	27	0	0	0	0	0	

S. 7. Sentence Skills: **Transformation**

Population	Grade	Number of students	1	2	3	4	5	6	7	8	9	10	11	12
GSP	3	12	58	33	25	25	8	8	8	0	8	0	8	0

P. 1. Paragraph Skills: **Form Convention**

Population	Grade	Number of students	1	2
GSP	4	12	75	50
	5	6–7	86	83

P. 2. Paragraph Skills: **Grammatical Patterns**

Population	Grade	Number of students	1	2	3	4
GSP	4	12	33	17	0	0
	5	6	0	0	0	0

P. 3. Paragraph Skills: **Phonological Patterns**

Population	Grade	Number of students	1	2	3	4	5
GSP	4	12	17	50	8	0	33
	5	6–7	43	0	0	0	0

P. 4. Paragraph Skills: **Universe of Discourse**

Population	Grade	Number of students	1	2
GSP	4	11–12	83	73
	5	7	57	29

continued

P. 5. Paragraph Skills: **Topic**

Population	Grade	Number of students	1	2	3	4	5
GSP (Fall)	4	11–12	83	70	55	64	36
	5	7	100	70	43	14	43

P. 6. Paragraph Skills: **Plot**

Population	Grade	Number of students	1	2	3	4	5	6	7	8
GSP (Fall)	4	8–10	50	55	33	25	29	50	30	25
	5	7–6	29	14	43	29	29	17	30	0

P. 7. Paragraph Skills: **Referential Links**

Population	Grade	Number of students	1	2
GSP (Fall)	4	8	37	0
	5	3–5	33	0

P. 8. Paragraph Skills: **Relational Links**

Population	Grade	Number of students	1	2	3	4	5	6
GSP (Fall)	4	8	—	0	—	—	25	12
	5	3–4	—	0	—	—	25	0
	6	22	64	—	27	14	—	—

P. 9. Paragraph Skills: **Information**

Population	Grade	Number of students	1	2	3	4	5	6	7	8	9
GSP (Fall)	4	8	87	75	75	62	37	37	37	62	37
	5	3	100	100	100	67	0	33	0	0	0

P. 10. Paragraph Skills: **Summarization**

Population	Grade	Number of students	1	2	3	4	5
GSP (Fall)	6	23	78	56	17	9	13

continued

Table 1.4 (*continued*)

P. 11. Paragraph Skills: **Induction**

Population	Grade	Number of students	1	2	3	4	5	6
GSP (Fall)	6	17	87	100	70	60	35	18

P. 12. Paragraph Skills: **Deduction**

Population	Grade	Number of students	1	2	3
GSP (Fall)	6	15	80	13	67

P. 13. Paragraph Skills: **Focus**

Population	Grade	Number of students	1	2	3	4	5
GSP (Fall)	6	14	84	50	14	0	0

P. 14. Paragraph Skills: **Point of View**

Population	Grade	Number of students	1	2	3	4
GSP (Fall)	6	13	84	100	100	92

P. 15. Paragraph Skills: **Mood**

Population	Grade	Number of students	1	2	3
GSP	6	12	92	83	33

P. 16. Paragraph Skills: **Oral Reading**

Population	Grade	Number of students	1	2	3	4
GSP (Fall)	6	15	100	86	60	40

tables, presents the data that so far exist pertaining to the difficulty of the various tests at different grade levels, among two different populations.

Knowledge of the relative difficulty of the tests is a powerful means of making the system efficient and capable of practical use: If the sequential dependencies within the structure of competencies can be firmly established, it will not be necessary to administer a large number of tests to an individual in order to construct a reasonably accurate profile of his probable instructional needs. One has simply to make hypotheses about present competencies and to check them by administering measures—each hypothesis becoming more informed and refined than the last, as the "data bank" for an individual student gradually builds.

Table 1.4 contains some gaps, some scarcities of data, and some apparent inconsistencies. Data gaps result from recent production of some of the material and rearrangements of tests based on theoretical or task analytic considerations. Inconsistencies result from the occasional convenience of grouping similar tests rather than ordering them on purely empirical grounds. Any serious and determined user will quickly become familiar both with the general patterns of difficulty reported here and with the ways in which local populations deviate from those patterns.

The cell entries in Table 1.4 are proportions of students who passed the particular test at the 100% criterion level. The abbreviation GSP stands for **general school population**—general because there was no systematic selection of students prior to administration of *STARS,* although obviously the various segments were administered to different numbers of students in a number of different locations. The abbreviation SPP stands for **special projects population**. Students in the latter population were selected for an ESEA Title I program based on educational need and were tested individually by paraprofessional teachers using *STARS* as an integral part of their work with the students.

C. Systemic Validity

How does an evaluator, measurement specialist, or teacher manage a system anchored by *STARS*? The seriousness of this question is attested by some data that, more than anything else we could say, testify to the power and danger of permitting well-designed criterion-based measures into an educational environment.

In 1972 field testing of the Letter level of *STARS* began in a small mid-Michigan community. Performance levels were recorded, and, in 1973, teachers were given the tests and permitted to use them routinely, although no special training or program requirements were imposed.

Table 1.5 shows the difference in end-of-year performance when, as far as we are aware, the only **treatment** difference was the availability of the *STARS* criterion-referenced tests. The percentages indicate the proportions of all tests administered that were passed at the 100% criterion level. The number of students exceeded 50 at each of the three grade levels. The data for the Cursive Form test category are shown in Figures 1.1 and 1.2.

Perhaps this demonstrates only that it is possible to "teach to the test." But if the test represents a valid job-sample (Gagné, 1975), then it shows also that "the power to test is the power to define the curriculum." The curriculum has

Table 1.5
Changes in Percentage of Tests Passed
from 1972 to 1973 with the Introduction of
Criterion-Based Tests of Reading and Writing
(*STARS:* **Letter Level**)

Test category	Number of tests administered	Grade	Percentage of tests passed		Change in percentage
			1972	1973	
1. Letter Shapes	6	1	74	90	+ 16
2. Letter Functions	5	1	62	86	+ 24
3. Letter Naming	8	1	57	85	+ 27
4. Letter–Sound Equivalents	12	3	80	84	+ 4
5. Cursive Form	11	3	33	72	+ 39
6. Cursive Form	11	4	58	94	+ 36

evidently been somewhat adjusted to take account of new performance expectations, which have been defined by the tests, acting as an influence on the attention of teachers and students.

Although the evidence cited is relevant to systemic validity—the capacity of an instrument to become a contributing part of the instructional ecosystem—it does

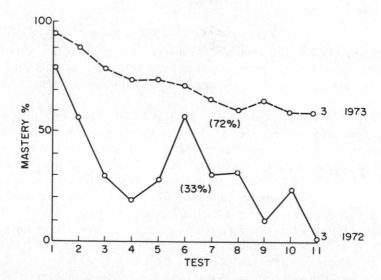

Figure 1.1. Proportion of third grade children who achieved 100% scores on tests of Cursive Form with (1973 data) and without (1972 data) use of criterion-referenced tests.

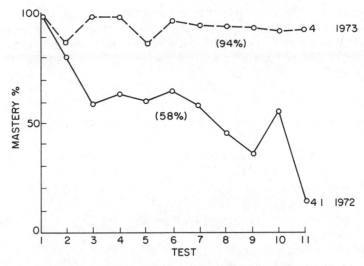

Figure 1.2. Proportion of fourth grade children who achieved 100% scores on tests of Cursive Form with (1973 data) and without (1972 data) use of criterion-referenced tests.

not go very far into the qualitative aspects of the incursion. For example, do the teachers agree that the *STARS* tests represent authentic curricular goals, or are we entering a curricular vacuum in which **any** standards are better than none? Is the change going to continue? Are the teachers searching for better instructional materials now that it is possible to gauge the effects of instruction directly and conveniently? What will happen when the entire set is introduced? Will the testing fall into place easily and gracefully, or will there be a forcible wrenching of priorities? How much information about performance can be used, and how much is too much? How can results be communicated? Who is responsible? Will it mean more work?

Since we have been suggesting that validity is, or should be, both a contextual matter and a matter of consequence, these questions need to be asked and answered in the process of installing a new system or system component such as *STARS.*

It is necessary to acknowledge also that an instrument of such monumental proportions is capable of great disruption if foolishly handled or carelessly installed. Much more needs to be understood about both the hazards and the productive potentials of the system before an adequate procedural manual can be completed.

Enough is known at least to make a number of procedural suggestions, and to propose with some confidence a set of categories with which to consider the issues involved in permitting *STARS* to become part of any instructional environment, whether it involves a student, a class, a school, or a school system.

The following outline will serve to introduce these systemic categories, provide occasions for tentative forays into some areas, and, eventually, shape the distillation of further experience into a more prescriptive explication of system management:

OUTLINE FOR A MANUAL FOR INSTALLING AND MANAGING *STARS*

(*I*) Characterization of the system from a management perspective
    (*A*) Uses and probable outcomes
    (*B*) Methods of use
        (*1*) Tutorial applications
        (*2*) Classroom and building applications
        (*3*) System-wide applications
        (*4*) Project applications
    (*C*) Resources and costs: the nature of the investment
(*II*) Orientation, training, and maintenance
    (*A*) Teacher
    (*B*) Principal
    (*C*) System manager
(*III*) Activity specifications for system managers
    (*A*) Production of materials and inventory control
    (*B*) Training and supervision
    (*C*) Feedback management (child, teacher, principal, central administration, parents)
    (*D*) Evaluation

The following discussion will be guided by the outline given, although, as we have noted, it makes no pretense of being complete. We assume that there are numerous persons and institutions oriented toward and experienced with criterion-based measures of one sort or another and whose energies and creativity are equal to the task of using *STARS* in proper and productive ways—some yet to be invented. They will be the contributors to whatever further specification of *STARS* from a management perspective may be developed.

CHARACTERIZATION OF THE SYSTEM

Uses and Probable Outcomes

Although at this writing no one has had the opportunity to use the entire system, parts of it have been used successfully as—

(*1*) a diagnostic aid to individual tutorial instruction;

(*2*) a device for pacing group instruction in classrooms;

(*3*) a program evaluation instrument in ESEA Title I (process and product);

(*4*) a diagnostic "needs assessment" instrument in ESEA Title I;

(*5*) a diagnostic battery to support instructional planning and the development of individual instructional objectives for students referred to a reading referral service affiliated with the University of Michigan;

(*6*) a research instrument to investigate correlates of auditory discrimination.

The list could be extended somewhat, but the point is that *STARS* can do a number of things that traditional achievement tests can do and a number of things that they cannot do. One item that is not yet on the list is the use of *STARS* as a system-wide accountability instrument. This is perhaps its most impressive potential, although laden with the most systemic or ecological problems as well. A system **adopted** may well be accepted, but a system **imposed** will most certainly be resisted.

All the uses cited can be summarized easily with reference to the character of the information produced. *STARS* produces information about student performance: Which performances (competencies) are present? Which are absent? To what degree? The question of degree **can** be answered comparatively, if that is deemed necessary. But the unique character of the *STARS* information is that the question can be answered in absolute terms. What proportion of the total domain of competencies (or that portion of the total domain appropriate to the student's present age or grade status) is present or absent?

Note that **nowhere** do we specify what that appropriate portion is! To beg the question is, in this instance, not at all cowardly. We simply believe that it is time to end the idolatry of actuarial norms as a way of establishing achievement aspirations in education enterprises. Before a persuasive task analysis appeared, perhaps we **had** to establish goals based on the average performance of a norm group, despite the logical absurdity of hoping that everyone could achieve a grade-level score that, by definition, was higher than that of exactly half the students.

With an operational specification of components, this nonsense is no longer necessary. What **is** necessary is to make two rather fundamental working assumptions. The first is that, although the development of competencies has a perceptible orderliness about it (Table 1.4), nevertheless everyone is different. Each person should do his or her best; no one can judge what that "best" is better than one's self. The second assumption is that the rate at which competencies emerge is at least to some degree dependent upon the quantity and the quality of instruction.

The probable consequences of using *STARS* (assuming good management and supervision, administrative support, communication among participants, and the like) are that students will begin to demolish many of our cherished ideas concerning what is possible and reasonable for them to achieve and teachers will begin to demand better instructional materials referenced to particular competencies and groups of competencies.

Methods of Use

Tutorial applications. A tutorial situation might take many forms: a cross-age tutorial project, a paraprofessional teacher or volunteer in a classroom, or a more clinical situation inside or outside the school. If the student's achievement status is initially unknown, it might be most efficient to administer a quick test such as the *Wide Range Achievement Test* in order to have some notion of where to start. The idea is to generate a **profile** of the students' competencies as quickly as possible so that the teacher will know what kind of instruction to make available. Nevertheless, it is very important **not** to move rigidly through the system or any considerable part of it making a vast catalog of instructional needs for the student. One need only find out **enough to begin the instructional program** and then test periodically to confirm progress and move into other levels and competency categories. Keeping a file gives both teacher and student a convenient way to measure and document gains and productivity. The file can include the profile sheet and tests that show missing competencies and are subsequently passed. In addition, the tests themselves can serve as guides for the generation of ad hoc instructional materials if needed.

Classroom and school applications. In addition to the considerations just listed, classroom and school use require consideration of (1) efficient handling of the testing materials, (2) coverage (everyone? or only those apparently having some problems?), (3) group versus individual use, (4) communication of results, and (5) methods of improving instruction systematically in response to the information produced.

With respect to materials, there are two methods that have been developed so far. The first is that all tests selected for a particular group are collected so that each student has his own "book" of tests. The tests are mastered in order and are removed from the book (and taken home by the child) one at a time. The second method is to keep two file drawers, one for the inventory of tests, and one for student records. Tests can be pulled from the inventory file and used one at a time or in groups as needed. Each test is to be scored immediately; if passed, it is given to the student (and the profile is updated). If not passed, the test is put into the student's file as an indication that instruction is needed. Each of these methods has advantages, but not even the authors agree about which is best. Obviously, if *STARS* is used in several classrooms in a building, keeping a central file from which teachers could draw materials as needed might save some work.

With respect to the issue of coverage, it is clear that *STARS* could be used either as a comprehensive pacing device for all students or as a troubleshooting instrument. One could make an analogy to preventive health care in order to argue for a systematic application of criterion-based measures in order to avoid "trouble." But trouble of the low-performance type is only one kind of problem. Insufficient challenge, boredom, and the lack of instruction tailored to rapid and wide-ranging intellectual growth are others. It might therefore be just as important to test the gifted in order to know what **not** to teach, and to whom not to teach it.

Finally, concerning communication of results, it appears very important to have students participate in the charting of their own progress and productivity (Chapman, 1973). And since everybody thrives on feedback, the principal should get a periodic report on classroom productivity so that he can properly acknowledge the good things that are happening. The measure that has been proposed for doing this is the Classroom Productivity Index (CPI), which is the number of tests passed per child for a given period, such as a month. It is computed by dividing the total number of tests passed during the period by the average daily attendance for the same period.

$$CPI = \frac{\text{Number of tests completed}}{\text{Average daily attendance}}$$

System-wide applications. In addition to the management elements already mentioned, a system-wide application will make possible a centralized method for inventory management. It will also necessitate careful provision for the participation of principals and teachers in the details of their local implementation, as well as another level of the communication of results—from principals to system-level managers or superintendents reporting on building-level productivity.

Our hopes, of course, that attempts to implement *STARS* on a system-wide basis will be confined to districts in which a reasonable level of rapport and political equanimity already exists among building and central-staff people. There are plenty of educational policy issues involved in this kind of enterprise; additional power struggles will doom the system before it starts.

It might be useful to mention also that it is perfectly possible for *STARS* to serve as an instrument for district-wide reading and writing assessment. Probably the best way to do this would be periodically to collect data consisting of the total number of mastery levels or competencies achieved by individual students, and to average these results for schools and for the total district. Once such a procedure is started, it is possible to compare rates of productivity for different years, and to generate local norms such as "standard scores" in order to display results clearly and even to compare results with other districts.

Project applications. The unique aspects of funded projects clearly fit very well with the unique aspects of a criterion-based assessment system. Although many funded-project evaluation formats still encourage the use of the long obsolete Grade Equivalent Score, there is a growing acceptance of reports based on the proportion of objectives attained. These reports will be much more acceptable to funding agencies if they are based on published instruments with known properties rather than on locally developed measures. Perhaps more important, it is now possible to use the same instrument, or some parts of it, for all the common uses of evaluation in projects—for needs assessment (identifying target populations), for diagnostic purposes pursuant to planning instruction, and for program evaluation and reporting of results. And it may be that a funded project could serve the district of which it is a part by demonstrating the viability of an instrument that has the potential of contributing to the overall quality of the district's services to students.

Resources and Costs: The Nature of the Investment

There are three points to be made here. First, the resources of the local school or district can be used to minimize the cost of installing *STARS*. Rather than purchasing large amounts of printed material, the user purchases a master set of materials and the rights of reproduction. Alternatively the school or district can produce its own version so that the printing can be handled within the school system or by local printers. For school systems with their own offset printing capabilities, this is a tremendous saving (approximately $50/pupil per year).

Second, secondary costs such as instructional materials necessitated by the exposure of competency deficits defined by *STARS* are a better investment than instructional materials usually are, simply because there is some assurance that they will be used for a purpose specifically related to achievement output, which can be measured. The same principle holds, of course, for the utilization of school staff insofar as they will tend to be somewhat more under the control of events related to measured learning and somewhat better able to provide evidence of their productivity.

Third, a compelling argument can be made that the vulnerability of educational agencies to reductions in public expenditures for education, to rejections of ballot bond issues, and the like, is related to the difficulty of providing persuasive evidence that such agencies are doing more than simply maintaining themselves. More specific and more powerful output measures than the usual actuarial comparisons are certain in the long run to provide means whereby schools and school systems can improve their services and thereby establish themselves in a more secure and respected place in the estimation of their fellow citizens.

ORIENTATION, TRAINING, AND MAINTENANCE

Training materials to accompany *STARS* are not yet available (with certain exceptions: See Chapter 2) but such materials constitute only one of several deficits that must be remedied for successful system use. One does not simply drop a thing of the dimensions of *STARS* onto the teacher's (or principal's) desk and expect anything good to happen. There are a number of installation dimensions that must not be left to chance. Some of these involve administrative aspects, such as materials, time schedules, and communication. Others cut deeply into educational policy and strategy. These relate to such matters as the degree of change *STARS* would necessitate in the ways goals are currently defined and measured, the degree of openness in the environment with respect to the use of materials, and grading practices and other methods of feedback to students. The training issue, in other words, is not that things have necessarily to be done in a certain way, but that all the really important dimensions of the installation of a new component have to be **considered.** The whole operation must be carried out with awareness of the meaning of the technology, and awareness of how it can be made an obedient servant of overall educational objectives.

The word *maintenance* in the title of this section refers to the maintenance of behavior and to the fact that training and orientation in the use of criterion-based measures will be effective only to the extent that provision is made either for external reinforcement or for self-shaping. The latter is, of course, much to be preferred.

ACTIVITY SPECIFICATIONS FOR SYSTEM MANAGERS

These specifications should appear separately as "job aids" to provide for the complexities of the task of facilitating the use of *STARS* by a number of teachers in a more or less coordinated effort, whether this involves adoption of the system by a school, a group of schools, a funded program, or a school district. Presumably a person appointed to take responsibility for the proper installation of the system would serve as a resource person for others and would set up the necessary mechanisms. The specifications themselves will consist of outlines of orderly actions ensuring that the necessary materials are in the right place at the right time, that orientation and training sessions are held for all participants, that feedback provisions are made and monitored, and that some form of supervision occurs, of the sort that provides an occasion for teachers to share and get solutions for whatever difficulties and discontinuities result from the installation of a new component.

* * * * *

This discussion of systemic validity has included so many caveats that one might conclude the system should not be used. To contradict that impression, we include, in the next chapter of this book, a teacher's manual that evolved over 3 years of developmental use of *STARS*. It includes brief sections on how the system may be used by superintendents and principals.

REFERENCES

Beutler, S. A. *Results from a criterion-referenced test model.* Unpublished Ph.D. dissertation, University of Michigan, 1974.

Brennan, R. L. *Some potential uses of decision–theoretic (confidence) testing in the analysis of criterion-referenced item data.* Paper presented at the annual meeting of the American Educational Research Association, Chicago, April 1974.

Carroll, J., Davies, P., & Richman, B. *Word frequency book.* New York: American Heritage and Houghton Mifflin, 1971.

Chapman, R. E. *Evaluation as feedback in innovative school programs.* Ph.D. dissertation, University of Michigan, 1973. (Univ. Microfilm No. *34,* 1472A, 1974.)

Coleman, E. B. Collecting a data base for a reading technology. *Journal of Educational Psychology Monograph,* 1970, *61,* (4, Pt. 2).

Cronbach, L. J. Test validation. In R. L. Thorndike (Ed.), *Educational measurement* (2nd ed.). Washington, D.C.: American Council on Education, 1971.

Davis, F. B. (Ed.), *The literature of research in reading with emphasis on models.* East Brunswick, New Jersey: Iris Corp., 1971.

EPIE: Educational Product Report. No. 58, Evaluating Instructional Systems. New York: Educational Products Exchange Institute, 1974.

Fillyaw, H. *Ecological correlates of auditory discrimination.* Unpublished Ph.D. dissertation, University of Michigan, 1975.

Gagné, R. M. Observing the effects of learning. *Educational Psychologist,* 1975, *11,* 144–157.

Glaser, R. Instructional technology and the measurement of learning outcomes: Some questions. *American Psychologist,* 1963, *18,* 519–521.

Guilford, J. P. *Psychometric methods.* New York: McGraw-Hill, 1954.

Guttman, L. Integration of test design and analysis. *Proceedings of the 1969 Invitational Conference on Testing Problems.* Princeton, New Jersey: Educational Testing Service, 1969.

Hively, W. An introduction to domain-referenced testing. *Educational Technology,* in press.

Horn, V. Using connectives in elementary composition. *English Langauge Teaching,* 1972, *26,* 154–159.

Katz, J., & Fodor, J. The structure of a semantic theory. *Language,* 1963, *30,* 170–210.

MacDonald, R. *Analysis of intelligence scores.* ERIC Document Reproduction Service No. EDO62016-71.

A manual of style (12th ed.). Chicago: University of Chicago Press, 1969.

Marshall, J., & Powers, J. *Correlates of achievement: Prediction and cross-validation for intermediate grade levels.* ERIC Microfiche, No. EDO64377.

Messick, S. The standard problem: Meaning and value in measurement and evaluation. *American Psychologist,* 1975, *30,* 955–966.

Millman, J. Criterion-referenced measurement. Prepublication draft, Cornell University, 1974.

Morrison, H. C. *The practice of teaching in the secondary school.* Chicago: University of Chicago Press, 1926, 1931.

Nunnally, J. C. *Psychometric theory.* New York: McGraw-Hill, 1967.

Osborne, J. B., & Lindsey, J. *A longitudinal investigation of change in the factorial composition of intelligence with age in young school children.* ERIC Document Reproduction Service No. EDO26149-65.

Pike, K. L., & Pike, E. *Grammatical analysis.* Santa Ana, California: Summer Institute of Linguistics, 1973.

Popham, W. J. *Measurement advances for educational evaluators.* Paper presented at the annual meeting of the American Educational Research Association, Chicago, April 1974.

Popham, W. J., & Husek, T. R. Implications of criterion-referenced measurement. *Journal of Educational Measurement,* 1969, *6,* 1–9.

Singer, H. *Substrata-factor reorganization accompanying development in speed and power of reading at the elementary school level.* U.S. Department of Health, Education, and Welfare, Office of Education, Cooperative Research Project 2011, 1965.

Smith, D. E. P., & Smith, J. M. *The Michigan language program.* New York: Random House, 1975.

Spearman, C. E. *The abilities of man: Their nature and measurement.* New York: AMS Press, 1970.

Vineyard, E., & Massey, H. The interrelationship of certain linguistic skills and their relationship with scholastic achievement when intelligence is ruled constant. *Journal of Educational Psychology,* 1957, *48,* 279–286.

Wide Range Achievement Test. Wilmington, Delaware: Guidance Associates, 1965.

Young, R., Becker, A., & Pike, K. *Rhetoric: Discovery and change.* New York: Harcourt, Brace, & World, 1970.

USE OF THE TESTS:
A TEACHER'S MANUAL

I. Teacher's Use

The *STARS* tests are used like any teacher-made tests—at the end of a unit, or on a particular day every week, or however the teacher sees fit. The primary difference between *STARS* tests and teacher-made tests is the requirement of a perfect score before the child takes the next test in a particular series.

A. *Procedure*

- Each child has a TEST BOOKLET with a PROGRESS CHART in the front.
- The teacher has a TEST BOOKLET with all directions and a LANGUAGE ARTS COMPETENCY PROFILE for each child.

(*1*) The first test in each series can be given a whole class. Read the directions and **do whatever is necessary to be sure children understand what they are to do.**

(*2*) Circulate among the children to score the papers. This procedure provides immediate feedback and guards against the piling up of tests.

STARS PROGRESS CHART

GRADE

	K	1	2	3	4	5	6
LETTER SKILLS							
MATCHING	1 2 3 4	5 6					
ALPHABET	1 2	3 4 5					
MANUSCRIPT WRITING	1 2 3	4 5 6 7 8 9 / 10 11 12 13 14					
NAMING	1 2	3 4 5 / 6 7 8					
LETTER-SOUND		1 2 3 4	5 6 7 / 8 9 10	11 12			
CURSIVE WRITING				1 2 3 4 / 5 6 7 8	9 10 11		
WORD SKILLS							
MATCHING		1 2 3 4	5				
AUDITORY SKILLS	1 2 3 4	5 6 7 8 / 9 10 11	12 13 14 / 15 16	17 18			
WORD RECOGNITION		1 2	3 4 5	6 7 8	9 10 11		
SPELLING		1	2	3	4	5	
VOCABULARY — RANGE			1 2 3 4	5 6 7 / 8 9	10 11 12	13 14 15 16	17 18 19 20
VOCABULARY — SEMANTIC FACTOR	1	2			3 4 5 6 / 7 8 9 10	11	
VOCABULARY — CLASSIFICATION FACTOR			1	2 3 4	5 6 7 8	9 10 11	
VOCABULARY — SYNTACTIC FACTOR	1	2 3 4	5	6 7 8	9 10	11	
VOCABULARY — FLUENCY		1 2 3	4 5 6	7			

(*3*) Scoring:

Arm yourself with a colored pencil and your Competency Profile folder.

(*a*) If a paper is perfect,

(*i*) Write 100% at the top.

(*ii*) Put a small check mark (✓) in the corresponding box on the child's progress chart.

(*iii*) Have the child black in the box immediately, tear out the perfect test, and take it home.

(*iv*) Note completion in the correct box on the Competency Profile.

(*b*) If a paper is not perfect,

(*i*) Indicate **number of items correct** at the top.[1]

(*ii*) Instruct as necessary.

(*iii*) Provide another opportunity for the child to take the test when he or she seems ready.

(*4*) Notes:

In all test series, the order of the tests should be changed to fit the curriculum.

MATCHING LETTERS

Three kinds of errors occur. The child may—

(*1*) circle the wrong letter;

(*2*) find only one letter when he should find two, or find the right letter on the wrong line;

(*3*) skip a whole item.

All these are viewed as **errors** (rather than carelessness).

MANUSCRIPT WRITING

Writing spaces include a gray zone on baseline and topline. Consider the baseline and topline to be the total width of the gray zone. If the child's letter is within the zone, it is viewed as satisfying the topline, baseline standard.

[1] The **number correct** tells the child how close he or she is to the goal.

LETTER–SOUND EQUIVALENCE

Order tests to reflect the curriculum.

B. Diagnosis

Most children will progress easily from test to test. When a performance problem occurs, however, it will tend to be either—

(*1*) a particular **response deficit,** common to several children (such as the *b–d* distinction); or

(*2*) a general **performance deficit,** specific to a very few children who seem to expect to fail.

RESPONSE DEFICITS

When scoring, you will notice that particular items will be missed by more than one child. For example, in Naming Letters, Test 8, 44% of first grade children in one school district failed to name the letter *b* correctly. Other problem letters were *t* (36%), *g* (32%), *d* (28%), and *q* (24%).

Furthermore, while 44% of first graders miscalled *b*, 40% of second graders also miscalled it. Such response deficits can be handled by special instruction.

PERFORMANCE DEFICITS

About three or four children in each classroom may demonstrate a performance deficit. These children, often called **learning disabled,** seem unable to complete a worksheet without error. Continued instruction seems to be of little use. When the target response is finally learned, another response seems to slip away, to be forgotten.

Although instruction needs to be available to such children, instruction alone is not enough. The essential technique is to **maintain the standard.** The child's paper is returned with the number correct written at the top. The child **may not advance** to another test in the **same series** until he achieves 100%. He may well act out—cry, tear up papers, even shout obscenities. These angry behaviors are best ignored. The teacher should remain obdurate and impassive. Eventually, the child will succeed. Thereafter he will require fewer and fewer tries before succeeding.

C. Prescriptions

Some tasks can be taught **directly**—for example, the height of the beginning stroke in cursive *p*. Other tasks are most efficiently handled **indirectly,** by systematic instruction in fundamental skills. For example, hearing beginning sounds in words is dependent on training in attending to words. Similarly, carelessness in identifying particular letters often results from inadequate training in attention to letters generally.

PERCEPTUAL TRAINING

Numerous learning and behavior problems result partly from deficits in perceptual training:

- "You aren't paying attention. How many times must I say the page number?"
- "Stephen, stop pestering Joe. Pay attention to your own paper."
- "*Poetic,* Susan, not *prehistoric.* All you looked at were the *p* and the *ic.* Look at the middle letters!"

These and many other problems are due, at least in part, to **attentional deficits.** They are best handled by systematic training in letter and sound discrimination. Often higher-level skills follow spontaneously. At any rate, instruction in higher-level skills is largely wasted when basic skills are missing. (See Geake & Smith, 1975; Smith & Smith, 1975a, 1975b; J. M. Smith, 1973.)

PRESCRIPTIVE TEACHING: TECHNIQUES

LETTER MATCHING

Problems:
- Finds one letter but overlooks the next one.
- Finds the right letter on the wrong line.

Reason:
Insufficient familiarity with letters in general ("primitive," "young," "perceptually retarded").

Correction:
(*1*) Search tasks:
"Find all the small *a*'s on this story page. Circle each one. There are 17 *a*'s." (Tomorrow, count all the *b*'s, etc. After the alphabet is completed, find two letters at a time—*a* and *o, c* and *e,* etc.).
(*2*) Individualized self-instruction:
Grades K, 1: *Letter Mastery* (J. M. Smith, 1973)
Grades 2+: *Visual Tracking* (Geake & Smith, 1975)

Problem:

- Confuses *h* : *n; i* : *l; d* : *a.*

Reason:

Length of vertical line (*l* : *i*).

Correction:

(1) Search tasks:

"Here is a row of *d*'s and *a*'s. Circle all the *d*'s."

Problem:

- Confuses *d* : *b; p* : *q.*

Reason:

Unique identity of *d* and *b, p* and *q* depends on a space cue: "It's *d* **because** the circle is toward the margin." A space cue is not necessary to the identity of *K* or *X* or *m* (Ʞ, x, m: a backwards Ʞ is still a *K*; a backwards *d* is a *b*).

Correction:

(1) Language of space relationships:

Page: Margin, top, bottom

Direction: Toward, away from, up, down (vertical)

"What is a *d*?"

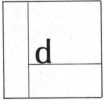

A *d* is a circle and a stick.

The stick is up and down.

The circle is at the bottom of the stick.

The circle is toward the margin.

(2) Search tasks:

"Find all *d*'s on this page. There are 12."

(3) Next, "What is a *b*?" etc., as for *d*.

Problem:

•   Letter matching skill is erratic: able to do tasks one day, but not the next.

Reason:

Discriminative skill is quite specific. Identifying the *d* in *dad* is not the same as identifying the *d* in *Sandy.* The letter must be found in a large variety of contexts.

Correction:

Search tasks (see preceding problems).

ALPHABET MASTERY

Problem:

•   When saying the alphabet:
leaves out *m, n*
reverses *m, n*
leaves out *u*
reverses *w, v*

Reason:

A letter is noticed if it has meaning.

Letters have little or no meaning within the alphabet—*"l-m-n-o"* tends to be said as one letter.

A letter becomes unique when there is a **payoff** for recognizing its **shape** or its **name.** For example, if I must find the letters of the alphabet **in order** within a paragraph, as in the one that follows, and I'm clocking myself—and if I miss one, I must start over—**then every letter becomes unique.**

Correction:[2]

a b c d e f g h i j k l m n o p q r s t u v w x y z.

Ifligger mort newqapto iblix morsn tstp flopi morcner.
Iglox ponur hloffdon strik hloffe ris zmo loox pliggirs.
Rafbag mort baqc trakt. Mort Klappi horatis ignori.
Dextro rotatre, obnojo mort dbra, rstv op oppa aklappa.
Grag ponur mortn dextr rexa zmo iffer diswit ponur hied ibbi.
Jeggle ijiffle abaced. Jakkeg Hiffle, hegda bced ieqb efrl.
Mini nowg klosspo. Oattle, nojjie foag baed nokel iunten ixv.
Fliwer reprixco ipyaz.

Min____ Sec____

Within **20** paragraphs of this sort, most children learn to say the alphabet perfectly.

[2] Reprinted, with permission, from *Visual tracking,* by R. Geake & D. E. P. Smith, 1975, p. 36.

69

Problems:
- Unable to order the alphabet without use of wall charts.
- Unable to draw letters in order without use of wall charts.

Reason:

The task is similar to memorizing a list of 26 numbers.

Correction:

Use **backward programming,** also called **mathetics.**

> Finish the alphabet:
> 1. *a b c d e f g h i j k l m n o p q r s t u v* _ _ _ _
> 2. *a b c d e f g h i j k l m n o p q r s t u* _ _ _ _ _

> Collect this

> 3. *a b c d e f g h i j k l m n o p q r s t* _ _ _ _ _ _
> 4. *a b c d e f g h i j k l m n o p q r* _ _ _ _ _ _ _ _
> And so on.

The child is allowed to look back for missing letters, but looking back must be made arduous. For example, you might take alphabet cards **starting at the end** (first *x y z;* then *u v w,* etc.) and mount them behind a door. The child must go to the door to find the next letter.

LETTER NAMING

Problem:

- Knows all letters except: *b, d, p, q, g, l, t*

Reason:

These are the most confusable letters because of their similarity in appearance to other letters:

$$b : d; p : q; g : q; l : i; t : f$$

Correction:

Naming depends on both:

- clear visual discrimination of letters
- clear auditory discrimination of letter names

Therefore,

(*1*) Use prescriptions for Letter Matching:
   (*a*) search tasks;
   (*b*) *Visual Tracking* (Geake & Smith, 1975)

(*2*) Provide auditory discrimination training:
   (*a*) Listening 1, *Michigan Language Program* (Smith & Smith, 1975b)

Problem:
  •   Knows very few letter names.

Reason:
      Letter naming is the best predictor there is for success in reading (better than IQ scores). Children lack a **storage procedure,** so that letter names can be pulled out at will.

Correction:
  (*1*) Each child learns—
        (*a*) to recognize
        (*b*) to spell
        these key words:

cat	*bell*	*zebra*
tree	*box*	*fish*
man	*dog*	*wave*
jet	*queen*	*key*
gun	*pie*	

      The child must have two responses to each word—

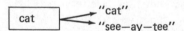

      Now, anytime he needs to name the letter *t,* he will think to himself, "*t* → cat → see—ay—tee → tee!"
  (*2*) Self-instruction: *DIDAC* (Smith & Smith, 1975b)

PRESCRIPTIVE TEACHING: EVALUATING MATERIALS

Commercially prepared materials can be evaluated using *STARS*. Two kinds of value can be determined:

(*1*) Effectiveness: number of tests passed, attributable to using materials.
(*2*) Cost: dollar cost of using those materials, based on price of the materials, cost of student time, and cost of teacher time.

Example

In a first grade class, the five lowest children were found deficient in Letter Matching.

Child	Tests Passed	Tests Failed
A	0	6
B	3	3
C	5	1
D	5	1
E	4	2

The children were trained using *Letter Mastery* booklets (J. M. Smith, 1973). Then they were tested again.

Child	Tests Passed	Training Time (minutes)	Tests Passed	Gain
A	0	90	6	6
B	3	90	6	3
C	5	90	6	1
D	5	90	6	1
E	4	90	6	2
		Teacher time = 75 minutes		13

Effectiveness is determined by:

(1) the number of tests passed (13);
(2) the percentage of mastery achieved:

$$\frac{\text{Average obtained}}{\text{Average possible}} = \frac{6.0}{6.0} = 100\%$$

Cost is determined as follows:

Price:	$0.75 (each) × 5 (children)	=	$3.75
Teacher time:	$10.00/hour × $1\frac{1}{4}$ hours	=	$12.50
Student time:	$2.00/hour × $7\frac{1}{2}$ hours	=	$15.00
		Total	$31.25

Therefore:

Effectiveness:	13 units or mastery
Cost:	$31.25
Cost/effectiveness:	$31.25/13 = $2.40/unit

The procedure yields an estimate of instructional cost—with these limitations:

(*1*) Instruction may affect achievement positively on other tests so that unit cost should be lower than it appears (e.g., Reading Letters 1 and 2 (Smith & Smith, 1975a) was used to teach Letter Naming at a unit cost of $1.64, even though it is designed only to teach Letter Matching.)

(*2*) The teacher's contribution may be considerable, either positively or negatively. In the data reported here, teachers were told, "Make the materials work. Do whatever you have to. Then report your modifications along with the data."

(*3*) Teachers may use materials to teach the wrong skill (as Reading Letters 1 and 2, just mentioned). If so, the reported unit cost may do a disservice to the materials.

About 20 titles have been evaluated to date. Those that have proved effective are listed in Table 2.1.

II. Superintendent's Use

The *STAR* System is an instructional aid for teachers and an accountability system for both principals and superintendents. The procedure used by the principal of each school yields a Classroom Productivity Index (CPI) for each classroom at each marking period (or each month).

$$CPI = \frac{\text{Number of tests completed}}{\text{Average daily attendance}} = \text{Number of tests per child}$$

Each principal computes a CPI for each classroom. The superintendent then requests a report from each school specifying the following:

(*1*) average CPI for the school;
(*2*) average CPI for each grade; or
(*3*) CPI for each teacher.

The first and second CPI would be most useful. The third is of concern to the principal.

Table 2.1

Cost Effectiveness of Instructional Materials[a]

Title	Publisher	Price	Number of children	Grade[b]	Mean mastery	Cost per unit of achievement	Notes
			LETTER MATCHING				
Letter Mastery, 1973	Tri-level	$ 0.75	5	1 (L)	100%	$2.40	Teacher taught. Supervision should be unnecessary.
Visual Tracking	Tri-level	1.40	5	2 (L)	100	3.80	
Symbol Tracking, 1967	Tri-level	1.40	5	1 (L)	70	3.61	Designed to train auditory memory.
Phonics Work-book A	Modern Curriculum Press	1.25	6	2 (L–H)	100	1.24	Selected pages, used self-instructionally.
			LETTER NAMING				
Reading Letters 1&2, Michigan Language Program	Random House	1.30 1.30	2	1 (L)	100	1.64	Teacher had children say names.
Alpha Boards	Educational Developmental Laboratories	45.00	6	1,2,3 (L)	100	3.62	Reusable; 3-year depreciation.

[a]These materials were also evaluated:

Letter Matching
  Read System, American Book Co. (1 study, 6 students)
Letter Naming
  Letter Names and Sounds, Craig Corp. (difficult letters missing: *b,d,p,q,f,h,j,g*)
Alphabet Mastery
  Manuscript Chart, Zaner-Bloser Co. (2 studies, 12 students)
  Primary Tracking, Ann Arbor Publishers (1 study, 4 students)
Cursive Writing
  Zaner-Bloser Program, Zaner-Bloser Co (1 study, 8 students)

[b]L, low group; H, high group.

continued

Table 2.1 (*continued*)

ALPHABET MASTERY

(Three options were evaluated; none were successful.)

Title	Publisher	Price	Number of children	Grade[b]	Mean mastery	Cost per unit of achievement	Notes
Signposts Wkbk.	Houghton Mifflin	.96	5	1 (H)	40	1.36	See p. 202.
Rainbow Teacher Edition	Houghton Mifflin	2.55	5				See pp. 9, 20, 23, 35, 50, 68, 72, 98, 108, 110.

LETTER–SOUND EQUIVALENCE

Title	Publisher	Price	Number of children	Grade[b]	Mean mastery	Cost per unit of achievement	Notes
Phonics Is Fun	Modern Curriculum Press	1.50	6	2 (H)	100	4.27	See pp. 25, 26, 28, 35, 33, 34, 9, 10, 49, 80, 125–127, 129, 136, 124.
Speech to Print Phonics	Harcourt Brace Jovanovich	32.00	9	4 (L)	0	2.56	Too elementary for Grade 4.

CURSIVE WRITING

Title	Publisher	Price	Number of children	Grade[b]	Mean mastery	Cost per unit of achievement	Notes
Basal Series Grade 3	Bobbs-Merrill	3.63	6	3 (L)	0	2.00	

III. Principal's Use

By following a simple recording procedure, the principal can keep track of the productivity of each classroom. He is in a position to provide recognition for improved achievement and to supply help for classrooms in trouble. Thus, the principal's role is to provide **feedback on success** and **resource material and services.**

LANGUAGE ARTS RECORD

GRADE   TEACHER   SCHOOL:_____   MARKING PERIOD_____

MARKING PERIOD

	Initial	I	2	3	4
TOTAL UNITS:	_____	___	___	___	___
CUMULATIVE UNITS:	_____				

A. Procedure

At regular intervals, each month or each marking period, the teachers are asked to report on student achievement. The report consists of two numbers:

(*1*) Total number of tests completed during the interval, e.g., number of tests = 170

(*2*) Average daily attendance for the interval, e.g., average daily attendance = 24.2

From these data, a clerk can compute the CPI, the Classroom Productivity Index:

$$\text{CPI} = \frac{\text{Number of tests}}{\text{Average daily attendance}} = \frac{170}{24.2} = 7.0 \quad \begin{array}{l}\text{(Number of tests per child,}\\\text{per marking period)}\end{array}$$

Each classroom achievement report is recorded on the school's Language Arts Record (see page 77).

References

Geake, R., & Smith, D. E. P. *Visual tracking* (rev. ed.) Ferndale, Michigan: Tri-Level Educational Materials, 1975.

Smith, D. E. P., & Smith, J. M. *DIDAC.* New York: Random House, 1975. (a)

Smith, D. E. P., & Smith, J. M. *The Michigan language program.* New York: Random House, 1975. (b)

Smith, J. M. *Letter mastery.* Ferndale, Michigan: Tri-Level Educational Materials, 1973.

STandard Achievement Recording System

STARs

Criterion-referenced Tests
of
Reading·Writing·Listening·Speaking
for
Grades K–6

1976 REVISION

Donald E. P. Smith & Judith M. Smith
The University of Michigan

developed by ED-VENTURES, inc.
Chelsea, Michigan

Name _____

LETTERS

PERCEPTUAL ASPECTS

Letter Shapes

Directions
Sample Pg-6

This set of tests contains six separate tests of letter discrimination. The tests are of increasing difficulty, the simplest being Test 1. In addition, there is a sample page on which children are taught to make the required response for this type of test. This page is not scored.

Following the six matching tests are two more, testing capital letter-lower case equivalence.

TEACHER:

<u>Sample Page:</u>

Find the line at the top. It says <u>name</u> next to the line.
Write your name on the line.   (pause)

Find number 1.   Point to it.   (Survey the room to see that all students are pointing to 1.) What is the letter next to number 1?.....Yes, it is O.   Next to the O are some dots.   Follow the dots with your finger until you come to a box with letters in it.   Point to the box.   There are some O's in the box, too.   How many can you find?....Yes, 2.   Finish the circle around each O.

Now find number 2.   Point to the letter next to number 2.   Follow the dots to the box ...How many times did you find it this time?   Yes, just once.   Draw a circle around it.

Find number 3.....Point to the letter.....Find the box.....Circle the letter. How many times did you find it?

Tests 1-6: Find the line at the top and write your name.   Find number 1 and point to it.   Look at the letter next to the number.   Point to it.   Follow the dots. Circle the same letter as many times as you find it there.   Sometimes you will find it once.   Sometimes you will find it two times.   Go on and finish the page by yourself.

Name _____

LETTERS

PERCEPTUAL ASPECTS

Letter Shapes

Sample
Page

1 O .... 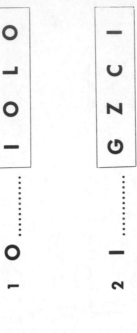 I O L O

2 I .... G Z C I

3 X .... X S X O

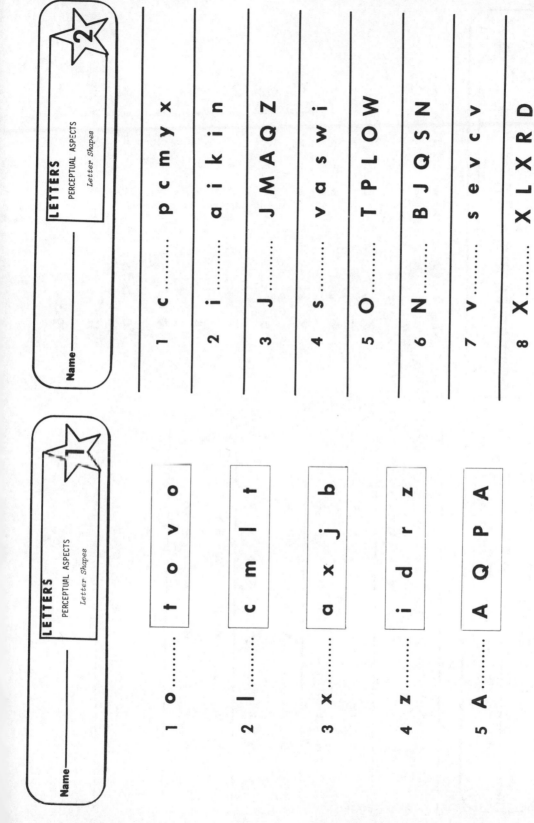

Name _____

2

1 c .... p c m y x

2 i .... a i k i n

3 J .... J M A Q Z

4 s .... v a s w i

5 O .... T P L O W

6 N .... B J Q S N

7 v .... s e v c v

8 X .... X L X R D

Name _____

1

1 o .... | t o v o |

2 l .... | c m l t |

3 x .... | a x j b |

4 z .... | i d r z |

5 A .... | A Q P A |

4

1	z	M	A	Z	T	X	O
2	m	a	m	e	r	v	u
3	y	p	w	c	b	y	l
4	e	e	o	x	e	r	s
5	s	c	S	R	W	S	G
6	d	d	k	g	y	m	i
7	U	P	D	E	U	V	J
8	t	x	l	k	d	s	t
9	g	s	p	g	k	g	v
10	u	v	u	l	m	i	u
11	L	L	D	T	Q	V	M
12	h	e	d	y	h	p	n

3

1	r	t	a	r	l	k	w
2	c	c	C	K	W	Z	T	L
3	j	s	h	c	j	z	t
4	a	i	a	m	x	a	z
5	P	A	L	W	O	N	P
6	k	n	a	p	k	o	s
7	Q	Y	A	Q	W	H	F
8	I	D	I	M	I	S	Q
9	w	e	l	w	s	a	w
10	T	D	T	G	S	T	D

82

Worksheet 5

Name _____

LETTERS

PERCEPTUAL ASPECTS

Letter Shapes

★ 5

1. s . . . . w c l e x s v
2. i . . . . o i a l d t m
3. f . . . . f b k h f x y
4. v . . . . A B V O N T l
5. a . . . . j o m a y k d
6. r . . . . k t n i c x r
7. Y . . . . Y Q A P S W E
8. c . . . . i c x o s c e
9. b . . . . y h k a t o b
10. n . . . . g p n v n k r
11. q . . . . c a q t g m
12. w . . . . w s m e v p d
13. k . . . . c b i k t x k
14. y . . . . v c y s b k j
15. j . . . . h j a i j y t

Worksheet 6

Name _____

LETTERS

PERCEPTUAL ASPECTS

Letter Shapes

★ 6

1. K . . . . . . A X Y K T H F Z
2. t . . . . . . f t x l i k t j
3. D . . . . . . O B D P Q C R G
4. d . . . . . . d p b g a q h
5. n . . . . . . m h u a r n h w
6. q . . . . . . q d p g b y a j
7. B . . . . . . P E R S D B B R
8. G . . . . . . C O D G O c h G
9. b . . . . . . p b d q q k o
10. f . . . . . . l x s j r k f
11. R . . . . . . P R B A D R K H
12. E . . . . . . F F H l E T R L
13. g . . . . . . b p g d q h g j
14. F . . . . . . T E J F H A L E
15. u . . . . . . m n o a v w u
16. H . . . . . . E F H i E H R L
17. P . . . . . . d g y P b y
18. w . . . . . . Y N W V Y W Z M
19. h . . . . . . n b r m u z d t h
20. M . . . . . . V W W Y N Z L M

LETTERS

PERCEPTUAL ASPECTS

Letter Shapes

(equivalents)

Name

Teacher: "Circle the capital letter that goes with the small letter."

1. p ...... D   B   P   R
2. c ...... O   C   U   Q
3. w ...... W   N   M   Y
4. o ...... D   Q   C   O
5. u V   J   U   Y
6. f ...... R   K   H   F
7. i L   I   T   K
8. x X   K   Y   Z
9. s ...... J   B   S   G
10. j C   G   J   L
11. y V   W   K   Y
12. t ...... F   T   J   I
13. z ...... Z   N   M   Y
14. v ...... Y   V   W   U
15. k V   X   Y   K

LETTERS

PERCEPTUAL ASPECTS

Letter Shapes

(equivalents)

Name

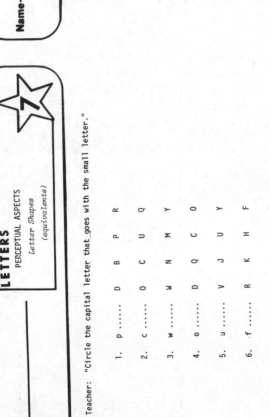

Teacher: "Circle the small letter that goes with the capital letter."

1. J ...... r   y   j   t
2. T x   l   h   t
3. H ...... b   h   k   r
4. E ...... e   f   t   l
5. A v   y   a   r
6. I ...... t   d   i   n
7. M ...... w   y   n   m
8. Q ...... d   q   c   o
9. R ...... r   h   w   n
10. B ...... p   b   g   f
11. N ...... y   z   v   n
12. L ...... t   v   l   k
13. G c   g   o   e
14. D ...... d   a   p   r
15. F ...... t   k   l   f

LETTERS

PERCEPTUAL ASPECTS

Manuscript Form

Directions Tests 1-2

Name _____

DESCRIPTION

Tests 1-6 measure a single characteristic of letter form or placement. For example:

Test 1: drawing a line which connects two points
Test 2: drawing a letter which touches the baseline
Test 5: drawing a letter which touches the top line.

Only one characteristic is evaluated.

If the child's drawing fulfills the single standard, the item is correct. On tests 7-14, two or more standards are used.

DIRECTIONS

Test 1: Teacher:

"Find a line at the top of the page. Point to it. Write your name on the line.

(Number 1). Now, find the box by number 1 [teacher holds up paper and points to box]. There are two little circles in the box ... and a line going from one circle to the other circle. We could say, "the line connects the circles." Say "connects the circles." Now follow the dotted line to another box. Find two little circles in this box. Draw a straight line to connect the circles... Now the boxes look alike.

(Number 2). Find the box by number 2. How many circles are there? Yes, three, a big one and two little ones. Are they connected? Yes. Follow the dotted line to the other box. Draw a big circle like the other one. Be sure the big circle touches the little circles. Do the others by yourself.

Test 2: Find number 1. Find the o. Make one like it in the next box. Be sure your o touches the baseline (or bottom line, or ground line). Now make another one ... Now make another one. Circle the best one. Do the rest yourself.

Tests 3-13. Explain the standard of correctness and illustrate on black-board as necessary. Use whatever terminology you wish (vertical= up and down, etc.)

SCORING

Test	Standard(s)	Right	Wrong
1	Line touches circles. (Evaluate the circled letter. If child omits circle, evaluate the best one.)		
2	Letter touches baseline. (Gray zone is considered part of baseline.)		
3	Bar on midline.		
4	Straight and curved lines touch: at one point at two points at three points		d, h, b p B
5	Letter touches topline.	(same as baseline)	
6	Letter touches midline: at one point at two points at three points		a, i n, u m
7	Descender extends below baseline and letters touch midline. (Both standards required for correctness.)		
8	Horizontal bar is straight on midline and parallel to baseline.	e	e

85

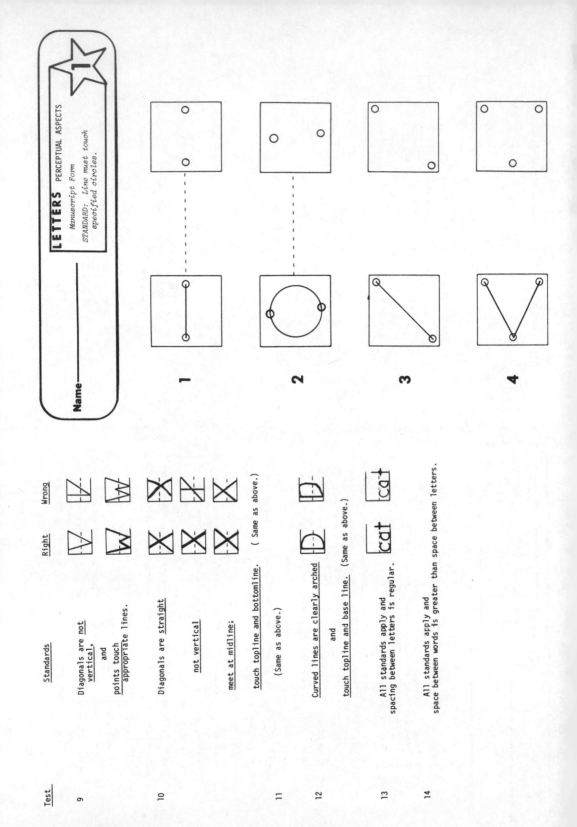

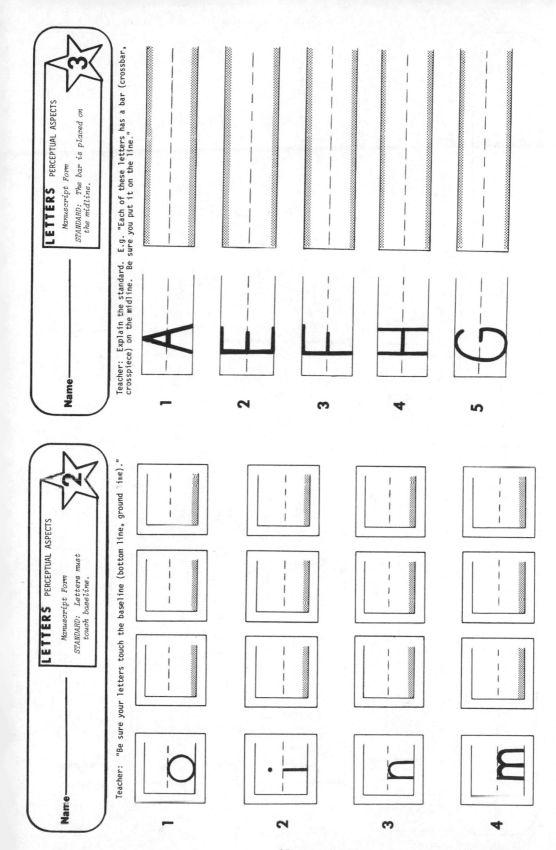

LETTERS PERCEPTUAL ASPECTS

Manuscript Form

STANDARD: Letters must touch baseline.

2

Teacher: "Be sure your letters touch the baseline (bottom line, ground line)."

1 o

2 i

3 n

4 m

LETTERS PERCEPTUAL ASPECTS

Manuscript Form

STANDARD: The bar is placed on the midline.

3

Teacher: Explain the standard. E.g. "Each of these letters has a bar (crossbar, crosspiece) on the midline. Be sure you put it on the line."

1 A

2 E

3 F

4 H

5 G

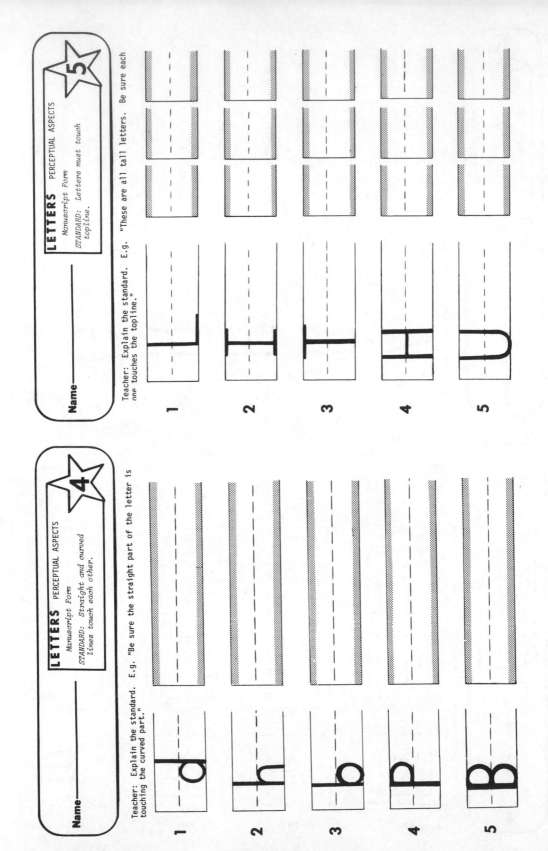

LETTERS PERCEPTUAL ASPECTS

Name _____

Manuscript Form

STANDARD: Straight and curved lines touch each other.

Teacher: Explain the standard. E.g. "Be sure the straight part of the letter is touching the curved part."

1 d
2 h
3 b
4 P
5 B

★ 4

LETTERS PERCEPTUAL ASPECTS

Name _____

Manuscript Form

STANDARD: Letters must touch topline.

Teacher: Explain the standard. E.g. "These are all tall letters. Be sure each one touches the topline."

1 L
2 I
3 T
4 H
5 U

★ 5

88

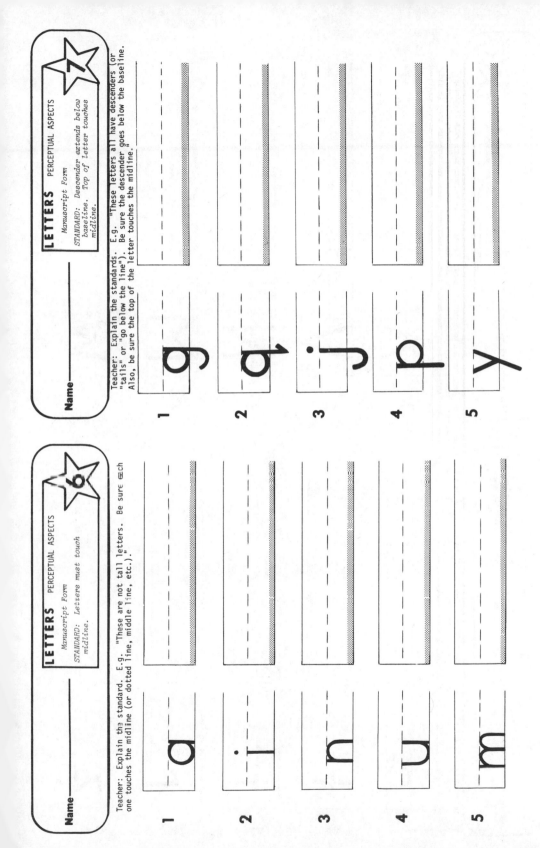

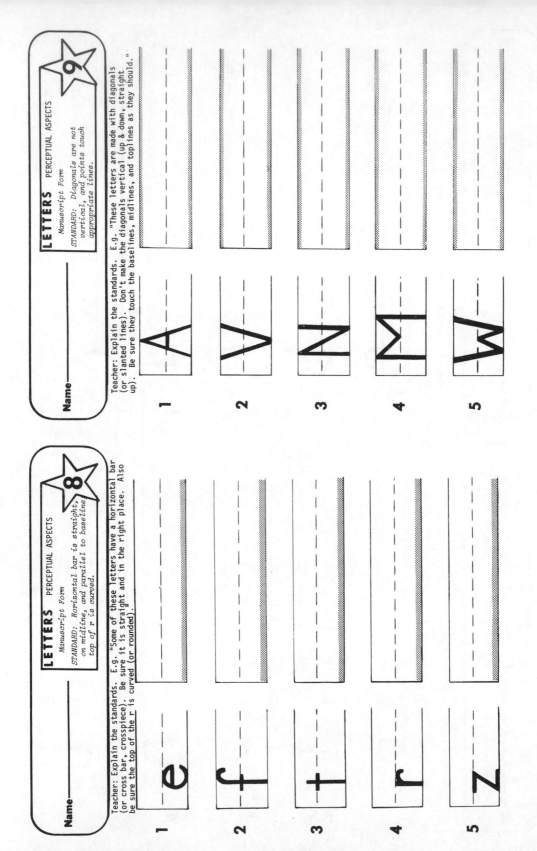

Name————

LETTERS PERCEPTUAL ASPECTS

Manuscript Form

STANDARD: *Horizontal bar is straight, on midline, and parallel to baseline; top of r is curved.*

Teacher: Explain the standards. E.g. "Some of these letters have a horizontal bar (or cross bar, crosspiece). Be sure it is straight and in the right place. Also be sure the top of the r is curved (or rounded)."

1. e
2. f
3. t
4. r
5. z

Name————

LETTERS PERCEPTUAL ASPECTS

Manuscript Form

STANDARD: *Diagonals are not vertical, and points touch appropriate lines.*

Teacher: Explain the standards. E.g. "These letters are made with diagonals (or slanted lines). Don't make the diagonals vertical (up & down, straight up). Be sure they touch the baselines, midlines, and toplines as they should."

1. A
2. V
3. N
4. M
5. W

90

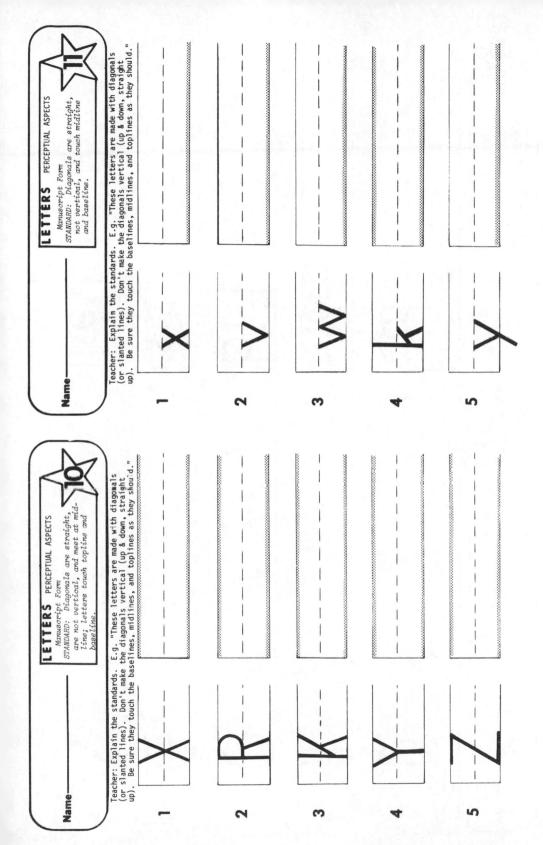

Name _____

LETTERS PERCEPTUAL ASPECTS

Manuscript Form
STANDARD: *Diagonals are straight,
are not vertical, and meet at midline; letters touch topline and
baseline.*

Teacher: Explain the standards. E.g. "These letters are made with diagonals
(or slanted lines). Don't make the diagonals vertical (up & down, straight
up). Be sure they touch the baselines, midlines, and toplines as they should."

1   X

2   R

3   K

4   Y

5   Z

Name _____

LETTERS PERCEPTUAL ASPECTS

Manuscript Form
STANDARD: *Diagonals are straight,
not vertical, and touch midline
and baseline.*

Teacher: Explain the standards. E.g. "These letters are made with diagonals
(or slanted lines). Don't make the diagonals vertical (up & down, straight
up). Be sure they touch the baselines, midlines, and toplines as they should."

1   x

2   v

3   w

4   k

5   y

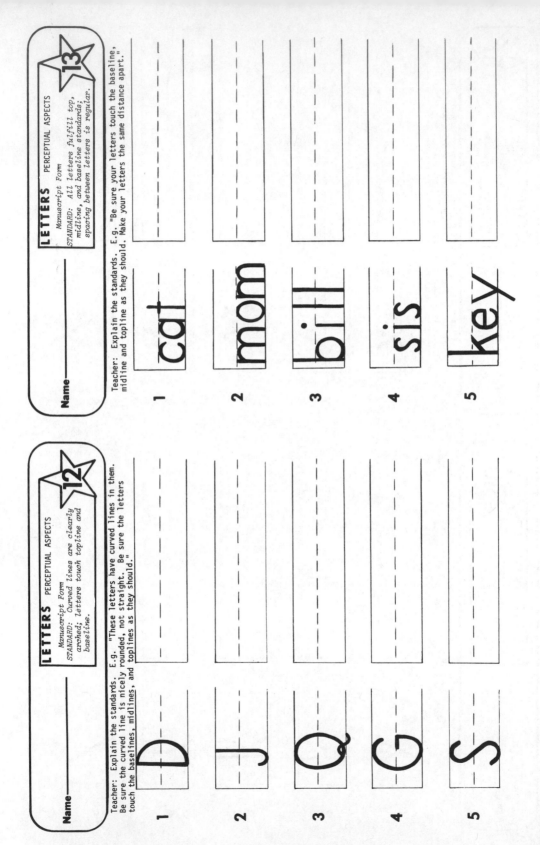

LETTERS PERCEPTUAL ASPECTS

Name _____

Manuscript Form
STANDARD: Curved lines are clearly
arched; letters touch topline and
baseline.

⭐ 12

Teacher: Explain the standards. E.g. "These letters have curved lines in them.
Be sure the curved line is nicely rounded, not straight. Be sure the letters
touch the baselines, midlines, and toplines as they should."

1   D

2   J

3   Q

4   G

5   S

LETTERS PERCEPTUAL ASPECTS

Name _____

Manuscript Form
STANDARD: All letters fulfill top,
midline, and baseline standards;
spacing between letters is regular.

⭐ 13

Teacher: Explain the standards. E.g. "Be sure your letters touch the baseline,
midline and topline as they should. Make your letters the same distance apart."

1   cat

2   mom

3   bill

4   sis

5   key

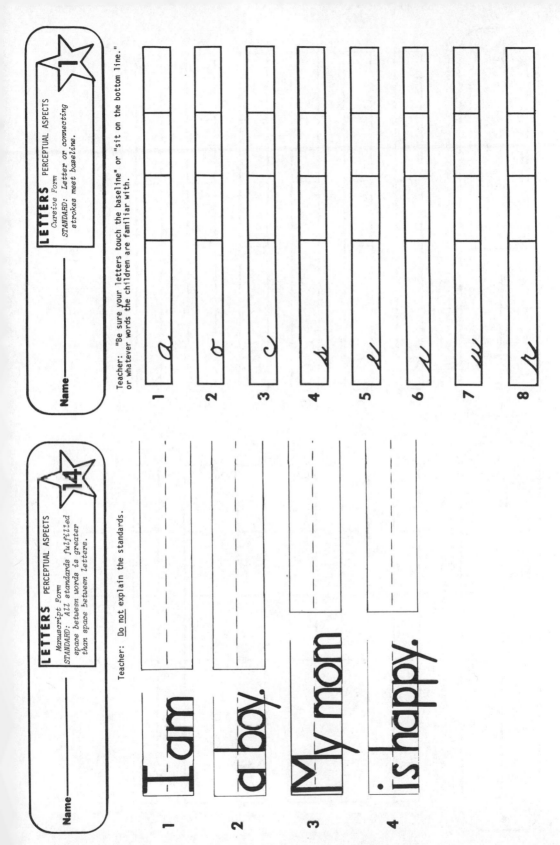

LETTERS PERCEPTUAL ASPECTS

Cursive Form

STANDARD: Letter or connecting strokes meet baseline.

Name _____

⭐ 1

Teacher: "Be sure your letters touch the baseline" or "sit on the bottom line." or whatever words the children are familiar with.

1 *a*

2 *o*

3 *c*

4 *d*

5 *e*

6 *u*

7 *w*

8 *r*

LETTERS PERCEPTUAL ASPECTS

Manuscript Form

STANDARD: All standards fulfilled space between words is greater than space between letters.

Name _____

⭐ 14

Teacher: Do <u>not</u> explain the standards.

1 I am

2 a boy.

3 My mom

4 is happy.

93

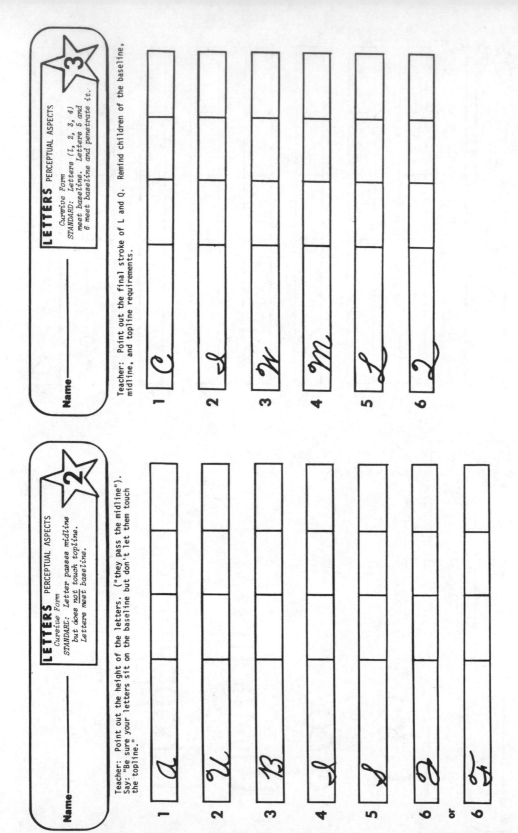

LETTERS PERCEPTUAL ASPECTS

☆2

Name _____

Cursive Form
STANDARD: Letter passes midline
but does not touch topline.
Letters meet baseline.

Teacher: Point out the height of the letters. ("they pass the midline").
Say: "Be sure your letters sit on the baseline but don't let them touch
the topline."

1
2
3
4
5
6
or
6

LETTERS PERCEPTUAL ASPECTS

☆3

Name _____

Cursive Form
STANDARD: Letters (1, 2, 3, 4)
meet baseline. Letters 5 and
6 meet baseline and penetrate it.

Teacher: Point out the final stroke of L and Q. Remind children of the baseline,
midline, and topline requirements.

1
2
3
4
5
6

94

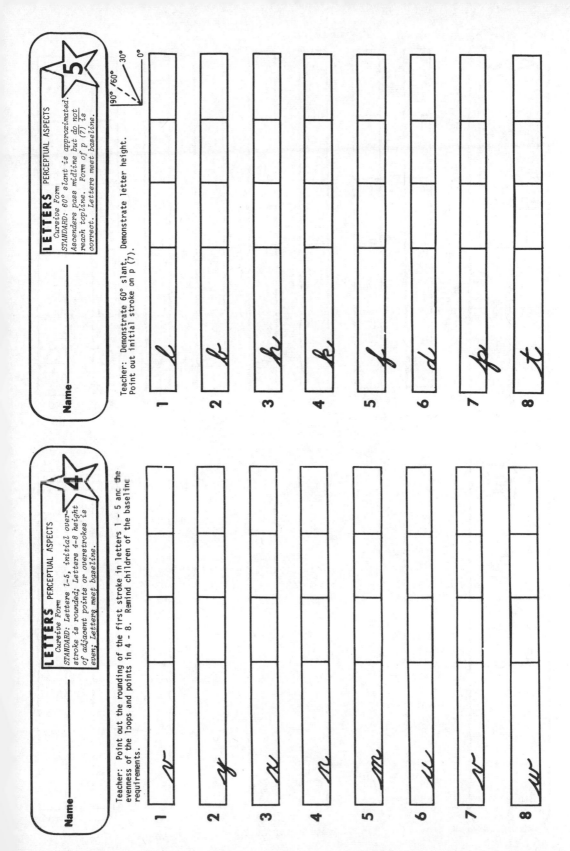

LETTERS PERCEPTUAL ASPECTS

Name _____

Cursive Form

STANDARD: Letters 1-5, initial over-
stroke is rounded; Letters 4-8 height
of adjacent points or overstrokes is
even; Letters meet baseline.

4

Teacher: Point out the rounding of the first stroke in letters 1 - 5 and the
evenness of the loops and points in 4 - 8. Remind children of the baseline
requirements.

1

2

3

4

5

6

7

8

LETTERS PERCEPTUAL ASPECTS

Name _____

Cursive Form

STANDARD: 60° slant is approximated.
Ascenders pass midline but do not
reach topline. Form of p (7) is
correct. Letters meet baseline.

5

90°/60° 30°
0°

Teacher: Demonstrate 60° slant. Demonstrate letter height.
Point out initial stroke on p (7).

1

2

3

4

5

6

7

8

95

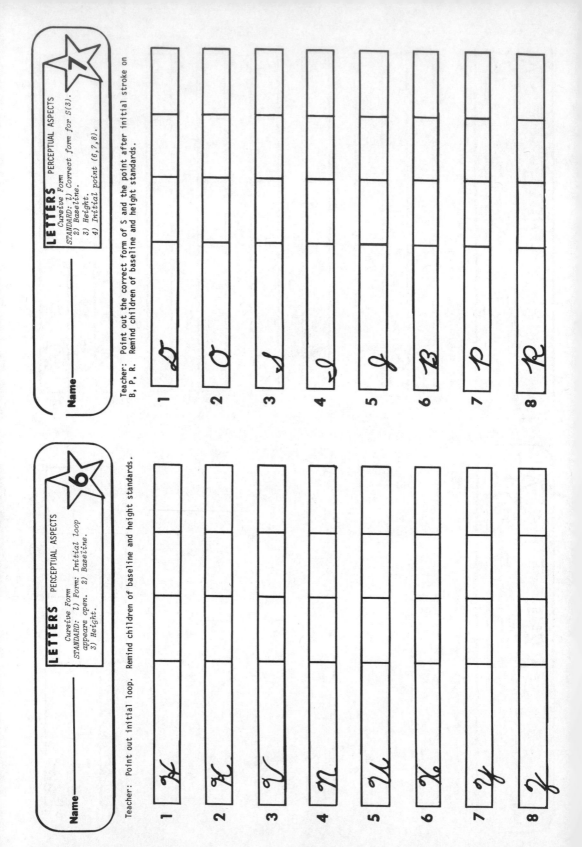

LETTERS PERCEPTUAL ASPECTS

Name _____

Cursive Form
STANDARD: 1) Form: Initial Loop appears open. 2) Baseline.
3) Height.

Teacher: Point out initial loop. Remind children of baseline and height standards.

1

2

3

4

5

6

7

8

LETTERS PERCEPTUAL ASPECTS

Name _____

Cursive Form
STANDARD: 1) Correct form for S(3).
2) Baseline.
3) Height.
4) Initial point (6,7,8).

Teacher: Point out the correct form of S and the point after initial stroke on B, P, R. Remind children of baseline and height standards.

1

2

3

4

5

6

7

8

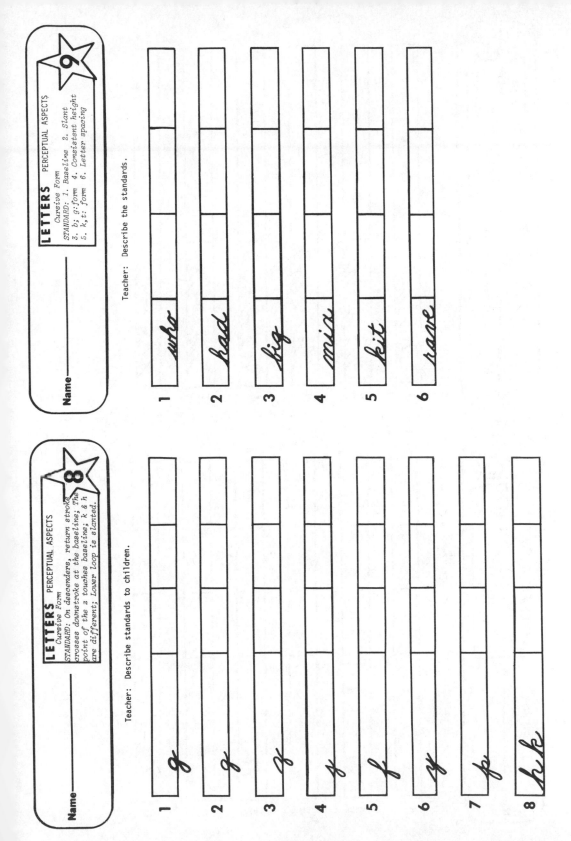

9

LETTERS PERCEPTUAL ASPECTS

Cursive Form
STANDARD: 1. Baseline 2. Slant
3. b; g:form 4. Consistent height
5. k,t: form 6. Letter spacing

Name _____

Teacher: Describe the standards.

1   *who*

2   *had*

3   *big*

4   *mix*

5   *kit*

6   *rare*

8

LETTERS PERCEPTUAL ASPECTS

Cursive Form
STANDARD: On descenders, return stroke
crosses downstroke at the baseline; The
point of the z touches baseline; k & h
are different; Lower loop is slanted.

Name _____

Teacher: Describe standards to children.

1   *g*

2   *g*

3   *z*

4   *z*

5   *f*

6   *x*

7   *p*

8   *h k*

97

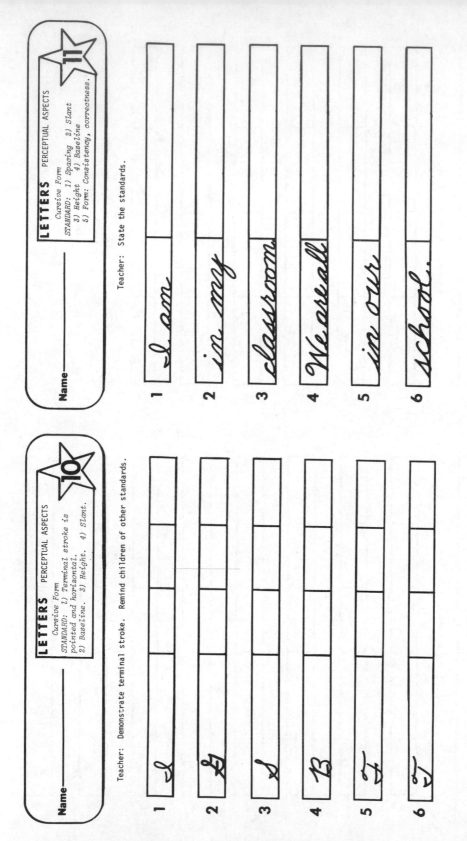

LETTERS PERCEPTUAL ASPECTS

★ **11**

Cursive Form
STANDARD: 1) Spacing 2) Slant
3) Height 4) Baseline
5) Form: Consistency, correctness.

Name ——————

Teacher: State the standards.

1. *l am*
2. *in my*
3. *classroom*
4. *We are all*
5. *in our*
6. *school.*

LETTERS PERCEPTUAL ASPECTS

★ **10**

Cursive Form
STANDARD: 1) Terminal stroke is
pointed and horizontal.
2) Baseline. 3) Height. 4) Slant.

Name ——————

Teacher: Demonstrate terminal stroke. Remind children of other standards.

1. *l*
2. *A*
3. *d*
4. *B*
5. *T*
6. *J*

Name _____

LETTERS EQUIVALENTS
Letter Names
Sample Page 6

1.   O   E   M   S

2.   i   h   x   p

3.   D   G   A   Q

TEACHER'S SCRIPT:

Sample Page:

Write your name at the top. (pause)

Find number 1. Point to it. There are some letters by number 1. Point to them.

Now, circle the letter I say... **O.**   Did you circle the first one?

Find number 2. Circle the...**X.**   Did you circle the third one?

Number 3. Circle the...**A.**   Did you circle the third one?

Test 1 and Test 2

Write your name at
the top.
Find number 1.
Circle the letter
I say.

1. Circle the o.

2. Circle the i.

3. Circle the x.

4. Circle the c.

5. Circle the a.

6. Circle the b.

Test 3 and Test 4

Write your name at
the top.
Find number 1.
Circle the letter
I say.

1. Circle the e.

2. Circle the m.

3. Circle the J.

4. Circle the g.

5. Circle the r.

6. Circle the p.

7. Circle the t.

8. Circle the z.

9. Circle the d.

10. Circle the s.

Test 5 and Test 6

Write your name at
the top.
Find number 1.
Circle the letter
I say.

1. Circle the y.

2. Circle the q.

3. Circle the k.

4. Circle the j.

5. Circle the v.

6. Circle the f.

7. Circle the w.

8. Circle the n.

9. Circle the h.

10. Circle the l.

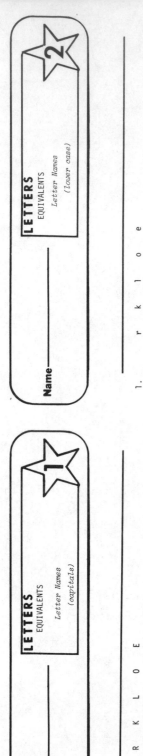

LETTERS
EQUIVALENTS
Letter Names
(capitals)

Name _____

1. R K L O E
2. S I U Z Q
3. G D X N H
4. F J M P C
5. A T V W Y
6. M U B S K

LETTERS
EQUIVALENTS
Letter Names
(lower case)

Name _____

1. r k l o e
2. s i u z q
3. g d x n h
4. f j m p c
5. a t v w y
6. m u b s k

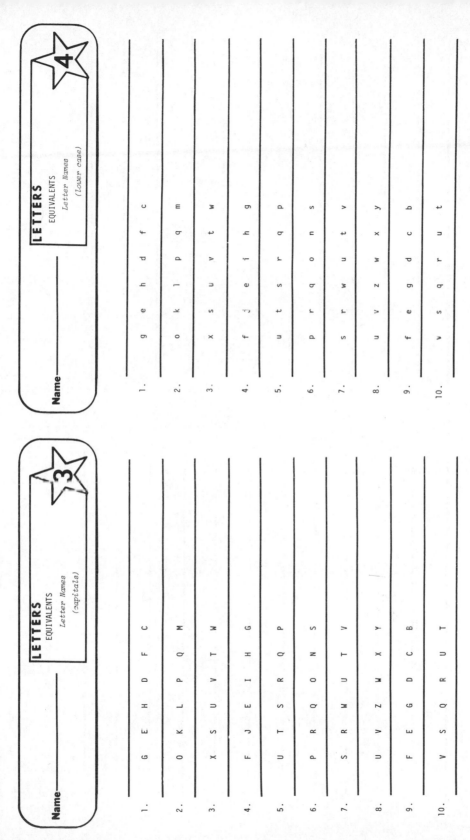

3

LETTERS

EQUIVALENTS

Letter Names
(capitals)

Name

1. G E H D F C
2. O K L P Q M
3. X S U V T W
4. F J E I H G
5. U T S R Q P
6. P R Q O N S
7. S R W U T V
8. U V Z W X Y
9. F E G D C B
10. V S Q R U T

4

LETTERS

EQUIVALENTS

Letter Names
(lower case)

Name

1. g e h d f c
2. o k l p q m
3. x s u v t w
4. f j e i h g
5. u t s r q p
6. p r q o n s
7. s r w u t v
8. u v z w x y
9. f e g d c b
10. v s q r u t

LETTERS

EQUIVALENTS

Letter Names
(capitals)

Name—————

1. T W Y Z X U S S V
2. N P R T S U V Q
3. K M L H G J N I
4. F L K H J E I G
5. Z S Y T X U V W
6. J F D I H C G H
7. R X S W T V U Q
8. S N L Q K O R T
9. K E D J F H G I
10. H O L K J N T M

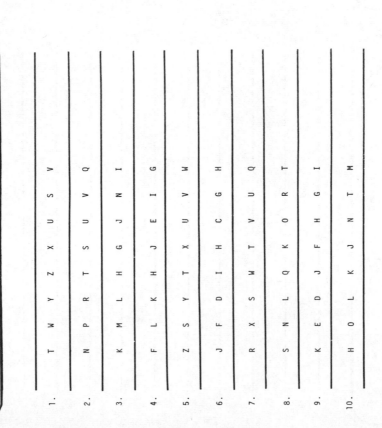

LETTERS

EQUIVALENTS

Letter Names
(lower case)

Name—————

1. t w y z x u s s v
2. n p r t s u v q
3. k m l h g j n ii
4. f l k h j e i g
5. z s y t x u v w
6. j f d l h c g h
7. r x s w t v u q
8. s n l q k o r t
9. k e d j f h g i
10. h o l k j n t m

LETTERS

EQUIVALENTS

Letter Names

(lower case)

Name _____

Teacher: "Name each letter as I point to it."

```
x    o    c    a
e    b    m    i
s    p    r    t    u    g
d    j    q    y    k    z
f    n    h    w    l    v
```

LETTERS

EQUIVALENTS

Letter Names

(capitals)

Name _____

Teacher: "Name each letter as I point to it."

```
O    X    A    C
B    I    E    M
U    G    R    P    T    S
Z    D    Y    K    Q    J
V    F    W    N    H    L
```

LETTERS EQUIVALENTS

Letter-Sound Equivalents
Sample Pages A & B

Sample Pgs. A+B

Name _____

SAMPLE PAGE A

1.   c-t   b-d

2.   m-n   d-g

3.   l--k   c-m-

....

SAMPLE PAGE B

1.   c a t ....   come   back   city

2.   s o ....   miss   wish   soon

3.   m a n ......   baby   ask   fat

LETTERS EQUIVALENTS

Letter-Sound Equivalents
Sample Pages A & B

Directions
Sample
Pgs. A+B

Name _____

TEACHER'S SCRIPT: (SAMPLE PAGE A)

(This page should be administered before giving Tests 1-10.)

Write your name at the top.

Find number 1. Point to it. There are two words by number one.
Each word has some letters missing. I will say one of those words.
Circle the one I say...cat. (pause)
Did you circle c-dash-t?
Does anyone know what letter is missing? (Elicit "a".)
Find number 2. Circle the one I say...dog. (pause)
Did you circle d-dash-g?
Does anyone know what letter is missing in dog? (Elicit "o".)
Find number 3. Circle the one I say...look. (pause)
Did you circle l-dash-dash-k?

....

TEACHER'S SCRIPT: (SAMPLE PAGE B)

(This page should be administered before giving Test 11 or Test 12.)

Write your name at the top.

Find number 1. Point to it. Point to the word by number 1.
Read the word...cat.
Notice that one sound is underlined in the word. Say that sound..."cuh."
Now read the other words.
Two of them contain the sound. One does not contain the sound.
Cross out the word that does not have that sound. (pause)
Did you cross out city? City does not have the "cuh" sound.
Find number 2. Read the word and say the underlined sound. (pause)
Read the other words. Cross out the one that does not have the sound. (pause)
Did you cross out wish? Wish does not have the "sss" sound.
Find number three. Read the word and say the underlined sound. (pause)
Read the other words. Cross out the one that does not have the sound. (pause)
Did you cross out baby? Baby does not have the "a" sound.

104

1. c--   m--   f--

2. t--   r--   h---

3. b--   l---   s---

4. t--   d--   r--

5. m---   p---   j---

6. z--   b--   w--

7. l---   v---   c---

8. d--   s---   n---

9. k-   l--   g--

10. n---   y---   p---

LETTERS EQUIVALENTS

Letter-Sound Equivalents
Tests 1-4

Directions
Tests
1 - 4

Name

TEACHER'S SCRIPT:

TEST 1:
Circle the one I say.

1. man
2. talk
3. soup
4. red
5. post
6. bear
7. coat
8. doll
9. leg
10. neck

TEST 2:
Circle the one I say.

1. kite
2. van
3. joke
4. hen
5. fire
6. game
7. yell
8. zoo
9. wore
10. show
11. chop
12. thin

TEST 4:
Circle the one I say.

1. hat
2. job
3. wet
4. gum
5. fit
6. bug
7. sled
8. jam
9. pig
10. shop

TEST 3:
Circle the one I say.

1. wet
2. hop
3. bus
4. crab
5. fun
6. pig
7. kid
8. car
9. gum
10. wish
11. hill
12. both
13. much
14. buzz
15. tack

Card 2

Name _____

LETTERS EQUIVALENTS
Letter-Sound Equivalents
(initial consonants)

1. b--- l--- k---
2. m-- v-- s--
3. w--- n--- j---
4. h-- k-- d--
5. t--- f--- p---
6. r--- v--- g---
7. h--- c--- y---
8. z-- g-- n--
9. p--- w--- j---
10. sh-- th-- qu--
11. ch-- kn-- th--
12. sh-- th-- ch--

Card 3

Name _____

LETTERS EQUIVALENTS
Letter-Sound Equivalents
(final consonants)

1. --r --m --t
2. --p --y --g
3. --m --r --s
4. --t --b --f
5. --l --n --r
6. --g --b --s
7. --n --d --f
8. --x --l --r
9. --b --s --m
10. --ck --ph --sh
11. --ch --ll --x
12. --th --zz --mb
13. --ch --ph --gn
14. --ll --ch --zz
15. --ck --ss --ld

LETTERS EQUIVALENTS

Letter-Sound Equivalents
(short vowel sounds)

★ 4

Name _____

1.   -a-   -i- _____

2.   -i-   -o- _____

3.   -o-   -e- _____

4.   -e-   -u- _____

5.   -i-   -a- _____

6.   -o-   -u- _____

7.   --e-   --u- _____

8.   -u-   -a- _____

9.   -a-   -i- _____

10.   --e-   --o- _____

LETTERS EQUIVALENTS

Letter-Sound Equivalents
Tests 5-8

★ Directions Tests 5-8

Name _____

TEST 5:
Circle the one I say.

1. dime
2. safe
3. feet
4. bike
5. tune
6. note
7. base
8. seed
9. rule
10. home

TEST 6:
Circle the one I say.

1. rain
2. goat
3. heat
4. book
5. soap
6. coin
7. wait
8. soil
9. look
10. meal

TEST 7:
Circle the one I say.

1. moon
2. fawn
3. loud
4. bread
5. howl
6. town
7. boot
8. crawl
9. dead
10. house

TEST 8:
Circle the one I say.

1. bring   9. flash
2. skin   10. spell
3. trash   11. black
4. swim   12. snack
5. print   13. clock
6. sleep   14. scat
7. drink   15. stand
8. glad

Card 5

Name _____

LETTERS EQUIVALENTS

Letter-Sound Equivalents
(long vowel sounds/silent E)

1. -o-e   -i-e
2. -a-e   -o-e
3. -ee-   -u-e
4. -a-e   -i-e
5. -ee-   -u-e
6. -p-e   -ee-
7. -u-e   -a-e
8. -ee-   -i-e
9. -u-e   -a-e
10. -i-e   -o-e

Card 6

Name _____

LETTERS EQUIVALENTS

Letter-Sound Equivalents
(advanced vowel sounds)

1. -ai-   -oo-
2. -oa-   -ea-
3. -ai-   -ea-
4. -oo-   -ai-
5. -ea-   -oa-
6. -oo-   -oi-
7. -oi-   -ai-
8. -oi-   -oa-
9. -ai-   -oo-
10. -oa-   -ea-

LETTERS EQUIVALENTS ☆7

Letter-Sound Equivalents
(advanced vowel sounds)

Name _____

1. -ai-   -oo-
2. -ea-   -aw-
3. -ou-   -ai-
4. --oa-   --ea-
5. -ow-   -ai-
6. -ea-   -ow-
7. -ai-   -oo-
8. --aw-   --oi-
9. -ea-   -oa-
10. -ou-   -ai--

LETTERS EQUIVALENTS ☆8

Letter-Sound Equivalents
(initial consonant blends)

Name _____

1. bl---   gr---   br---
2. sm--   sk--   sh--
3. tr---   th---   cr---
4. sp--   tw--   sw--
5. pr---   sp---   fr---
6. sm---   sl---   cl---
7. gr---   dr---   bl---
8. sr---   gr---   gl--
9. bl---   fr---   fl---
10. pr---   sp---   sn---
11. bl---   sl---   br---
12. sn---   sw---   sh---
13. bl---   cl---   cr---
14. sl--   cr---   sc--
15. st---   sl---   tr---

1.	bi----	ka----	ba----	nai---	see---	nee---
2.	do----	to----	de----	go----	lo----	ga------
3.	bi----	fi----	fa----	su----	si----	wi----
4.	ca---	na---	ce---	ze---	me---	zo---
5.	ki----	ku----	fi----	ni---	va---	vi---
6.	hu---	bo---	ho---	sto---	sha---	shi---
7.	ja----	yu---	ju----	re---	ro---	mo---
8.	de---	le---	li---	ta---	ti---	bi---
9.	ta---	ra---	ru---	po----	pi---	go----
10.	ri----	mo---	mi----	wa----	si---	wi----

Name _____

LETTERS

Letter-Sound Equivalents
Tests 9 & 10

Directions
Tests
9-10

TEACHER'S SCRIPT:

TEST 9:
Circle the one I say.

1. basket	11. needle
2. doctor	12. goldfish
3. fifteen	13. silent
4. camel	14. zebra
5. kitten	15. visit
6. hotel	16. shadow
7. jungle	17. robin
8. letter	18. tiger
9. rabbit	19. popcorn
10. mitten	20. winter

TEST 10:
Circle the one I say.

1. sing	11. gift
2. rent	12. sack
3. bank	13. belt
4. hand	14. mask
5. bell	15. catch
6. fish	16. help
7. neck	17. flash
8. rock	18. hunt
9. camp	19. milk
10. nest	20. dust

LETTERS EQUIVALENTS

Letter-Sound Equivalents (word bases)

Name _____

Star 10

1.	-ill	-ing	-end	11.	-ift	-arf	-isk
2.	-ist	-ent	-erb	12.	-esk	-uch	-ack
3.	-ash	-ock	-ank	13.	-ift	-elt	-all
4.	-and	-ord	-ast	14.	-uck	-esh	-ask
5.	-eck	-ale	-ell	15.	-osh	-amp	-atch
6.	-ish	-ind	-uch	16.	-elp	-urp	-est
7.	-eck	-ask	-end	17.	-and	-ash	-ith
8.	-ach	-cck	-ort	18.	-ush	-art	-unt
9.	-ome	-amp	-isp	19.	-ird	-eck	-ilk
10.	-int	-est	-ach	20.	-ust	-ash	-ent

LETTERS EQUIVALENTS

Letter-Sound Equivalents (allographs (consonants))

Name _____

Star 11

Teacher: "Read the first word and say the underlined sound.
Read the other words and cross out the one that does not have the sound."

1. h a s .... buzz   bus   does
2. f u n .... phone   laugh   ghost
3. y e s .... cry   you   yard
4. b u t .... tub   lamb   back
5. k i t e .... sick   key   know
6. h i m .... who   hour   how
7. l o o k .... long   talk   alone
8. w e .... write   away   wood
9. t o p .... catch   into   what
10. g o .... finger   give   high

LETTERS — EQUIVALENTS

12

Name _____

Letter-Sound Equivalents
(allographs (vowels))

Teacher: "Read the first word and say the underlined sound.
Read the other words and cross out the one that does not have the sound."

1. f u n .... mule   love   what

2. s a w .... haul   small   sand

3. t oo .... new   book   rule

4. b o y .... boil   day   toys

5. ou t .... tough   down   loud

6. t r ee .... even   tent   any

7. b oa t .... toes   rode   rock

8. p ie .... pig   mile   try

9. n e t .... tie   bread   said

10. s a y .... they   bake   said

LETTERS — LETTER FUNCTIONS

1

Name _____

LETTER FUNCTIONS
Personal Name

Teacher: "Circle every letter that is in your first name."

A   B   C   D   E   F   G   H   I   J   K

L   M   N   O   P   Q   R   S   T   U   V

W   X   Y   Z

Teacher: "Circle every letter in your last name."

A   B   C   D   E   F   G   H   I   J   K

L   M   N   O   P   Q   R   S   T   U   V

W   X   Y   Z

Teacher: "Write your first and last names."

_____

LETTERS

LETTER FUNCTIONS

Alphabet

(ordering)

Name _____

⭐ 3

Teacher: (Give child the gummed letter stickers.) "Place the letters of the alphabet in order on the chart. That is, paste A on the first square, B on the second square, and so on."

Test conditions:
Be certain that alphabet charts and posters are not in view.

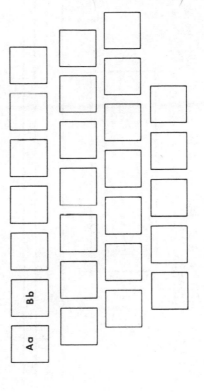

| Aa | Bb | | | | | |

LETTERS

LETTER FUNCTIONS

Alphabet

(reciting)

Name _____

⭐ 2

Teacher: "Say the letters of the alphabet, starting with a."

(On the alphabet below, mark any letters that are misplaced or omitted.)

Test Conditions:
Ee certain that alphabet charts and posters are not in view.
Singing the alphabet is not acceptable.

a b c d e f g h i j k l m
n o p q r s t u v w x y z

113

Name _____

LETTER FUNCTIONS
Writing the Alphabet
(Printing standards do not apply.)

Teacher: "On the lines below, write the letters of the alphabet. Write them in order, beginning with a. By number 1, write the small letters. By number 2, write the capital letters. The first letter is done for you."

Test Conditions:
Be certain that alphabet charts and posters are not in view.
Learners may choose to write the alphabet on regular school paper instead of using this test paper. This alternative is completely acceptable.

1 — a

2 — A

Name _____

LETTERS

LETTER FUNCTIONS
Alphabet
(ordering)

Cut these squares apart, and paste them on the chart (in order).

Ff	Aa	Qq	Ee	Rr	Tt	Hh	Ii	Oo
Xx	Dd	Ww	Ss	Zz	Uu	Yy	Vv	Jj
Gg	Kk	Pp	Ll	Mm	Cc	Nn	Bb	

Cut these squares apart, and paste them on the chart (in order).

Ff	Aa	Qq	Ee	Rr	Tt	Hh	Ii	Oo
Xx	Dd	Ww	Ss	Zz	Uu	Yy	Vv	Jj
Gg	Kk	Pp	Ll	Mm	Cc	Nn	Bb	

114

LETTERS
LETTER FUNCTIONS
Alphabet
(alphabetical order)

6

Write these names in alphabetical order.

Black
Greenway
Brown
MacDonald
Smith
McHenry
Bronson
Jackson
Smedley
Reston
Jacobson
Green
Woods
Krest
Blake
Smithe
Reese
Cameron
Blair
Jakobson

LETTERS
LETTER FUNCTIONS
Alphabet
(alphabetical order)

5

Write these words in alphabetical order.

great
drink
apple
up
when
there
know
fair
junk
salt

1
2
3
4
5
6
7
8
9
10

* *

Write these names in alphabetical order.

Smith...Brown...McNeil...Clark...Walters...Meyers...Reid...Johnson

1
2
3
4

5
6
7
8

This set of tests contains five separate tests of word discrimination.
The tests are of increasing difficulty. The directions are the same
for all tests and do not need to be repeated after Test 1.

TEACHER'S SCRIPT:

Find the line at the top and write your name.

Find number 1 and point to it. Look at the word next to the number.
Point to it. Look at the other words in that line. Find two words
just like the first word and circle them. One is partly done.

Did you find two words?

Circle the same word as many times as you find it. Sometimes you will
find it once...sometimes twice...sometimes three times.

Go on and finish the page by yourself.

WORDS

PERCEPTUAL ASPECTS

Word Shapes
(endings)

Name _____

1.	called :	caller	(called)	recall	called
2.	working :	working	worker	working	worked
3.	looked :	looking	looks	looker	looked
4.	asked :	asked	asked	asks	asker
5.	parts :	parts	parting	partner	parted
6.	turned :	turns	return	turned	turning
7.	helping :	helper	helping	helps	helped
8.	smaller :	small	smallest	smaller	smaller
9.	sounds :	sounds	sounded	sound	soundly
10.	usually :	unusual	usually	usual	usually
11.	following :	follows	followed	follower	following
12.	numbers :	numbers	numbered	number	numbers
13.	bigger :	bigger	biggest	bigger	big

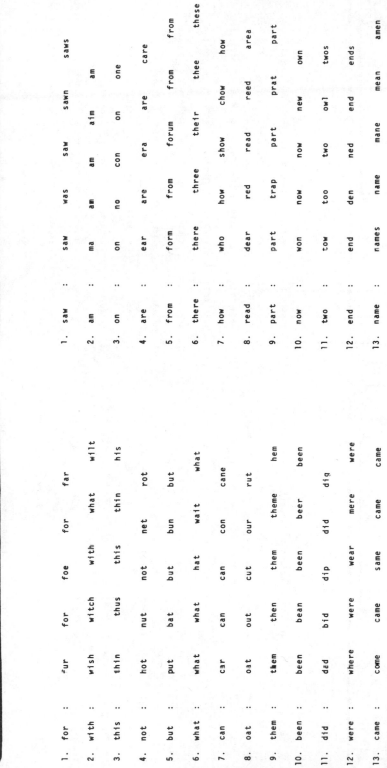

Card 2

WORDS

PERCEPTUAL ASPECTS

Word Shapes

(similar words)

Name _____

1.	for	:	fur	for	foe	for	far
2.	with	:	wish	witch	with	what	wilt
3.	this	:	thin	thus	this	thin	his
4.	not	:	hot	nut	not	net	rot
5.	but	:	put	bat	but	bun	but
6.	what	:	what	what	hat	wait	what
7.	can	:	car	can	can	con	cane
8.	oat	:	oat	out	cut	our	rut
9.	them	:	them	then	them	theme	hem
10.	been	:	been	bean	been	beer	been
11.	did	:	dad	bid	dip	did	dig
12.	were	:	where	were	wear	mere	were
13.	came	:	come	came	same	came	came

Card 3

WORDS

PERCEPTUAL ASPECTS

Word Shapes

(letter order)

Name _____

1.	saw	:	saw	was	saw	sawn	saws
2.	am	:	ma	am	am	aim	am
3.	on	:	on	no	con	on	one
4.	are	:	ear	are	era	are	care
5.	from	:	form	from	forum	from	from
6.	there	:	there	three	their	thee	these
7.	how	:	who	how	show	chow	how
8.	read	:	dear	red	read	reed	area
9.	part	:	part	trap	part	prat	part
10.	now	:	won	now	now	new	own
11.	two	:	tow	too	two	owl	twos
12.	end	:	end	den	ned	end	ends
13.	name	:	names	name	mane	mean	amen

1.	he said	:	he said	hesaid	he said	hesa id
2.	you and I	:	youand I	you and I	you andI	youandI
3.	one or two	:	one or two	oneortwo	oneor two	
4.	too big	:	toobig	too big	to obig	too big
5.	what is it	:	what isit	whatis it	what is it	
6.	we can go	:	wecan go	we can go	wecango	we can go
7.	all of us	:	all of us	allofus	allof us	all ofus
8.	I see him	:	Isee him	I see him	I see him	I seehim
9.	they did not	:	they did not	theydid not	they didnot	
10.	very far away	:	very faraway	veryfar away	very far away	

1.	people	:	paple	people	people	poeple	peopel
2.	different	:	different	diffrent	diffrent	deffirent	different
3.	because	:	becuse	becase	because	because	becasue
4.	through	:	through	though	through	thorough	
5.	another	:	anoter	another	anothel	anotheir	another
6.	something	:	something	somethnig	soemthing	somthing	
7.	animals	:	aniamls	ainmals	animals	aminals	
8.	children	:	chidren	children	childern	children	
9.	important	:	impotant	improtant	important	important	imprtant
10.	together	:	together	togther	toghter	together	toegether
11.	however	:	howeer	however	hovewer	however	
12.	without	:	witout	without	withot	withuot	
13.	thought	:	thouth	thought	thought	thought	throught

5

4

118

WORDS 1

Name _____

PERCEPTUAL ASPECTS

Phonological Features

(auditory memory)

Teacher: I will say a sentence. Then you repeat the sentence,
just the way I said it.

Check here if response is correct.

1. They drink water.   ( )

2. The flowers are red.   ( )

3. My old coat is lost.   ( )

4. We should leave.   ( )

5. Another man brought things.   (·)

6. Where could he work?   ( )

WORDS 2

Name _____

PERCEPTUAL ASPECTS

Phonological Features

(auditory memory)

Teacher: Say the letters I say. (Say the letters slowly, regularly.
In items 5 and 6, group letters as indicated).

Check here if response is correct.

1. m...o...l   ( )

2. a...c...y   ( )

3. x...t...u...n   ( )

4. s...r...h...e   ( )

5. b l ...c k ...t   ( )

6. r u ...t h ...l   ( )

Teacher: I will say some words that rhyme (end the same).
Then, you tell me another word that rhymes with them.
It does not have to be a real word.

Check here if response is correct.

1. mat...fat...sat...   ( )

2. sop...cop...lop...   ( )

3. ill...mill...till...   ( )

4. hock...frock...stock...   ( )

5. wheat...neat...sleet...   ( )

Teacher: I will say some words that start the same. Then,
you tell me another word that starts the same way.

Check here if response is correct.

1. bean...bird...bunch...   ( )

2. face...fall...five...   ( )

3. man...me...milk...   ( )

4. tail...top...ten...   ( )

5. sad...soon...seal...   ( )

Name _____

WORDS
PERCEPTUAL ASPECTS
Phonological Features
Sample Page A

Sample Page A

1      NO

2   ●   NO

3   run   NO

4   look   NO

5   jump   NO

6   little   NO

Name _____

WORDS
PERCEPTUAL ASPECTS
Phonological Features
Sample Page A

Directions: Sample Page

TEACHER'S SCRIPT:

(This page should be administered before giving Tests 5-7).

Write your name at the top.

In this test you are going to listen to words.

Find Number 1. Point to it. Point to the cat. Point to the NO.
I will say some words. CAT...CAT...CAT
Were they the same? Yes, so circle the cat.

Now find Number 2. Listen to these words.   BALL...CAKE...BALL
Were they the same? No, so circle the NO.

Find Number 3. Listen. RUN...RUN...RUN. If they are the same,
circle the word "run." Did you circle "run?"

Find Number 4. Listen. LOOK...HELP...LOOK. If they are not the same,
circle the NO. Did you circle NO?

Number 5. JUMP...WORK...JUMP. Circle. Which one did you circle?
You should have circled NO.

Number 6. LITTLE...LITTLE...LITTLE. Circle. Which one did you circle?
You should have circled the word "little."

121

WORDS

PERCEPTUAL ASPECTS

Phonological Features
(word matching)

Name _____

1. fat·············NO

2. road·············NO

3. deer·············NO

4. lake·············NO

5. tub·············NO

6. moon·············NO

7. hedge·············NO

8. dig·············NO

9. loaf·············NO

10. dime·············NO

WORDS

PERCEPTUAL ASPECTS

Phonological Features
(word matching)

Directions Tests 5, 6, 7

Name _____

TEST 5:

I will say some words. If they are the same, circle the word.
If they are not the same, circle the NO.

1. fat...fan...fat
2. road...roll...road
3. deer...deer...deer
4. lake...lake...lake
5. tub...tub...tub

6. moon...move...moon
7. hedge...hedge...hedge
8. dig...dip...dig
9. loaf...loaf...loaf
10. dime...dice...dime

TEST 6:

I will say some words. If they are the same, circle the word.
If they are not the same, circle the NO.

1. red...bed...red
2. game...game...game
3. hole...hole...hole
4. top...hop...top
5. man...can...man

6. pool...pool...pool
7. jug...dug...jug
8. fire...fire...fire
9. need...need...need
10. let...wet...let

TEST 7:

I will say some words. If they are the same, circle the word.
If they are not the same, circle the NO.

1. ran...rain...ran
2. nut...net...nut
3. wig...wig...wig
4. fire...fear...fire
5. dock...dock...dock

6. moon...moon...moon
7. soap...soup...soap
8. hall...hall...hall
9. bait...bet...bait
10. lid...lad...lid

122

WORDS

PERCEPTUAL ASPECTS

Phonological Features
(word matching)

Name _____

1 red ········· NO

2 game ········· NO

3 hole ········· NO

4 top ········· NO

5 man ········· NO

6 pool ········· NO

7 jug ········· NO

8 fire ········· NO

9 need ········· NO

10 let ········· NO

WORDS

PERCEPTUAL ASPECTS

Phonological Features
(word matching)

Name _____

1 ran ········· NO

2 nut ········· NO

3 wig ········· NO

4 fire ········· NO

5 dock ········· NO

6 moon ········· NO

7 soap ········· NO

8 hall ········· NO

9 bait ········· NO

10 lid ········· NO

WORDS
PERCEPTUAL ASPECTS
Phonological Features
(words in sentences)

Name _____

Directions
Tests 8-9

TEST 8:

I will say a word. Then I will say a sentence. If you hear the word in the sentence, circle the word. If the word is not in the sentence, circle the NO.
(Use normal phrasing when reading items).

1. Listen for home. I will go home after school.

2. Listen for boy. I see a child on a bike.

3. Listen for sun. It is a lovely bright day.

4. Listen for school. I go to school every day.

5. Listen for children. How many children are here?

6. Listen for light. Turn on the light, please.

7. Listen for animals. The farmer grows corn.

8. Listen for picture. I made a picture of a house.

TEST 9:

I will say a word. Then I will say a sentence. If you hear the word in the sentence, circle the word. If not, circle the NO.

1. Listen for that. Who was on the phone?

2. Listen for with. He stays with me sometimes.

3. Listen for from. Here is a letter for you.

4. Listen for said. The teacher said to be quiet.

5. Listen for were. We are late for school.

6. Listen for been. Have you been eating apples?

7. Listen for did. I hope we can find them.

8. Listen for just. I just have four marbles.

124

WORDS
PERCEPTUAL ASPECTS
Phonological Features
(words in sentences)

Name _____

8

1. _____ home..........NO

2. _____ boy...........NO

3. _____ sun...........NO

4. _____ school........NO

5. _____ children......NO

6. _____ light.........NO

7. _____ animals.......NO

8. _____ picture.......NO

Name _____

WORDS

PERCEPTUAL ASPECTS

Phonological Features

(Tests 10 & 11)

Direction Tests 10·11

TEST 10:
Listen for the sound I say. If you hear the sound in the word, circle yes. If you don't hear the sound, circle no.

1. Listen for ēep...jeep.
2. Listen for ĭsh...fin.
3. Listen for ĕnd...bet.
4. Listen for ăm...ham.
5. Listen for ŭs...buck.
6. Listen for īle...while.
7. Listen for ŏt...got.
8. Listen for īnd...mile.
9. Listen for ŭmp...jump.
10. Listen for ōld...mold.

11. Listen for āsh...leash.
12. Listen for ōne...cane.
13. Listen for ĭck...sick.
14. Listen for ēam...feet.
15. Listen for āke...cake.
16. Listen for ŏp...lip.
17. Listen for ūle...rail.
18. Listen for ĕst...best.
19. Listen for āil...maid.
20. Listen for ūle...rule.

TEST 11:
Listen for the sound I say. If you hear the sound in the word, circle yes. If you don't hear the sound, circle no.

1. Listen for că...cat.
2. Listen for nī...fire.
3. Listen for wē...weep.
4. Listen for tū...tune.
5. Listen for jō...soap.
6. Listen for bĕ...bed.
7. Listen for sĭ...pig.
8. Listen for mī...mine.
9. Listen for dŭ...luck.
10. Listen for chĕ...wet.

11. Listen for rō...road.
12. Listen for lē...lake.
13. Listen for shŏ...shot.
14. Listen for gŏ...gate.
15. Listen for thă...thin.
16. Listen for zŭ...zip.
17. Listen for fĭ...fist.
18. Listen for hă...hide.
19. Listen for pŭ...pup.
20. Listen for bā...bake.

1. that..........NO
2. with..........NO
3. from..........NO
4. said..........NO
5. were..........NO
6. been..........NO
7. did..........NO
8. just..........NO

1. eep......yes   no
2. ish......yes   no
3. end......yes   no
4. am.......yes   no
5. us.......yes   no
6. ile......yes   no
7. ot.......yes   no
8. ind......yes   no
9. ump......yes   no
10. old......yes   no

11. ash......yes   no
12. one......yes   no
13. ick......yes   no
14. eam......yes   no
15. ake......yes   no
16. op.......yes   no
17. ule......yes   no
18. est......yes   no
19. ail......yes   no
20. ule......yes   no

1. ca.......yes   no
2. mi.......yes   no
3. we.......yes   no
4. tu.......yes   no
5. jo.......yes   no
6. be.......yes   no
7. si.......yes   no
8. mi.......yes   no
9. du.......yes   no
10. che......yes   no

11. ro.......yes   no
12. le.......yes   no
13. sho......yes   no
14. go.......yes   no
15. tha......yes   no
16. zu.......yes   no
17. fi.......yes   no
18. ha.......yes   no
19. pu.......yes   no
20. ba.......yes   no

WORDS

PERCEPTUAL ASPECTS

Phonological Features

Sample Page B

Name _____

★ Directions Sample Page E

TEACHER'S SCRIPT:

(This page should be administered before giving Tests 10-12).

Find Number 1 in a circle. Point to the numbers by it, 1-2-3-4-5.
I will say some words. You count to find out how many words I say.
When I say the first word, point to 1, when I say the next word,
point to 2, and so on. When I finish, you will know how many words
I have said.

Do it now with me. (Demonstrate by writing numbers on the board,
and pointing as you say the words below).

1. boy...girl   How many words did I say? Yes, two.
   Circle the 2.

2. pig..horse...cow   How many words did I say? Yes, three.
   Circle 3.

3. jump...run   How many words did I say? Yes, two.
   Circle 2.

4. arm...leg...head...foot   How many words did I say? Yes, four.
   Circle the 4.

127

WORDS

PERCEPTUAL ASPECTS

Phonological Features

Sample Page B

Name _____

★ Sample Page B

1.   1   2   3   4   5

2.   1   2   3   4   5

3.   1   2   3   4   5

4.   1   2   3   4   5

(1.) _____

    1   2   3   4   5   6   7   8

(2.) _____

    1   2   3   4   5   6   7   8

(3.) _____

    1   2   3   4   5   6   7   8

(4.) _____

    1   2   3   4   5   6   7   8

(5.) _____

    1   2   3   4   5   6   7   8

(6.) _____

    1   2   3   4   5   6   7   8

_____

WORDS

PERCEPTUAL ASPECTS

Phonological Features

(word junctures)

Directions
Tests
12-15

Name _____

TEST 12:

Point to the numbers as I say the words. Then circle the number that tells how many words I said.

1. bell...drum   4. hat...rat...sat

2. dog...cat...fish   5. red...blue...green...black

3. flower...tree   6. bread...butter...jam

TEST 13:

Point to the numbers as I say the words. Then circle the number that tells how many words I said. (Use normal phrasing when reading items).

1. My dog...   4. He can run fast.

2. She is here.   5. Do you read books?

3. I-like to drink milk.   6. Play with me.

TEST 14:

Point to the numbers as I say the words. Then circle the number that tells how many words I said.

1. Our country...   4. Where are my boots?

2. She is reading.   5. The dog is following us.

3. My mother is not home.   6. Is it important?

TEST 15:

I will say some words. If they rhyme (end the same), circle the YES. If they do not rhyme, circle the NO.

1. boat...coat...goat   6. think...mink...rink

2. Sam...ham...gum   7. rain...cane...gain

3. seed...feed...need   8. bird...third...board

4. cut...shut...mitt   9. soon...moon...loon

5. whip...lip...lap   10. fill...still...fall

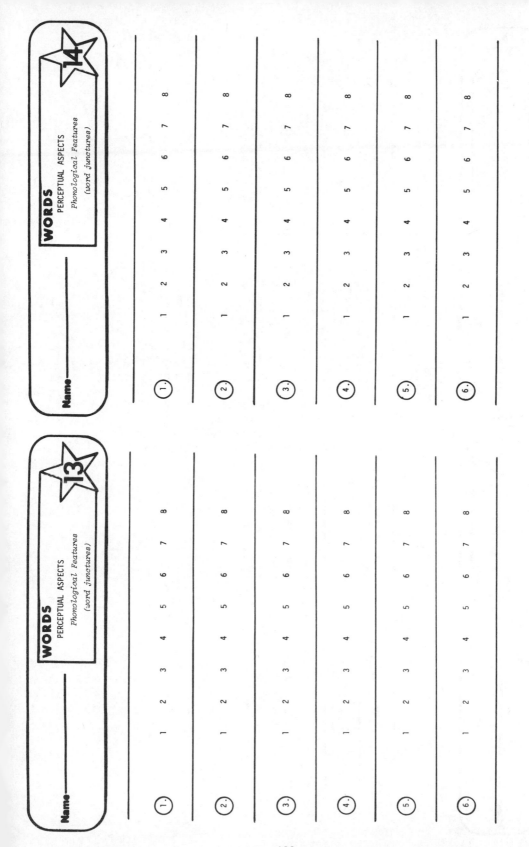

WORDS

PERCEPTUAL ASPECTS

Phonological Features
(word junctures)

Name

13

1. 1 2 3 4 5 6 7 8

2. 1 2 3 4 5 6 7 8

3. 1 2 3 4 5 6 7 8

4. 1 2 3 4 5 6 7 8

5. 1 2 3 4 5 6 7 8

6. 1 2 3 4 5

WORDS

PERCEPTUAL ASPECTS

Phonological Features
(word junctures)

Name

14

1. 1 2 3 4 5 6 7 8

2. 1 2 3 4 5 6 7 8

3. 1 2 3 4 5 6 7 8

4. 1 2 3 4 5 6 7 8

5. 1 2 3 4 5 6 7 8

6. 1 2 3 4 5 6 7 8

1. YES   NO

2. YES   NO

3. YES   NO

4. YES   NO

5. YES   NO

6. YES   NO

7. YES   NO

8. YES   NO

9. YES   NO

10. YES   NO

WORDS

Directions
Tests
16-18

PERCEPTUAL ASPECTS

Phonological Features
(initial sounds and syllables)

Name

TEST 16:

I will say some words. If they start the same, circle the YES.
If they do not start the same, circle the NO.

1. mat...man...mash   6. sand...sack...band

2. fish...fit...dish   7. bean...beat...mean

3. tooth...tool...booth   8. line...light...like

4. shop...shock...shot   9. rug...run...rub

5. net...neck...nest   10. gate...game...late

TEST 17:

I will say a word. Listen and count the syllables in the word. On your
answer sheet, circle the number of syllables you hear in each word.

1. people   6. again

2. another   7. world

3. before   8. under

4. through   9. sometimes

5. together 10. animals

TEST 18:

I will say a word. Listen and count the syllables in the word. On your
answer sheet, circle the number of syllables you hear in each word.

1. probably   6. several

2. however   7. automobile

3. electricity   8. misunderstanding

4. usually   9. important

5. remember   10. refrigerator

WORDS ★ 17

PERCEPTUAL ASPECTS

Phonological Features
(syllables)

Name _____

1. 1 2 3 4 5 6
2. 1 2 3 4 5 6
3. 1 2 3 4 5 6
4. 1 2 3 4 5 6
5. 1 2 3 4 5 6
6. 1 2 3 4 5 6
7. 1 2 3 4 5 6
8. 1 2 3 4 5 6
9. 1 2 3 4 5 6
10. 1 2 3 4 5 6

WORDS ★ 16

PERCEPTUAL ASPECTS

Phonological Features
(initial sounds)

Name _____

1. YES NO
2. YES NO
3. YES NO
4. YES NO
5. YES NO
6. YES NO
7. YES NO
8. YES NO
9. YES NO
10. YES NO

131

1. 1 2 3 4 5 6

2. 1 2 3 4 5 6

3. 1 2 3 4 5 6

4. 1 2 3 4 5 6

5. 1 2 3 4 5 6

6. 1 2 3 4 5 6

7. 1 2 3 4 5 6

8. 1 2 3 4 5 6

9. 1 2 3 4 5 6

10. 1 2 3 4 5 6

Directions

Tests
1, 2, 3

WORDS

EQUIVALENTS

Word-Sounds

(word recognition)

Name

TEST 1

Find number 1. Point to it.
There is a sentence by number 1
I will say one of the words.
Circle the word I say. (Pause 3 seconds between items.)

1.	the	6.	I
2.	to	7.	are
3.	is	8.	an
4.	it	9.	her
5.	on	10.	we

TEST 2

I will say two words. (Pause 1 second between words.
Circle the two words I say.   Pause 5 seconds between items.)

1.	they...and	6.	will...you
2.	what...she	7.	his...him
3.	this...new	8.	have...no
4.	at...them	9.	was...he
5.	who...said	10.	can...from

TEST 3

I will say two words. (Pause 1 second between words.
Circle the two words I say.   Pause 5 seconds between items.)

1.	mother...home	6.	six...days
2.	going...school	7.	think...big
3.	how...little	8.	don't...street
4.	men...work	9.	your...name
5.	did...something	10.	look...boy

1. Look at the people.

2. I go to school.

3. That is my mother.

4. It was too big.

5. Don't work on that.

6. I will go home.

7. We are very good.

8. I have an old car.

9. Do you see her?

10. When can we go?

1. They come and go.

2. What did she say?

3. This book is new.

4. Don't look at them.

5. Who said he went home?

6. When will you go?

7. His mother called him.

8. I have no water.

9. When was he going?

10. We can see from here.

133

WORDS

EQUIVALENTS

Word-Sounds

(word recognition)

Name ____

3

1. My mother went home today.

2. I am going to school.

3. How old is the little girl?

4. I can see men at work.

5. Did you get something there?

6. I went for six days.

7. They think I am too big.

8. What is your name?

9. Don't run into the street.

10. I will look for the boy.

WORDS

EQUIVALENTS

Word-Sounds

(word recognition)

Name ____

Directions Tests 4,5,6

TEST 4

(No directions. Children read sentences aloud.)

TEST 5

I will say a word.
Circle the word I say. (Pause 3 seconds between items.)

1.	has	6.	cut
2.	any	7.	set
3.	man	8.	use
4.	way	9.	own
	saw	10.	why

TEST 6

I will say two words. (Pause 1 second between words.
Circle the two words I say. Pause 5 seconds between items.)

1.	only...them	7.	city...town
2.	well...done	8.	door...open
3.	both...same	9.	very...much
4.	last...year	10.	want...more
5.	hand...feet	11.	gone...west
6.	eyes...face	12.	full...turn

134

1. our   has   yet   boy

2. any   got   now   two

3. old   big   car   man

4. end   far   way   put

5. all   say   saw   did

6. ask   off   air   cut

7. set   how   men   too

8. see   use   let   day

9. six   run   own   get

10. why   art   red   top

Read these sentences:

1. The man went to work.

2. I can see the little children.

3. My book is red.

4. Tell me who called today.

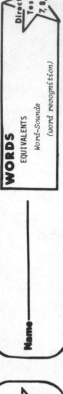

Name _____

WORDS
EQUIVALENTS
Word-Sounds
(word recognition)

Directions
Tests
7, 8, 9

TEST 7

I will say two words.
Circle the two words I say.   (Pause 1 second between words.
Pause 5 seconds between items.)

1. before...after
2. music...sound
3. another...number
4. never...believe
5. nothing...better

6. almost...always
7. different...place
8. should...change
9. around...across
10. early...morning

TEST 8

(No directions. Children read phrases aloud.)

TEST 9

I will say a word.
Circle the word I say.   (Pause 3 seconds between items.)

1. important
2. sentence
3. however
4. country

5. picture
6. children
7. enough
8. answer

9. family
10. ground
11. nothing
12. perhaps

1. were   only   them   been   even
2. well   most   each   done   long
3. both   know   same   must   part
4. made   take   last   does   year
5. high   hand   told   feet   head
6. eyes   face   road   show   find
7. kind   came   city   town   five
8. door   past   left   knew   open
9. seen   very   gave   some   much
10. need   best   give   want   more
11. real   gone   miss   west   feel
12. sure   plan   full   says   turn

136

WORDS
EQUIVALENTS
Word-Sounds
(word recognition)

Name _____

1. five long years
2. our first idea
3. find real money
4. got left behind
5. far down the road
6. wanted to go outside
7. found every part

WORDS
EQUIVALENTS
Word-Sounds
(word recognition)

Name _____

1. which before their after other
2. music first sound could these
3. might would under another number
4. never great believe where those
5. right nothing better three behind
6. until almost again because always
7. different brought front whole place
8. outside should every change church
9. above wanted around table across
10. early thought really morning money

WORDS
EQUIVALENTS
Word-Sounds
(word recognition)

Name _____

TEST 10

I will say two words.
Circle the two words I say.

(Pause 1 second between words.
Pause 5 seconds between items.)

1. modern...houses
2. strange...weather
3. machine...trouble
4. growing...business

5. suddenly...stopped
6. someone...decided
7. simple...problems
8. walked...alone

9. famous...scientists
10. couldn't...travel
11. taking...pictures
12. written...language

TEST 11

I will say two words.
Circle the two words I say.

(Pause 1 second between words.
Pause 5 seconds between items.)

1. interesting...stories
2. wrong...answers
3. pretty...garden
4. busy...afternoon

5. forest...areas
6. various...materials
7. sharp...teeth
8. especially...fresh

9. quiet...engine
10. feeling...afraid
11. radio...control
12. necessary...rule

WORDS
EQUIVALENTS
Word-Sounds
(word recognition)

9

Name _____

1. inside   important   instead   idea   Indian

2. special   sometimes   sentence   second   started

3. however   hundred   horse   himself   heard

4. complete   could   close   country   cannot

5. piece   picture   places   paper   people

6. course   certain   common   change   children

7. earth   either   example   enough   early

8. answer   animals   among   anything   animal

9. finally   father   friends   follow   family

10. group   green   ground   game   going

11. night   nothing   numbers   needed   notice

12. person   plants   parts   perhaps   problem

1. island | interesting interest stands stories states
2. weight | works wrong amount answered answers
3. pretty | practice party garden greater general
4. busy | beyond bought anyone addition afternoon
5. farmers | forward forest areas ancient arms
6. village | various developed minute months materials
7. stars | sharp shape teeth test team
8. especially | opposite examples formed fresh fingers
9. period | guess quiet eight engine edge
10. fields | fight feeling afraid age action
11. radio | record raised century control cattle
12. needs | necessary missing return result rule

1. music | moment modern horses human houses
2. straight | strange speed wrote weather window
3. moving | teacher mountain machine thousands trouble
4. growing | grass groups bottom business building
5. suppose | sides suddenly stopped spring store
6. someone | srow seven distance difference decided
7. single | simple square problems present pattern
8. woman | walked worked alone added although
9. famous | farm scientists figure sent sleep
10. couldn't | correct carried trying travel tall
11. takes | taking talking pieces pictures products
12. within | writing written leaves listen language

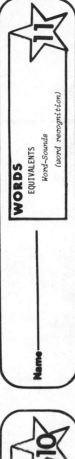

139

STARS Spelling Tests
and
Supplementary Teacher-Made Tests

The words which a child learns to spell should be highly relevant words. They should be limited to those:

(1) which the child can read

(2) which he will use in written work

(3) which reflect the content of the current curriculum.

Therefore, the best criterion-referenced tests for spelling are constructed by individual teachers to reflect the interests and learning experiences of the child.

The spelling tests included in STARS should be accompanied by such teacher-made tests. They may be helpful as diagnostic instruments, in determining a child's present level of ability, and they may serve as periodic summary tests, following several months of instruction. Field tests have shown that these tests represent the developmental sequence in which most children seem to master spelling skills.

Construction of Teacher-Made Tests*

While individual teachers are free, of course, to construct any sort of spelling test to accompany the STARS tests, we do submit the following recommendations for consideration.

*For teachers interested in constructing their own spelling curriculum, several booklets may be of interest:
Smith, J. M. Curriculum Developer's Handbook for Spelling. Chelsea, Mich.:Ed-Ventures, Inc., 1972.
Smith, D. E. P. Spelling: A Digest of Current Literature. Chelsea, Mich.:Ed-Ventures, Inc., 1972.
Wolter, J. B. Word Domains. Chelsea, Mich.:Ed-Ventures, Inc., 1972.
Drob, C. A. How to Program a Word for Spelling. Chelsea, Mich.: Ed-Ventures, Inc., 1972.

Domain

The lists of words covered by various spelling series are quite similar to one another. A series which takes a "phonic" approach, however, may include relatively more unusual words, which, nevertheless, have desirable phonic features (e.g., rhyming words such as rat, bat, mat, vat). The domain of words used in any published series is probably adequate as a base. Several word lists are also available which might serve this function. The STARS tests are based on the Rinsland-Horn List* of 1000 words used most frequently by children in their written work. This list is somewhat different from those based on a child's reading or speaking vocabulary.

Developmental Sequence

In general, common words are easier to spell than uncommon words; short words are easier than long words; phonically regular words are easier than irregular words. Thus, in the construction of the STARS tests, a sample of words was selected from the Rinsland-Horn List in order to balance these factors.

(1) Test 1 consists of very easy, mostly short words, frequency 1-100.

(2) Test 2 consists of short words from the first 300 words on the list.

(3) Test 3 consists of the longer words from the same domain as Test 2, frequency 1-300.

*Rinsland, H. D. A Basic Vocabulary of Elementary School Children. New York:Macmillan, 1945.(Reported in Coleman, E. B. "Collecting a data base for a reading technology." Journal of Educational Psychology Monograph. 61, 4, Part 2, August 1970.)

(4) Test 4 is based on frequency 301-600 words, but does not include any very easy words in that list.

(5) Test 5 is based on frequency 601-1000 words, and does not include easy words.

Format

STARS utilizes a "copyediting" format in its spelling tests. This format has the advantage of being easily administered in an individualized setting, since no script need be read by the teacher. It is also a highly relevant skill for students. It is not, however, the optimal test of spelling ability. To provide that test, the teacher-made tests should require that a child write a word from an auditory stimulus (dictated or auto-dictated). The usual method of administering spelling tests is adequate for this purpose: dictate the word, using it in a sentence (e.g., "Fast...The boy runs fast...fast.") Alternatively, a sentence might be constructed which prompts the student to dictate the word to himself (e.g., "The boy runs ____/not slow/.") Problems may arise with this format (a) if the child cannot read all the words in the prompting sentence, or (b) if the sentence is ambiguous.

When designing dictated or auto-dictated tests, the teacher would be wise to limit the length of the test. Since mastery is the goal, as in other STARS tests, it is reasonable to test students on a small number of words; from 5-10 is usually optimal, even for older students.

A response sheet is provided for use with teacher-made tests. These need not be used, however, if the teacher prefers to use regular school paper. The Spelling Record should, however, be kept by all children so that they may record their achievement on the teacher-made tests.

Standards

Like the other tests included in the STARS system, teacher-made spelling tests should be considered "mastery" tests, i.e., mastery is required. Most spelling tests are administered once with a final score recorded. In this case, the entire test should be readministered if a child makes an error. The process is repeated until mastery is attained. (Relevant instruction precedes testing, of course.) Similarly, if a pretest is utilized before instruction, and no errors occur, further testing is deemed unnecessary.

the ( )	kat ( )	big ( )
go ( )	yes ( )	heee ( )
aam ( )	be ( )	upp ( )
it ( )	look ( )	and ( )
bedd ( )	a ( )	we ( )

WORDS

EQUIVALENTS

Spelling

Name _____

Directions Tests 1-5 ★

DIRECTIONS FOR TEST 1

Point to the words in the box. I will read the words.

the...cat...big. Are any of those words spelled wrong?

Yes, cat is spelled wrong. It should be c-a-t. Mark an x

in the brackets next to the word, to show that it is wrong.

Don't mark the brackets by the other words, because they are

right. (Demonstrate marking an x in the brackets on the

blackboard if that seems necessary.)

Now look at the rest of the words on the page. Mark an x

in the brackets next to any word that is spelled wrong.

Go on by yourself.

DIRECTIONS FOR TESTS 2-5

Mark an x in the brackets next to any word that is spelled wrong.

142

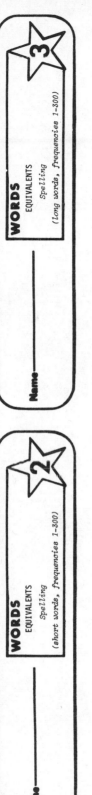

me ( )	can ( )	hte ( )
buy ( )	all ( )	wus ( )
not ( )	out ( )	hiz ( )
nue ( )	big ( )	bed ( )
did ( )	put ( )	hoo ( )
her ( )	sie ( )	but ( )
eat ( )	car ( )	olb ( )
let ( )	aer ( )	yuo ( )
cow ( )	cut ( )	tuo ( )
one ( )	red ( )	box ( )

another ( )	littel ( )	pritty ( )
around ( )	today ( )	right ( )
where ( )	funney ( )	paper ( )
white ( )	childen ( )	think ( )
yellow ( )	kiten ( )	yesterday ( )
water ( )	please ( )	scool ( )
about ( )	write ( )	agin ( )
mother ( )	morning ( )	house ( )
gess ( )	becaouse ( )	bring ( )
coud ( )	people ( )	brother ( )

Star 5

WORDS EQUIVALENTS
Spelling
(frequencies 601-1000)

Name _____

hungry ( )	hasn't ( )	garaje ( )	vaction ( )
oranges ( )	tonigth ( )	everybody ( )	toast ( )
listen ( )	goldfich ( )	autobile ( )	remember ( )
cousin ( )	elifant ( )	tried ( )	beleeve ( )
building ( )	spelling ( )	hunderd ( )	hosptal ( )
frends ( )	colored ( )	number ( )	breakfast ( )
mashine ( )	asleep ( )	bicycle ( )	fingre ( )
stopped ( )	raining ( )	early ( )	kindegarden ( )
behine ( )	upstairs ( )	electric ( )	reely ( )
balloon ( )	absent ( )	fense ( )	answer ( )
suppost ( )	swimming ( )	learnd ( )	clime ( )
coffee ( )	tiny ( )	nock ( )	without ( )
circle ( )	lettus ( )	kichen ( )	twelf ( )
sugar ( )	anybody ( )	second ( )	telaphone ( )
woman ( )	shirt ( )	scware ( )	sisters ( )

Star 4

WORDS EQUIVALENTS
Spelling
(frequencies 301-600)

Name _____

room ( )	gardin ( )	clean ( )	round ( )
storey ( )	reddy ( )	street ( )	tomorro ( )
enuf ( )	window ( )	allmost ( )	before ( )
sleep ( )	should ( )	mony ( )	whole ( )
wach ( )	leaves ( )	airplane ( )	purple ( )
sissors ( )	allways ( )	peice ( )	wanted ( )
playing ( )	robin ( )	happy ( )	breid ( )
dinner ( )	myself ( )	caught ( )	cuntry ( )
spring ( )	pincil ( )	chimney ( )	paented ( )
squirel ( )	afraid ( )	nothing ( )	siven ( )
farmer ( )	afternoon ( )	riting ( )	aminals ( )
broken ( )	football ( )	diffrent ( )	eight ( )
wenter ( )	pony ( )	dirty ( )	finnish ( )
brije ( )	having ( )	break ( )	hered ( )
mouth ( )	minute ( )	shue ( )	truck ( )

WORDS

Name _____

EQUIVALENTS
Spelling
(teacher-made tests)

I have mastered these tests:

1	2	3	4	5	6	7	8	9	10
11	12	13	14	15	16	17	18	19	20
21	22	23	24	25	26	27	28	29	30
31	32	33	34	35	36	37	38	39	40
41	42	43	44	45	46	47	48	49	50
51	52	53	54	55	56	57	58	59	60
61	62	63	64	65	66	67	68	59	70
71	72	73	74	75	76	77	78	79	80
81	82	83	84	85	86	87	88	89	90
91	92	93	94	95	96	97	98	99	100

(STARS TESTS)

WORDS

Name _____

EQUIVALENTS
Spelling
(teacher-made test form)

1.
2.
3.
4.
5.
6.
7.
8.
9.
10.

Name _____

| WORDS |
| GRAMMATICAL MEANING |
| *Syntactic Factor* |

Directions
Sample
Page
A

SAMPLE PAGE A

Find Number 1. Point to it.

How many pictures are by number 1? Yes, two.

I will say a sentence that goes with one of the pictures.

"I have a ball." Which picture goes with that sentence?

Yes, the first one, where the girl is holding a ball. Put an x
on that picture. (pause)

Find number 2. Choose which picture goes with this sentence.

"I am sitting down." Make an x on the right picture. (pause)

Which picture did you choose? Yes, the second one.

Number 3. "I am a boy." (pause) Which one did you mark?
Yes, the first one.

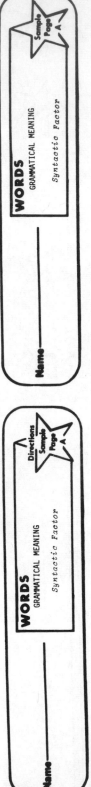

Name _____

| WORDS |
| GRAMMATICAL MEANING |
| *Syntactic Factor* |

Sample
Page
A

Vocabulary-Syntactic Contrast

Introductory Test A

1.

2.

3.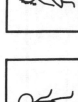

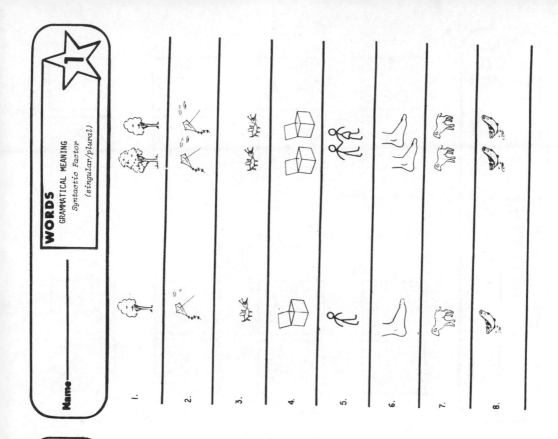

WORDS

GRAMMATICAL MEANING

Syntactic Factor

(singular/plural)

Name

Directions
Test

TEST 1

Find number 1. Point to the picture of one tree.
Point to the picture of two trees.
Listen to the sentence I say.

The trees have green leaves.
Is that sentence about one tree or two trees? Listen again.
The trees have green leaves.
Circle the picture that shows how many trees.

Number 2. Listen to find out how many. My kite is flying high.
Circle the right picture.

3. I saw some bugs on the window. Circle the right picture

4. There is food in the box.

5. Look at the children under the tree.

6. I hurt my feet.

7. The sheep is eating the grass.

8. The fish are good to eat.

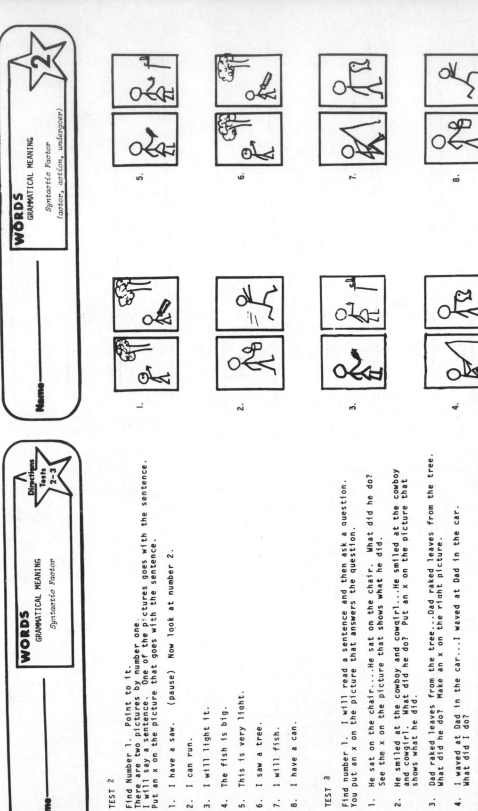

Name ___

WORDS
GRAMMATICAL MEANING
Syntactic Factor
(actor, action, undergoer)

2

5.

6.

7.

8.

1.

2.

3.

4.

Name ___

WORDS
GRAMMATICAL MEANING
Syntactic Factor

Directions
Tests
2-3

TEST 2

Find Number 1. Point to it.
There are two pictures by number one.
I will say a sentence. One of the pictures goes with the sentence.
Put an x on the picture that goes with the sentence.

1. I have a saw.   (pause)   Now look at number 2.

2. I can run.

3. I will light it.

4. The fish is big.

5. This is very light.

6. I saw a tree.

7. I will fish.

8. I have a can.

TEST 3

Find number 1. I will read a sentence and then ask a question.
You put an x on the picture that answers the question.

1. He sat on the chair...He sat on the chair. What did he do?
   See the x on the picture that shows what he did.

2. He smiled at the cowboy and cowgirl...He smiled at the cowboy
   and cowgirl. What did he do? Put an x on the picture that
   shows what he did.

3. Dad raked leaves from the tree...Dad raked leaves from the tree.
   What did he do? Make an x on the right picture.

4. I waved at Dad in the car...I waved at Dad in the car.
   What did I do?

5. The dog ate meat from the dish...The dog ate meat from the dish.
   What did it do?

148

TEST 3

Find number 1. I will read a sentence and then ask a question. You put an x on the picture that answers the question.

1. The boy will throw the ball over the fence.... The boy will throw the ball over the fence. Which one throws?

2. My dog chews bones and shoes...My dog chews bones and shoes. Which one chews?

3. The truck carried pigs and sheep...The truck carried pigs and sheep. Which one carries?

4. Trees are bigger than bushes or flowers.... Trees are bigger than bushes or flowers. Which one is bigger?

5. The box is full of apples and pears. The box is full of apples and pears. Which one is full?

TEST 4

Find number 1. I will read a sentence and ask a question. You put an x on the picture that answers the question.

1. Mom put the glass on the table...Mom put the glass on the table. What did she put?

2. The boy will take his book to school...The boy will take his book to school. What will he take?

3. She washed her socks in the sink...She washed her socks in the sink. What did she wash?

4. The box contained apples from our tree...The box contained apples from our tree. What did it contain?

5. The cat caught the mouse under the bed...The cat caught the mouse under the bed. What did it catch?

6. The dog found a bone behind the chair...The dog found a bone behind the chair. What did it find?

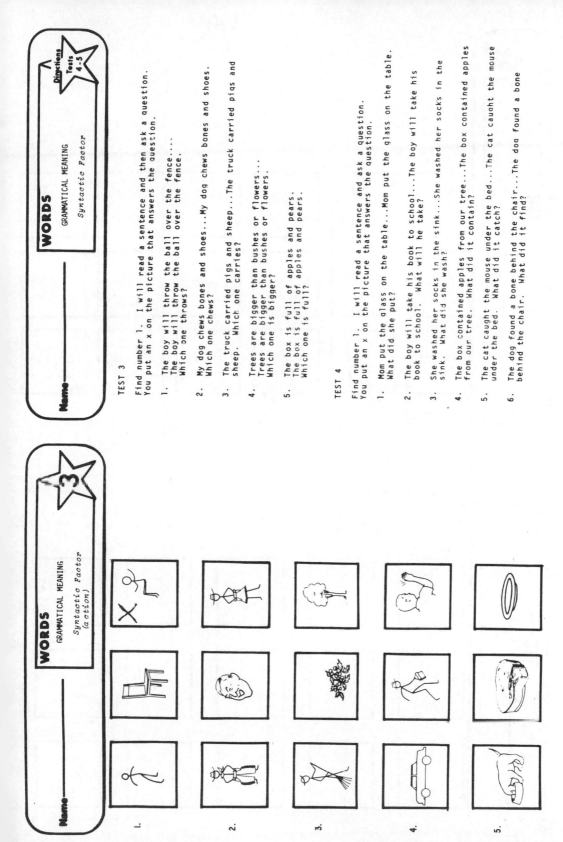

1.

2.

3.

4.

5.

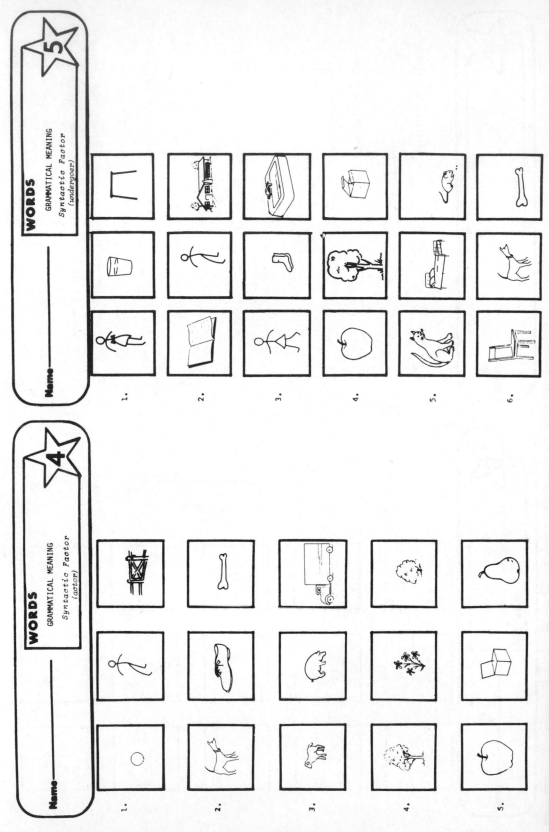

WORDS

6

GRAMMATICAL MEANING

Syntactic Factor
(tense)

Directions: Read each sentence. Decide when it is happening.
Circle the right answer.

When is it happening?

	already happened	happening now	has not happened yet
1. Joe is cooking dinner.	already	now	not yet
Dad cooked breakfast	already	now	not yet
Mom will cook a steak.	already	now	not yet
2. The dog ran home.	already	now	not yet
Those dogs run fast.	already	now	not yet
This dog will run faster.	already	now	not yet
3. I am reading a book	already	now	not yet
He will be reading it next.	already	now	not yet
Joe was reading the comics.	already	now	not yet
4. He has a cold.	already	now	not yet
He had dinner at my house.	already	now	not yet
He is going to have a party.	already	now	not yet
5. I see the picture.	already	now	not yet
I saw the picture.	already	now	not yet
I am seeing the picture.	already	now	not yet
I was seeing the picture.	already	now	not yet
I have seen the picture.	already	now	not yet
I will see the picture.	already	now	not yet
I did see the picture.	already	now	not yet
I do see the picture.	already	now	not yet

WORDS

7

GRAMMATICAL MEANING

Syntactic Factor
(actor)

Directions:

In most sentences, a person or thing does something.

"The boy ran home."   Who did something?   <u>boy</u>...home
"The cat ate the mouse."   What did something?   mouse...<u>cat</u>

1. The child plays in the street.
    Which one did?   street.....child.....plays

2. Faster and faster Dad drove the car.
    Which one did?   faster.....car.....Dad

3. The boy took a picture of his dog.
    Which one did?   boy.....picture.....dog

4. Yesterday we heard a loud sound.
    Which one did?   sound.....yesterday.....we

5. Into the hole ran the little mouse.
    Which one did?   mouse.....hole.....ran

6. His mother told Jack a story.
    Which one did?   Jack.....mother.....story

7. I asked Father about school.
    Which one did?   Father.....I.....school

8. In the dark forest lived wild animals.
    Which one did?   forest.....lived.....animals

WORDS — 8

GRAMMATICAL MEANING
Syntactic Factor
(undergoer)

Name _____

Directions:

In many sentences a person or thing does something to <u>another person or thing</u>.

"The cat ate the mouse."   Ate what?   cat.....mouse
"The boy saw the house."   Saw what?   <u>house</u>.....boy

1. The girl will catch the ball.
   Catch what?   girl....will.....ball

2. My mother can make a cake for me.
   Make what?   me.....cake.....mother

3. The animals ate food from the forest.
   Ate what?   food.....animals.....forest

4. Father read a book about cars.
   Read what?   cars.....Father.....book

5. We drove the car to the city.
   Drove what?   car.....we.....city

6. The boy cut the paper into little pieces.
   Cut what?   boy.....pieces.....paper

7. The dog bit the mailman in the yard.
   Bit what?   dog.....mailman.....yard

8. The children left their coats at home.
   Left what?   home.....children.....coats

WORDS — 9

GRAMMATICAL MEANING
Syntactic Factor
(scope)

Name _____

Directions:

In many sentences, we know more than who did it, what was done, and what it was done to.

"The boy ran home."   Ran where?   boy.....home
"The cat gave me the mouse."   Gave to whom?   cat.....<u>me</u>

1. We ran home before dinner.
   Ran where?   we.....dinner.....home

2. The boy threw his dog a bone.
   Threw to whom?   boy.....dog.....bone

3. His mother told Jack a story.
   Told to whom?   Jack.....story.....mother

4. The man paid me some money.
   Paid to whom?   man.....me.....money

5. We have lived here for two years.
   Lived where?   we.....years.....here

6. Dad ordered me to wait here.
   Ordered whom?   Dad.....me.....wait

7. The teacher brought her a new book.
   Brought to whom?   her.....teacher.....book

8. I asked Father about school.
   Asked whom?   I.....school.....Father

Name

WORDS
GRAMMATICAL MEANING
Syntactic Factor

Directions
Sample
Page
B

SAMPLE PAGE B

Sometimes a word can mean different things.

Look at the sentences in box 1.
  ...I saw a boy.
  ...The saw is sharp.
What word is underlined? Yes, <u>saw</u>.
Does saw have different meanings in those sentences? Yes, they are different.

Now read the three sentences by number 2. What word is underlined in the sentences? (pause) Yes, hand is underlined. In two of the sentences, hand means about the same thing. In one sentence the meaning is different. Put an x in front of the two sentences where the meaning of <u>hand</u> is about the same.

(pause)

Did you put an x in front of the second and third sentences? (Discuss the reasons for this choice if there appears to be confusion. Ask learners to justify their choices, i.e., what does hand mean in the second and third sentences; what does it mean in the first sentence?)

Now do number 3 and number 4.

(pause)

Check your answers.
Number 3...you should have put an x in front of the first and second sentences.
Number 4...you should have put an x in front of the first and third sentences.

(Discuss these items until it is clear that learners have a grasp of the task requirements. If necessary, make up more items, or ask students to generate sentences in which words have different meanings.)

Directions:

In most sentences, a person or thing does something.

  "The boy ran home." What did he do? home.....<u>ran</u>
  "The cat ate the mouse." What did it do? <u>ate</u>.....<u>cat</u>

1. Yesterday we heard a loud sound.
   What was done? we.....heard.....yesterday

2. We drove the car to the city.
   What was done? car.....city.....drove

3. I asked Father about school.
   What was done? asked.....school.....about

4. The girl will catch the ball.
   What was done? catch.....girl.....ball

5. My dog bit the mailman.
   What was done? mailman.....dog.....bit

6. Into the hole ran the little mouse.
   What was done? mouse.....ran.....hole

7. My mother made a cake.
   What was done? mother.....cake.....made

8. I learned about plants and animals.
   What was done? plants.....learned.....I

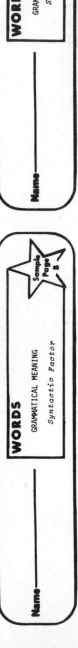

Name _____

WORDS

GRAMMATICAL MEANING
Syntactic Factor

Sample
Page
B

Vocabulary-Syntactic Contrast

Introductory Test B

---

1. I <u>saw</u> a boy.

    The <u>saw</u> is sharp.

---

2. ( ) <u>Hand</u> me that ball.

    ( ) I hurt my <u>hand</u>.

    ( ) I see his <u>hand</u>.

3. ( ) I like to <u>play</u> games.

    ( ) Will you <u>play</u> with me?

    ( ) I saw a <u>play</u>.

4. ( ) We walk on <u>land</u>.

    ( ) I saw the ball <u>land</u> on the floor.

    ( ) Trees grow on the <u>land</u>.

Name _____

WORDS

GRAMMATICAL MEANING
Syntactic Factor

Directions
Tests
11-12

TEST 9 and 10

For each item, put an x in front of two sentences where the
underlined word means about the same thing.

154

1. ( ) I must <u>water</u> the flowers.
   ( ) Give me a drink of water.
   ( ) The glass is full of <u>water</u>.

2. ( ) What <u>time</u> is it?
   ( ) Joe will <u>time</u> the race.
   ( ) The <u>time</u> is three o'clock.

3. ( ) Mary has a <u>long</u> string.
   ( ) I <u>long</u> for a candy bar.
   ( ) Joe has <u>long</u> hair.

4. ( ) Today my <u>back</u> hurts.
   ( ) Joe's <u>back</u> is sunburned.
   ( ) Dad will <u>back</u> the car into the garage.

5. ( ) Joe saw an old <u>man</u>.
   ( ) I can <u>man</u> the ship by myself.
   ( ) There is a <u>man</u> on the bridge.

6. ( ) I eat breakfast with my <u>right</u> hand.
   ( ) A cat will <u>right</u> itself when it falls.
   ( ) The cat hurt its <u>right</u> foot.

7. ( ) I like to <u>look</u> at TV.
   ( ) I don't like the <u>look</u> of that TV.
   ( ) I will <u>look</u> under the TV.

1. ( ) Dad is <u>working</u> in the yard.
   ( ) Joe is a good <u>worker</u>.
   ( ) Mom <u>worked</u> in the kitchen.

2. ( ) We will <u>part</u> tomorrow.
   ( ) They <u>parted</u> at three o'clock.
   ( ) There are three <u>parts</u> missing.

3. ( ) This book is too <u>wordy</u>.
   ( ) I can't read this long <u>word</u>.
   ( ) I can spell three <u>words</u>.

4. ( ) Joe is <u>numbering</u> his problems.
   ( ) Big <u>numbers</u> are hard to add.
   ( ) Mary <u>numbered</u> the pages of her story.

5. ( ) I can write my <u>name</u>.
   ( ) I <u>named</u> my dog Spot.
   ( ) Some boys' <u>names</u> are Tom, John, and Joe.

6. ( ) I heard a <u>sound</u> in the kitchen.
   ( ) He <u>sounded</u> his horn.
   ( ) Those <u>sounds</u> are loud.

7. ( ) Please <u>show</u> me your cat.
   ( ) We go to the cat <u>shows</u>.
   ( ) He is <u>showing</u> his new cat.

Sample:

Find number 1. Point to it. Read the sentence in the box.

"Joe likes to ___blank___." What word could go in the blank?

What could Joe like to do?

Look at the words under the box. Let's try each word in the blank to see if it makes sense. The first word is (pause) help.

Joes likes to help. Does that make sense? Yes, so draw a circle around it.

The next word is and. Joe likes to and. Does that make sense?

No, so do not draw a circle around it.

The next word is will. Joe likes to will. Does that make sense? (No)

Should you circle it?

The last word is see. Joe likes to see. Does that make sense? (Yes)

Should you circle it?

Now try the next sentence, by number 2. "Joe sees a ___blank___."

Try each of the words below. Circle the words that make sense in the sentence. (Pause approximately 2 minutes.)

Which words did you circle? Did you circle ball..(1 sec)..car..(1 sec).. boat? (Discuss the choices with the students if there is any uncertainty. Demonstrate by reading correct and incorrect choices in the sentence, if necessary.)

Directions:

A made up word is used in each item below.

Guess which form of the word belongs in the blank.

1. I have a gump. My gump is my pet.

   It eats a lot of food. I do not want two _____.

        gumps   gumpy   gumping

2. Mary likes to bort. She will bort in the morning and at night.

   She _____ whenever she can.

        bortly   borting   borts

3. My dog is very rilty. He is more rilty than my cat.

   But my rabbit is _____ of all.

        riltiest   rilter   rilted

4. Today it is my turn to grek. I grek every Monday.

   Tomorrow Joe will be _____.

        greking   greks   grekly

5. I have a tosh car. Joe has a tosh bike. Mary has a tosh

   wagon. We all ride _____.

        toshed   toshily   tosher

6. The boy tried to bink. He could not bink at first.

   He tried again. Then he _____.

        binking   binked   binkest

Name ——————

WORDS

GRAMMATICAL MEANING

Range

Directions
Tests
8-20

Tests 8, 9, 10, 11, 12, 13, 14, 15, 16, 17, 18, 19, 20

Look at the first set of words on the left side of the page.
Point to them. How many words are in that set? (pause) Yes, five.
There are four sentences next to the words. Point to them.
Each sentence has a blank where there is a word missing.
Put one of the five words in each blank. Be sure that it makes
sense in the sentence.
You will find there is one word left over.

Then do the same thing for the other sets of five words.

Name ——————

WORDS

GRAMMATICAL MEANING

Range

Directions
Tests
1-7

Tests 1, 2, 3, 4

Read the sentence in the box. Then read the words under the box. Circle
each word that could make sense in the blank. Score = Rights - Wrongs.

Test 5

Find number 1. Point to it. Look at the word by number 1.
 yourself "What is it?" Then circle the answer...FOOD, COLOR, NUMBER,
PERSON, or ANIMAL.
Do the same on the rest of the page.

Test 6

Point to the word by number 1. Ask yourself "What could it do?"
Then circle each answer that is correct. You will often circle more
than one answer. Score = Rights - Wrongs.

Test 7

Look at the word by number 1. Ask yourself "How could you describe it?"
Then circle each answer that is correct. You will often circle more
than one answer.

157

WORDS

GRAMMATICAL MEANING

Range _____

Name _____

1. | Joe likes to ____. |

help   and   will   see

2. | Joe sees a ____. |

no   ball   said   this

you   are   car   boat

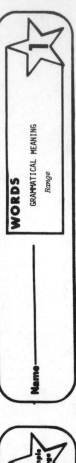

WORDS ⭐ 1

GRAMMATICAL MEANING

Range _____

Name _____

1. | Joe likes to ____. |

jump   blue   ride   did

me   dog   for   run

who   sit   paint   that

eat   you   about   look

2. | Joe sees a ____. |

house   around   dog   from

want   take   bike   fish

now   book   has   father

tree   man   away   thank

Passing = 12

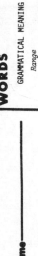

WORDS

GRAMMATICAL MEANING

Range

Name

1. Joe has a _____ toy.

soon   big   is   blue

red   for   green   new

all   funny   they   fast

2. Joe looked _____ a box.

for   cake   funny   in

good   at   on   home

3. Joe looks at _____ toy.

the   show   that   us

have   this   call   a

my   word   your   from

Passing = 15

WORDS

GRAMMATICAL MEANING

Range

Name

1. Joe rides in a _____ .

car   hat   bus   truck   wish

after   wagon   four   game   rocket

2. The animal is a _____ .

back   bear   wagon   goat   kitten

rabbit   walk   turtle   stay   window

fox   hat   hello   pony   horse

3. Joe has no _____ .

began   food   under   then   money

water   two   sister   our   just

along   friends   could   picture   maybe

4. Look at _____ .

them   next   why   him   over

got   her   us   took   these

Passing = 22

WORDS
GRAMMATICAL MEANING
Range

Name _____

What is it? Circle only one.

1. daddy......... food color number (person) animal
2. blue.......... food color number person animal
3. five.......... food color number person animal
4. horse......... food color number person animal
5. peanut........ food color number person animal
6. sister........ food color number person animal
7. fox........... food color number person animal
8. two........... food color number person animal
9. yellow........ food color number person animal
10. mother........ food color number person animal
11. cake.......... food color number person animal
12. turtle........ food color number person animal
13. one........... food color number person animal
14. duck.......... food color number person animal
15. girl.......... food color number person animal

WORDS
GRAMMATICAL MEANING
Range

Name _____

1. [_____ are you working?]

other   where   party   kind   time
why   grass   hold   when   gave

2. [We _____ .]

morning   sang   shoe   stopped   rocket
came   kind   went   those   lost

3. [We _____ go.]

nothing   should   kitten   brown   will
didn't   head   could   won't   as

4. [We walked _____ the box.]

behind   surprise   around   by   three
other   under   wish   over   any

5. [Joe hurt his _____ .]

gave   back   rain   head   hand
sister   where   leg   along   talk

Passing = 21

160

WORDS

GRAMMATICAL MEANING

Range

Name _____

What could it do?

1. boy......... fly (laugh) (see) walk
2. hat......... think try fall talk
3. tree........ walk guess come fall
4. girl........ help think hear fly
5. wagon....... eat stop go sleep
6. rabbit...... jump eat talk fly
7. father...... sit build guess read
8. airplane.... bark fly fall go
9. children.... fight hurry jump fly
10. baby........ sleep laugh fly eat
11. balloon..... fly wish build fall
12. dog......... run fight bark fly
13. bear........ eat fight sing run
14. bird........ fly sing guess stop
15. shoe........ fall try talk hear

Passing = 33

WORDS

GRAMMATICAL MEANING

Range

Name _____

How could you describe it?

1. sister........ big three blue happy
2. window........ little kind old fast
3. car........... red fast four kind
4. book.......... long kind funny old
5. man........... kind black five white
6. coat.......... green big wet happy
7. road.......... blue long new wet
8. peanut........ good brown kind little
9. letter........ funny four old long
10. truck......... three old last big
11. rain.......... happy wet long red
12. story......... two long funny last
13. duck.......... funny wet cold white
14. box........... green happy red old
15. town.......... big yellow kind four

Passing = 36

161

Worksheet 8

Name _____

WORDS
GRAMMATICAL MEANING
Range

the
or
them
who
get

same
put
set
often
enough

high
hard
change
body
kinds

space
hands
yes
can't
quickly

1. _____ little boys ran home.
2. _____ saw the boys?
3. I saw _____.
4. Did they walk _____ run?

5. Does he run home very _____?
6. He is strong _____ to run.
7. I saw the _____ boys.
8. They _____ on their shoes.

9. Did you _____ your shoes?
10. That bird flies _____.
11. What _____ of birds can fly?
12. It is _____ to tie my shoes.

13. I have two _____.
14. There is no more _____ in my toy box.
15. Pick up your toys _____!
16. I _____ find my toy box.

Worksheet 9

Name _____

WORDS
GRAMMATICAL MEANING
Range

instead
follow
third
wild
books

tall
heat
straight
teacher
trying

tail
blood
dead
son
method

playing
century
send
adding
wear

1. He is in _____ grade.
2. The cat will _____ me home.
3. The lion is a _____ animal.
4. I like to read _____.

5. My _____ is a man.
6. Draw a _____ line.
7. Joe is a _____ boy.
8. I am _____ to do a good job.

9. Your _____ is red.
10. The dog wags his _____.
11. His _____ is Jack.
12. The flowers in the vase are _____.

13. Jack is _____ outside.
14. Did he _____ his coat?
15. I am _____ 3 + 5.
16. I will _____ grandmother a letter.

WORDS 10

Name ___

GRAMMATICAL MEANING

Range

1. Please ___ the lost dog.
2. I was ___ the television.
3. That bug is one ___ long.
4. This bug is ___ as long.

5. We are ___ about Indians.
6. I go to ___ on Sunday.
7. The farmer plants his ___.
8. That ___ is shining in the sky.

9. I like to go ___.
10. He is ___ happy.
11. I can ___ very high.
12. What are the ___ between a dog and a cat?

13. I will drink a ___ of pop.
14. I am ___ it until later.
15. Did the ___ ring?
16. ___ your apple until later.

describe
inch
movement
watching
twice

hill
church
learning
crops
star

jump
fishing
differences
completely
captain

keeping
industry
bottle
save
bell

WORDS 11

Name ___

GRAMMATICAL MEANING

Range

1. This candy is ___.
2. I am careful ___ I cross the street.
3. The clown is ___.
4. Mom put an ___ in my lunch.

5. The President belongs to a ___ party.
6. What is the ___ of this coat?
7. Mom will ___ pie for dessert.
8. Can you ___ this heavy box?

9. The prisoner did not try to ___.
10. The miner takes ___ from the earth.
11. I keep my money in my ___.
12. There was too much ___ to sleep.

13. The fog makes it ___ to see.
14. Twelve donuts make one ___.
15. I like to ride in an ___.
16. Do you belong to the ___?

sweet
apple
cases
whenever
funny

serve
plays
political
lift
price

pocket
escape
represents
excitement
minerals

automobile
impossible
club
angles
dozen

WORDS — 13

Name _____

GRAMMATICAL MEANING
Range

travels
pleasure
industrial
false
anybody

raced
powder
handsome
articles
stems

skills
managed
private
plastic
checked

whistle
sink
shine
camera
constant

1. Dad _____ in an airplane.
2. That story is _____.
3. It is a _____ to meet you.
4. Did you see _____ in the hall?
5. I read some good _____ in the newspaper.
6. I cut the flowers with long _____.
7. The movie star is _____.
8. We _____ from the house to the corner.
9. We learn reading _____ at school.
10. These toy cars are made of _____.
11. That is the door to his _____ office.
12. The teacher _____ my school work.
13. Did the sun _____ today?
14. Joe likes to _____ as he works.
15. I washed the dishes in the _____.
16. He took my picture with his _____.

WORDS — 12

Name _____

GRAMMATICAL MEANING
Range

flies
pole
listening
somewhere
shirt

ought
silence
pound
cheese
citizens

influence
elephant
knees
touched
collect

beans
wherever
becoming
trained
visitors

1. The cat climbed up the telephone _____.
2. Are you _____ to the music?
3. I left my books _____.
4. That bird _____ high.
5. You _____ to stay home.
6. We put _____ in the mouse trap.
7. There must be _____ in the halls.
8. The _____ vote for the President.
9. The _____ is a large mammal.
10. Did you _____ the money?
11. I fell and scraped my _____.
12. Joe _____ the hot stove and burned himself.
13. My dog is _____ to sit up.
14. He follows me _____ I go.
15. He barks at _____.
16. Mom fixed hot dogs and _____ for supper.

Card 14

Name ____

WORDS
GRAMMATICAL MEANING
Range

opinion
occasionally
garage
rocky
species

complicated
grandmother
writers
chose
lungs

good-by
otherwise
chocolate
characteristic
midnight

combinations
selling
selected
adventures
underneath

1. ____ we go to the park to play.
2. What is your ____ of my poem?
3. This ground is ____.
4. What ____ of insect is this?

5. This story is very ____.
6. The author is one of my favorite ____.
7. ____ likes the story, too.
8. I ____ to read it for my book report.

9. My favorite candy is ____.
10. On New Year's Eve we stayed awake until ____.
11. When he left, he said, "____."
12. Long hair is a ____ of Persian cats.

13. We had some exciting ____ this summer.
14. The man was ____ hot dogs.
15. I looked ____ the table for my shoes.
16. We ____ the best books to read.

Card 15

Name ____

WORDS
GRAMMATICAL MEANING
Range

poems
gentlemen
breaks
committee
storms

ribbon
described
rats
mistakes
permanent

grand
westward
dairy
puzzled
races

diamond
trust
structures
electronics
assume

1. I am afraid of thunder ____.
2. Joe and Mary are on the ____.
3. Everyone in the class wrote ____.
4. We saw three ____ walking down the hall.

5. Dad set traps to catch the ____.
6. Mary tied a ____ in her hair.
7. I ____ Mary as a pretty, blond girl.
8. I made three ____ on my test.

9. The pioneers moved ____ in wagons.
10. It's a ____ day for a picnic.
11. We saw cows when we visited the ____.
12. I was ____ by the missing letter.

13. Mother has a ____ ring.
14. My brother made three tall ____ from blocks.
15. I ____ my friend to tell me the truth.
16. Did you ____ that I would bring the paper?

Card 17

WORDS
GRAMMATICAL MEANING
Range

Name _____

1. Mr. Smith is an _____ businessman.
2. This bottle is _____ "poison."
3. The men poured _____ to make a sidewalk.
4. In math class, we solved an _____.

5. Santa has a long, white _____.
6. Santa brings _____ of gifts.
7. We enjoy a _____ Christmas.
8. The roof _____ the reindeer and sleigh.

9. Mom _____ me to wear my new shoes today.
10. Our teacher _____ how to do hard problems.
11. I love to watch a colorful _____.
12. I saw the sun _____ behind the clouds.

13. The _____ fixed the bridge.
14. Joe was afraid of _____ on his spelling test.
15. He _____ the football over the goal.
16. The man took two _____ of the bridge.

equation
grasses
labeled
honest
cement

beard
supported
traditional
ridges
bundles

explains
permitted
sunset
disappear
inventions

workmen
failure
kicked
apparent
photographs

Card 16

WORDS
GRAMMATICAL MEANING
Range

Name _____

1. Mom _____ in my direction.
2. The dog _____ the robber.
3. I _____ out the answer.
4. My dog runs at a fast _____.

5. I don't know the _____ of the new word.
6. I go to church _____.
7. The rider used a _____ to make the horse run.
8. The _____ spent three weeks in space.

9. What _____ should I use at the end of this sentence?
10. The candy bar cost a _____.
11. I broke the _____ of my glasses.
12. I made two _____ on my test.

13. Sight and hearing are two of man's _____.
14. Do you have _____ money to buy lunch?
15. The tree _____ the path.
16. A _____ is a dangerous fish.

pace
attacked
figured
attract
glanced

pronunciation
wondering
whip
regularly
astronauts

lens
punctuation
errors
dime
contract

catches
senses
shaded
sufficient
shark

WORDS 18

Name _____

GRAMMATICAL MEANING
Range

1. I like movies better than television _____
2. Joe is trying to _____ a new kind of machine.
3. If you can solve this problem, you are _____
4. The artist paints on _____
5. I like stories with happy _____
6. The cook _____ the potatoes.
7. The artist _____ red and yellow to make orange.
8. The _____ stole the money.
9. _____, he broke his leg.
10. Mom told her to _____ the medicine.
11. Joe _____ he was a jet pilot.
12. Most boys and girls in school belong to _____
13. Joe wore a _____ costume.
14. He showed great _____ when he was president of the club.
15. He is always _____ to adults.
16. He learned to _____ a canoe.

invent
intelligent
leaning
drama
canvas

thief
endings
jewels
boiled
combines

intervals
unfortunately
swallow
clubs
imagined

frightening
polite
leadership
rectangle
paddle

WORDS 19

Name _____

GRAMMATICAL MEANING
Range

1. Mary _____ at the beautiful scenery.
2. That duck built his nest in a _____.
3. Eat the rest of that chicken; otherwise it will _____.
4. Mary _____ the weights on the scale.
5. Joe _____ a load of hay with his truck.
6. Mary always wears _____ clothes.
7. All of the information was entered into the _____.
8. Can you _____ whether it will rain?
9. Joe swallowed a _____ of vitamins.
10. I will _____ the sugar in my coffee.
11. Joe _____ the ball very hard.
12. King Henry VIII had six _____.
13. I tried in _____ to spell the word correctly.
14. My favorite children's game is _____.
15. Mary _____ her milk.
16. Is this story fantasy or _____?
17. The horse's _____ was long and silky.
18. Can you guess the _____ of the killer?
19. There were several deep _____ beneath the waterfall.
20. Which _____ should sign this permission slip?

balanced
openings
spoil
swamp
gazed
computer
dip
predict
sensible
hauled
throws
wives
capsule
servant
dissolve
reality
oars
tag
vain
spilled
pools
mane
supporting
parent
identity

Left worksheet

Name _____

WORDS ★20

GRAMMATICAL MEANING
Range

outfit
chapters
grasped
blades
assignment
safer
hesitated
plate
cloudy
bride
curves
den
patients
succeed
plowed
nectar
spices
supports
illustrations
remark
stanza
distribution
draws
sorrow
shrugged

1. Joe was proud of his new cowboy _____.
2. Mary read three _____ of her book.
3. She finished her math _____ in ten minutes.
4. As he started to fall, he _____ the branches of the tree.
5. Mary _____ before accepting the invitation.
6. Joe ate everything on his _____.
7. Sometimes it is _____ to run than to walk.
8. It was a dull, _____ day.
9. Dad slowed the car as he drove around the _____.
10. It's important to _____ in school.
11. The farmer _____ his field.
12. Bears usually live in a _____.
13. Joe made a nasty _____ to me.
14. Bees collect _____ from the flowers.
15. Ginger and cinnamon are both _____.
16. Our science book has many _____.
17. Joe handles the _____ of newspapers to his customers.
18. I felt a great _____ at the news of his death.
19. We have to learn the second _____ of the poem.
20. Mary _____ better than anyone else in class.

Right worksheet

Name _____

WORDS ★1

REFERENTIAL MEANING
Semantic Factor
(noun)

1. ( ) There are three feet in a yard.
   ( ) I wear shoes on my feet.
   ( ) He ran fifty feet.
2. ( ) This side of the rug is furry.
   ( ) Did you look on the other side of the page?
   ( ) Joe spoke on my side of the argument.
3. ( ) I broke my fishing line yesterday.
   ( ) The line is straight.
   ( ) Did you draw that line?
4. ( ) I learned the multiplication table.
   ( ) I set the dining room table for Mom.
   ( ) Please put your books on the table.
5. ( ) You gave me quite a turn!
   ( ) My turn is after Mary finishes.
   ( ) Every child must wait for his turn.
6. ( ) Joe has a cut on his finger.
   ( ) Mom made a cut in my allowance.
   ( ) This cut has healed quickly.
7. ( ) This knife has a sharp point.
   ( ) You made your point quite well.
   ( ) I made a point on the stick.

1. ( ) School begins tomorrow.
   ( ) I saw a <u>school</u> of fish.
   ( ) He left <u>school</u> when he was sixteen.

2. ( ) <u>Rain</u> is wet.
   ( ) <u>Rain</u> is good for the crops.
   ( ) A <u>rain</u> of ashes came from the chimney.

3. ( ) That <u>man</u> is wearing a coat.
   ( ) <u>Man</u> cannot understand everything.
   ( ) We saw a <u>man</u> on the hill.

4. ( ) My <u>church</u> is on Oak Street.
   ( ) I go to <u>church</u> on Sunday.
   ( ) Mom enjoys <u>church</u> very much.

5. ( ) <u>Color</u> is beautiful to see.
   ( ) My favorite <u>color</u> is blue.
   ( ) This <u>color</u> is too bright.

6. ( ) The astronauts flew in <u>space</u>.
   ( ) There is a <u>space</u> between my front teeth.
   ( ) Put the book in that <u>space</u> on the shelf.

7. ( ) Mom baked two <u>legs</u> of lamb for dinner.
   ( ) <u>Legs</u> should be washed weekly.
   ( ) <u>Legs</u> are very important to runners.

1. ( ) He had a funny look on his <u>face</u>.
   ( ) Jack climbed up the <u>face</u> of the cliff.
   ( ) There were green shutters on the <u>face</u> of the house.

2. ( ) The <u>rest</u> of the bottles are empty.
   ( ) Mom takes a <u>rest</u> after lunch.
   ( ) I ate three and left the <u>rest</u> of the cookies.

3. ( ) Bill is the <u>head</u> of the club.
   ( ) Mary bumped her <u>head</u> today.
   ( ) This cap does not fit my <u>head</u>.

4. ( ) I ate <u>part</u> of the pie.
   ( ) Joe has a <u>part</u> in his hair.
   ( ) This is my favorite <u>part</u> of the house.

5. ( ) There is a label on the <u>side</u> of the box.
   ( ) The <u>side</u> of the car is dented.
   ( ) Jack has a pain in his <u>side</u>.

6. ( ) Don't touch that coat of paint!
   ( ) My <u>coat</u> is red and black.
   ( ) Don't forget to wear your <u>coat</u>!

7. ( ) The <u>body</u> of this letter is too long.
   ( ) Joe's <u>body</u> is covered with spots.
   ( ) The <u>body</u> of the car is rusty.

1. ( ) I will <u>save</u> these bubble gum cards.
   ( ) I will <u>save</u> money when I can.
   ( ) He will <u>save</u> the drowning boy.

2. ( ) She <u>picked</u> apples from the tree.
   ( ) She <u>picked</u> Joe to be the leader.
   ( ) She <u>picked</u> the prettiest doll to be her own.

3. ( ) We <u>miss</u> our dog since he ran away.
   ( ) If we are late, we <u>miss</u> the train.
   ( ) We <u>miss</u> lunch if we don't hear Mom call.

4. ( ) Our car <u>works</u> best on dry days.
   ( ) Dad <u>works</u> in the garden on Saturday.
   ( ) Joe <u>works</u> at the factory.

5. ( ) Jack will <u>saw</u> this wood.
   ( ) Tom may <u>saw</u> down the tree.
   ( ) Bill <u>saw</u> the boys in the street.

6. ( ) Mary <u>beat</u> Joe in the race.
   ( ) Jack <u>beat</u> the dog with a stick.
   ( ) I hurried, but Sally <u>beat</u> me.

7. ( ) Mom <u>passed</u> the salt.
   ( ) The train <u>passed</u> the car.
   ( ) The black horse <u>passed</u> the brown horse.

1. ( ) I <u>have</u> a dime.
   ( ) I <u>have</u> seen you before.
   ( ) You <u>have</u> a new coat.

2. ( ) I <u>keep</u> some cookies in the cupboard.
   ( ) I <u>keep</u> marbles in a bag.
   ( ) I <u>keep</u> trying to remember.

3. ( ) I can <u>do</u> this puzzle.
   ( ) You <u>do</u> sing nicely.
   ( ) We <u>do</u> like our new teacher.

4. ( ) I will <u>swim</u> in the lake.
   ( ) Jack <u>will</u> go home today.
   ( ) I shall <u>will</u> you my gold watch.

5. ( ) It <u>was</u> raining yesterday.
   ( ) She <u>was</u> a pretty child.
   ( ) He <u>was</u> running away.

6. ( ) He <u>did</u> like ice cream when he was little.
   ( ) I <u>did</u> my job very well.
   ( ) She <u>did</u> see a blue car on the street.

7. ( ) Mother <u>can</u> cook dinner now.
   ( ) Mother <u>can</u> bake a cake for the party.
   ( ) Mother will <u>can</u> these tomatoes.

170

WORDS

REFERENTIAL MEANING
Semantic Factor
(verb)

Name _____

1. ( ) The sun shines in the daytime.
   ( ) Dad shines his shoes at night.
   ( ) That star shines brightly.

2. ( ) I got cold in the snow.
   ( ) I got meat from the store.
   ( ) I got my sweater from the drawer.

3. ( ) The bell's sound beautiful.
   ( ) The dogs sound unhappy.
   ( ) The boy will sound the horn.

4. ( ) The meat is cooking in the oven.
   ( ) Joe is cooking a stew.
   ( ) I am cooking dinner.

5. ( ) We looked for the lost book.
   ( ) He looked tired yesterday.
   ( ) The children looked in the closet.

6. ( ) The road runs through our town.
   ( ) My horse runs in the first race.
   ( ) Joe runs to school every morning.

7. ( ) Did you take your book to school?
   ( ) Did he take his pill?
   ( ) Did she take her doll with her?

WORDS

REFERENTIAL MEANING
Semantic Factor
(modifier)

Name _____

1. ( ) This door is stuck fast.
   ( ) Joe can run fast.
   ( ) That duck is swimming fast.

2. ( ) On Saturday we are having a big dance.
   ( ) Tom likes to climb big trees.
   ( ) In New York we saw big buildings.

3. ( ) That turtle is too slow to win the race.
   ( ) This train is so slow that I will be late.
   ( ) Mary is slow in math.

4. ( ) The boy climbed down from the roof.
   ( ) The amount of rainfall is down this year.
   ( ) The cup fell down off the table.

5. ( ) He will go far in life.
   ( ) The school is far from my home.
   ( ) We traveled far on our vacation.

6. ( ) The candy is free for little children.
   ( ) The bird is free to fly away.
   ( ) This game was free with a box of cereal.

7. ( ) She is a good girl.
   ( ) These are good cookies.
   ( ) Mom makes good pies.

WORDS

REFERENTIAL MEANING

Semantic Factor
(modifier)

Name _____

1. ( ) The boy hit the ball __hard.__
   ( ) This is a __hard__ job for a child.
   ( ) I have a __hard__ problem to do for math.

2. ( ) The bird flies __high__ in the sky.
   ( ) He jumped so __high__ that he won the prize.
   ( ) There is a __high__ water tower in our town.

3. ( ) He ran __straight__ for the door.
   ( ) Jane has __straight__ hair.
   ( ) I tried to draw a __straight__ line.

4. ( ) The __late__ show begins at 12:00 p.m.
   ( ) I came too __late__ for breakfast.
   ( ) The __late__ train has left already.

5. ( ) This is a __light__ red dress.
   ( ) This bag of feathers is __light.__
   ( ) The baby is __light,__ but I am heavy.

6. ( ) Mark and Fred came __too.__
   ( ) He is __too__ heavy for that chair.
   ( ) You run __too__ fast for me to catch you.

7. ( ) Jill is wearing a __pretty__ dress.
   ( ) Jack is __pretty__ big for a seven year old.
   ( ) There is a __pretty__ picture on the wall.

WORDS

REFERENTIAL MEANING

Semantic Factor
(usage)

Name _____

Directions: Read each sentence below. Look at the words after the
sentence. One or both words may make sense in the sentence.
Underline the word that makes sense in the sentence. If
both make sense, underline BOTH.

1. The sun _____ at 7:00 AM today. | rises | appears | BOTH
   That word _____ four times on the page. | rises | appears | BOTH
   Cream _____ to the top of the bottle. | rises | appears | BOTH

2. Mom will _____ a party for me. | give | hand | BOTH
   Please _____ me that package. | give | hand | BOTH
   The bandit said, "_____ over your money." | give | hand | BOTH

3. He made a _____ for the train. | dash | run | BOTH
   She has a _____ in her stocking. | dash | run | BOTH
   There is a _____ between the words. | dash | run | BOTH

4. The statue is made from gold _____. | dish | plate | BOTH
   My _____ has blue flowers on it. | dish | plate | BOTH
   Mom made a delicious _____ for dinner. | dish | plate | BOTH

5. Mary is a _____ girl | good | delicious | BOTH
   These cookies taste _____. | good | delicious | BOTH
   The most _____ flavor is chocolate. | good | delicious | BOTH

6. Mary _____ the roses. | sniffs | smells | BOTH
   She _____ to clear her nose. | sniffs | smells | BOTH
   The flower _____ nice. | sniffs | smells | BOTH

7. He has hair on his _____. | chest | dresser | BOTH
   My clothes are kept in a _____. | chest | dresser | BOTH
   She is a stylish _____. | chest | dresser | BOTH

172

Directions:
Circle the word that is most nearly the same as the underlined word.

1. My room is <u>below</u> the roof.

   across   under   above   often

2. We lived in the <u>city</u> last year.

   town   earth   world   house

3. I lost the <u>top</u> of the paint can.

   picture   bottom   part   lid

4. The <u>tip</u> of the knife broke off.

   part   handle   point   side

5. Don't forget to <u>close</u> the door.

   find   shut   fix   open

6. You may <u>begin</u> work now.

   like   stop   want   start

7. That was <u>great</u> ice cream!

   good   cold   my   bad

8. This jar <u>holds</u> grape jam.

   wants   makes   contains   means

9. She is a very <u>beautiful</u> girl.

   ugly   kind   pretty   big

10. I want to sail on the <u>sea</u>.

    river   earth   air   ocean

Directions:

Circle the word that is most nearly the same as the underlined word.

The baby is <u>little.</u>

long   (small)   good   kind

1. My <u>house</u> is in the country.

   school   room   home   work

2. This is a story <u>of</u> a cat.

   about   for   over   in

3. Our <u>dad</u> went to work.

   animals   father   people   mother

4. That dog is very <u>big.</u>

   funny   mean   small   large

5. My <u>mother</u> helps me read.

   dog   school   mom   dad

6. I <u>must</u> go home.

   did   have to   can   won't

173

Circle the right word.

1. I _____ three dogs.   sea   see

2. Have you _____ this book?   read   red

3. I will _____ my new shoes.   wear   where

4. I have _____ feet.   two   too

5. Try to give the _____ answer.   write   right

6. He does not _____ happy.   seem   seam

7. My eyes are _____.   blew   blue

8. Cars go fast on this _____.   rode   road

9. I _____ that old man.   know   no

10. In the _____ I lived here.   past   passed

Look at the first word. Circle the one that is the opposite.

boy: dog   (girl)   man

before: (after)   then   morning

1. stop: write   go   say   come

2. up: in   at   over   down

3. out: around   on   in   back

4. yes: no   all   never   sure

5. over: against   under   across   before

6. little: same   big   small   few

7. work: help   look   find   play

8. good: bad   kind   right   high

9. always: almost   enough   never   same

10. right: sure   good   new   wrong

11. hot: cold   sun   big   great

12. long: big   new   short   old

174

Directions:
Circle the word that is most nearly the same as the underlined word.

1. He drives his <u>car</u> to work.
   family   horse   automobile   bicycle

2. Is your poem <u>ready</u>?
   finished   beautiful   special   short

3. My favorite season is <u>fall</u>.
   winter   autumn   spring   summer

4. He is going to <u>buy</u> a new car.
   purchase   need   draw   start

5. Did you <u>find</u> where I hid the cookies?
   notice   remember   discover   wonder

6. We know the <u>right</u> answer to the problem.
   wrong   difficult   following   correct

7. How much milk is <u>necessary</u> for the cake?
   missing   required   especially   free

8. I am afraid to <u>talk</u> to the teacher.
   return   complain   read   speak

9. Mom won't let us <u>fight</u> at the table.
   argue   talk   eat   laugh

10. I will be <u>happy</u> when school is over.
    sad   finished   glad   busy

Look at the first word. Circle the one that is the opposite.

day: man   tree   (night)
yes: fine   (no)   good

1. back: front   side   form
2. first: next   last   second
3. many: some   enough   few
4. left: place   north   right

5. start: stop   turn   ride
6. high: slow   under   low
7. far: here   near   short
8. true: false   never   no

9. open: turned   closed   empty
10. early: noon   night   late
11. full: empty   blank   open
12. find: search   lose   take

13. buy: need   want   sell
14. strong: small   weak   little
15. slowly: often   quickly   first
16. heavy: light   low   small

17. life: sickness   birth   death
18. arrive: leave   bring   start
19. beautiful: ugly   bad   mean
20. dry: warm   dirty   wet

175

Name _____

REFERENTIAL MEANING

Classification Factor
(class members)

Cross out the one that does not belong with the others.

Mary   ~~girl~~   Ann   Jane

1. pine   maple   tree   oak
2. poodle   dog   collie   bulldog
3. left   north   south   west
4. over   under   beside   place
5. rose   petal   daisy   tulip
6. bird   robin   bluejay   sparrow
7. small   large   size   tiny
8. kitten   cow   puppy   lamb
9. move   walk   skip   run
10. father   mother   family   sister
11. fish   robin   bird   insect
12. size   shape   amount   big
13. ear   leg   eye   nose
14. number   five   three   ten
15. morning   night   afternoon   day

Name _____

REFERENTIAL MEANING

Classification Factor
(class members)

Cross out the one that does not belong with the others.

two   four   ten   ~~cat~~   spoon
knife   fork   ~~red~~

1. dog   cat   horse   tree
2. flower   dress   leaf   stem
3. boy   home   church   school
4. truck   carrot   car   train
5. shirt   pants   socks   bug
6. stone   apple   pear   banana
7. table   chair   bed   house
8. bike   ant   fly   bee
9. glass   metal   wood   cow
10. run   lamp   walk   hop
11. red   blue   seed   green
12. yellow   sing   talk   whisper

176

REFERENTIAL MEANING
Classification Factor
(synonyms)

Name _____

Directions:
Circle the word that is most nearly the same as the underlined word.

1. Joe's decision to tell the truth showed great <u>courage</u>.

   progress   ignorance   bravery   cowardice

2. We had a long <u>discussion</u> about the coming election.

   argument   message   lecture   conversation

3. Mother is always <u>worried</u> when I come home late.

   concerned   interested   pleased   curious

4. Mary lives on a <u>distant</u> farm

   remote   neighboring   rural   restored

5. Dad <u>attached</u> a light to the fender of my bike.

   carried   fastened   turned   assigned

6. We used different <u>materials</u> in our chemical experiments.

   machines   procedures   minerals   substances

7. Her <u>normal</u> costume is a sweat shirt and jeans.

   first   original   usual   previous

8. I <u>sometimes</u> ride my bike to school.

   usually   occasionally   naturally   willingly

9. Joe <u>traded</u> his marbles for a frog.

   destroyed   melted   exchanged   replaced

10. This is <u>perhaps</u> the most crowded classroom in school.

    possibly   certainly   usually   generally

REFERENTIAL MEANING
Classification Factor
(synonyms)

Name _____

Directions:
Circle the word that is most nearly the same as the underlined word.

1. Do you <u>like</u> your music lessons?

   enjoy   miss   finish   study

2. I missed the <u>last</u> question on the test.

   difficult   first   final   easiest

3. Show me the <u>correct</u> way to set the table.

   scientific   wrong   easy   proper

4. Mary <u>came</u> home after Joan and Betty.

   left   arrived   started   rode

5. We finally <u>found</u> my shoe under the bed.

   lost   put   dropped   located

6. We are not <u>allowed</u> to skate on that pond.

   afraid   going   permitted   planning

7. On your map, be sure to <u>show</u> state borders.

   notice   indicate   erase   avoid

8. I <u>particularly</u> wanted Mary to come home early.

   never   frequently   sometimes   especially

9. Joe left on a long <u>trip</u>.

   journey   vacation   train   climb

10. Can you <u>name</u> this flower?

    diagram   destroy   identify   describe

11

WORDS

REFERENTIAL MEANING
Classification Factor
(emphasis)

Name _____

Put an (X) by the one that is more.
( ) little   (X) big
( ) great   (X) greatest
(X) delicious   ( ) good

1. ( ) wet   ( ) damp
2. ( ) warm   ( ) hot
3. ( ) cool   ( ) cold
4. ( ) bright   ( ) dim
5. ( ) red   ( ) pink
6. ( ) grey   ( ) black
7. ( ) great   ( ) good
8. ( ) mean   ( ) vicious
9. ( ) ancient   ( ) old
10. ( ) thin   ( ) slender
11. ( ) beautiful   ( ) pretty
12. ( ) afraid   ( ) terrified
13. ( ) laugh   ( ) smile
14. ( ) walk   ( ) run
15. ( ) jump   ( ) leap
16. ( ) slam   ( ) close
17. ( ) exploded   ( ) broke
18. ( ) demand   ( ) ask
19. ( ) higher   ( ) high
20. ( ) fresh   ( ) freshest
21. ( ) darker   ( ) darkest
22. ( ) hard   ( ) harder
23. ( ) sweetest   ( ) sweet
24. ( ) hottest   ( ) hotter

WORDS

REFERENTIAL MEANING
Classification Factor
(analogies)

Name _____

A. big : little..........hot :
B. cake : food..........red :
C. hat : head..........shoe :

green	water	cold
color	warm	house
arm	foot	brown

Circle the right word.

1. flower : plant..........table :   tree   furniture   chair
2. door : knob..........face :   knock   arm   eyes
3. letter : w..........number :   four   write   g
4. some : all..........part :   nothing   whole   any
5. east : west..........head :   south   foot   hair
6. rose : flower..........saw :   tree   tool   hammer
7. nose : trunk..........hand :   tail   foot   paw
8. pound : hammer..........cut :   nail   paper   scissors
9. stop : go..........light :   dark   start   white
10. hot : cold..........free :   warm   slave   liberty

Left form (Student Record Sheet)

Name _____

WORDS

VOCABULARY FLUENCY

★ Student Record Sheet

TESTS 1-7

TEST 1 (Approximately 10 seconds/question)

1. ( )   3. ( )   5. ( )   7. ( )
2. ( )   4. ( )   6. ( )   8. ( )

Number of correct responses ____

TEST 2 (Time: 30 seconds   Standard: Ten different items)

Number of correct responses ____

TEST 3 (Time: 30 seconds/sentence   Standard: Ten different items.)

Number of correct responses ____

TEST 4 (Time: 30 seconds/sentence   Standard: Three different items for each sentence.)

1. Number of correct responses ____
2. Number of correct responses ____
3. Number of correct responses ____

TEST 5 (Time: 30 seconds/question   Standard: Ten different items for each letter.)

1. Letter: ____   Responses ____
2. Letter: ____   Responses ____

TEST 6 (Time: 30 seconds/question   Standard: Five different items for each ending.)

1. Ending: ____   Responses ____
2. Ending: ____   Responses ____

TEST 7 (Time: 30 seconds/question   Standard: Five different items for each blend.)

1. Blend: ____   Responses ____
2. Blend: ____   Responses ____

Right form (Directions/Test)

Name _____

WORDS

VOCABULARY FLUENCY

★ Directions/Test

Directions: This test must be administered individually. Standards for correct responses are listed below.

1. To be correct, responses must be given within ten (10) seconds. Count slowly to ten (to yourself). A stopwatch, while more accurate, tends to intimidate some children. A different time standard may be established for children with severe speech impediments, or for those with serious learning difficulties.

2. Correct responses must be grammatically correct.
   Items 1 and 2 require a verb or verb phrase.
   Eg. eat, swim, go to school, play with Joe.
   Items 3 and 4 require a noun or noun phrase.
   Eg. (3) tree, bunch of kids;
   (4) bookcase, room in her house
   Items 5 and 6 require an adverb or adverb phrase.
   Eg. slowly, well, much faster than me
   An adjective form, colloquially used as an adverb, is also acceptable if it is normal in the speech of that child.
   Eg. "That boy is walking very good." (well)
   "That boy is walking very slow." (slowly)
   The word "so" in sentence 6 is intended as a qualifier. However, it is ambiguous, and might be interpreted as a conjunction. Therefore, a clause is an acceptable response for that item.
   Eg. "She usually doesn't do her work so I do it."
   Items 7 and 8 require an adjective or adjective phrase.
   Eg. pretty, hot, nice to look at

3. Correct responses should make some conceivable sense, but need not be obviously sensible. If a response is grammatical, but not sensible, repeat the sentence with the child's choice. Ask him if it makes sense. If he can give a plausible explanation, it is acceptable.
   Eg. "When he is home, Jack can ___.
   "When he is home, Jack can fly. Does that make sense?"
   "Fly."
   "Yes, he can pretend to fly."

I will read a sentence, but I will not finish it. You tell me a word to finish the sentence as fast as you can.

1. In the morning I like to ____.   (verb, verb phrase)
2. When he is home, Jack can ____.   (verb, verb phrase)
3. Look over there! I see a ____.   (noun, noun phrase)
4. Mary keeps her books in a ____.   (noun, noun phrase)
5. That boy is walking very ____.   (adverb, adv. phrase)
6. She usually doesn't do her work so ____.   (adv., adv. phr., clause)
7. That picture is very ____.   (adj., adj. phrase)
8. This food is too ____.   (adj., adj. phrase)

Directions: The tests below must be administered individually. Since timing must be accurate, a stop watch or a clock with a second hand are required. Since some children panic on timed exercises, it is advisable that they be given an opportunity to practice timed exercises of this sort before being tested. The teacher might, for example, allow children to test one another, using a stop watch or wall clock, on exercises similar to these tests.

TEST 2

Time: 30 seconds   **Standard:** Ten different items

When I say go, tell me the names of as many things as you can.

Go........(30 seconds).........Stop.

TEST 3

Time: 30 seconds   **Standard:** Ten different items

When I say go, tell me the names of all the things you can do.

Go........(30 seconds).........Stop.

TEST 4

Time: 30 seconds for each sentence.   **Standard:** Three different items for each sentence.

I will say a sentence with a blank. Listen and tell me different words that could go in that blank.

1. The blank is on the floor. (30 seconds).

2. This is a blank toy. (30 seconds)

3. The book is blank the table. (30 seconds)

Name _____

WORDS

VOCABULARY FLUENCY

Directions
Tests
5-7

TEST 5

Time: 30 seconds/question   **Standard:** Ten different items for each letter.

(Select two (2) of the following letters for each student: s, b, r, t, m.)

1. When I say go, tell me as many words as you can that start with _____.
   Go........(30 seconds).........Stop.

2. When I say go, tell me as many words as you can that start with _____.
   Go........(30 seconds).........Stop.

TEST 6

Time: 30 seconds/question   **Standard:** Five different items for each ending.

(Select two (2) of the following endings for each student: ay, ill, ing, ow.)

1. When I say go, tell me as many words as you can that end with the sound _____. (Pronounce the ending, do not spell it.)
   Go........(30 seconds).........Stop.

2. When I say go, tell me as many words as you can that end with _____.
   (Pronounce, do not spell the ending.)
   Go........(30 seconds).........Stop

TEST 7

Time: 30 seconds/question   **Standard:** Five different items for each blend.

(Select two (2) of the following blends for each student: st, tr, br, fl, cr, gr)

1. When I say go, tell me as many words as you can that start with _____.
   Go........(30 seconds).........Stop

2. When I say go, tell me as many words as you can that start with _____.
   Go........(30 seconds).........Stop

Name _____

SENTENCES

PERCEPTUAL   Oral Reading
*Standard: No more than 3 words
mispronounced. Sentences read
with appropriate intonation.*

⭐ 1

1.   Can you come out to play?

2.   What a nice surprise!

3.   I go to school every day.

4.   Bill is a good reader.

5.   What color did you paint the sky?

6.   The little dog played with the bone.

7.   What is your name?

8.   I can see something red.

9.   This is a very good book!

10. Take the candy out of the box.

11. Come and see me swim, Mother.

12. Jack, where is your book?

Name _____

SENTENCES

PERCEPTUAL   Oral Reading
*Standard: No more than 3 words
mispronounced. Sentences read
with appropriate intonation.*

⭐ 2

1.   Jack went outside, dressed in his warmest clothes.

2.   When the rabbits reached the woods, they ran right through.

3.   "Mary," asked Mr. Brown, "where is your mathematics book?"

4.   I looked through my purse, and I found four shiny dimes!

5.   Just as I turned the corner, I saw the dog racing across the street.

6.   "You may open your eyes now," said the magician.

7.   We took the train to New York, more than two hundred miles away.

8.   Up, up, up went the balloon, until we could hardly see it.

9.   "I'll try harder," I whispered, "even though it won't help."

10. "I suppose," said old Andrew, "that you tried as hard as you could."

181

Name _____

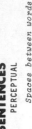

SENTENCES

PERCEPTUAL

Spaces between words

Decide if each sentence is correct or not correct.

1. This is a surprise! ( ) correct ( ) not correct

2. Thehouse iswhite. ( ) correct ( ) not correct

3. My doghas abone. ( ) correct ( ) not correct

4. I go to school every day. ( ) correct ( ) not correct

5. M y little boo k is red. ( ) correct ( ) not correct

6. Jack will find the ball. ( ) correct ( ) not correct

7. What did you have for lunch? ( ) correct ( ) not correct

8. Ihave anew jacket. ( ) correct ( ) not correct

9. I like white flowers. ( ) correct ( ) not correct

10. Write a sentence using five or six words. Be sure that the spaces are correct.

_____

_____

Name _____

SENTENCES

PERCEPTUAL   *Oral Reading*

Standard: No more than 3 words
mispronounced. Sentences read
with appropriate intonation.

1. Very carefully he went over the directions and made me repeat them until he was certain I knew them.

2. Joe was very much annoyed that it was raining, because today of all days he wanted to go to baseball practice.

3. Mark arranged the kindling in the fireplace and struck a match, with a small prayer that it would not go out.

4. Jane's role in the play meant that she must put on an old doggie costume and crawl around on the floor making bow-wow sounds.

5. "Jim!" Tom gasped, "Throw me a rope and yell for help!"

6. "Ah-ha," said the coyote, "so you thought that this fat, luscious feast of old mutton was for you, did you?"

7. The children took the cookies without so much as a "Thank you ma'am" and hurried out the door.

8. The fox, wary though she is, may show real courage in protecting her five or six cubs from dangers that may arise.

9. If you have nothing else to do this morning, would you mind taking care of the children until lunch?

10. The rabbit hated those cars that flung paper and cans onto the roadside--at least litter was flung from them, so presumably by them.

182

SENTENCES

PERCEPTUAL *Sentence Memory*

Standard: Sentences should be repeated without prompting with 100% accuracy.

TEST 1

Teacher: Repeat each sentence after me. (Teacher should say sentence only once.)

	Alternative form
1. She walks fast.	1. He came home.
2. I have three books.	2. Jane lost her book.
3. I can cook chicken.	3. I waited for you.
4. The tree has red leaves.	4. The bush has red flowers.
5. How did you get here?	5. Why did you go home?

TEST 2

Teacher: Repeat each sentence after me. (Teacher should say sentence only once.)

1. My blue boat 's broken.	1. The white dog is older.
2. I must look for my shoes.	2. She must drink all her milk.
3. The small black mouse ran away.	3. The big white horse likes apples.
4. Don't forget to bring some paper.	4. Don't forget to tell my sister.
5. Tom has to know if you like apples.	5. Dick wants to know if you have paper.
6. Ann found the treasure under the table.	6. Jane pulled her wagon over the mountain.

SENTENCES

PERCEPTUAL *Dictation*

(Frequencies 1-300)

TEST 1 (Frequencies 1-100)

Teacher:

I will say a sentence only once. Write down the sentence that I say. Be sure to use a capital letter and a period.

1. We look.
2. I am up.
3. He is it.
4. Look at me.
5. Yes I am.

TEST 2 (Frequencies 1-300)

Teacher:

I will say a sentence only once. Write down the sentence that I say. Be sure to use a capital letter and a period.

1. Let me eat.
2. We are out.
3. She did not.
4. The car is red.
5. His bed is old.

TEST 3 (Frequencies 1-300)

Teacher:

I will say a sentence only once. Write down the sentence I say. Be sure to use a capital letter and a period.

1. Please write to me.
2. My little brother went.
3. Today I can't come.
4. My paper was right.
5. I could bring mother.

SENTENCES PERCEPTUAL *Dictation*

Standard: Sentence starts with capital and ends with period. All words present and spelled correctly.

1. _____

2. _____

3. _____

4. _____

5. _____

SENTENCES

PERCEPTUAL *Dictation*
(Frequencies 1-1000)

Directions
Tests
4-6

TEST 4 (Frequencies 1-300)

Teacher:

I will say a sentence only once. Write down the sentence that I say.
Be sure to use a capital letter and a period.

1. The small boy found something.
2. The thing was very small.
3. It was near our house.
4. He almost took it home.
5. But it began to move.

- -

TEST 5 (Frequencies 301-600)

Teacher:

I will say a sentence only once. Write down the sentence that I say.
Be sure to use a capital letter and a period.

1. The streets are almost clean.
2. The happy farmer painted pictures.
3. Tomorrow afternoon we play football.
4. The animals live in the country.
5. She always wanted a purple room.

- -

TEST 6 (Frequencies 601-1000)

Teacher:

I will say a sentence only once. Write down the sentence that I say.
Be sure to use a capital letter and a period.

1. We built an electric fence yesterday.
2. Everybody tried to fix the automobile.
3. After breakfast, the kindergarten went swimming.
4. My sister believes she owns the telephone.
5. Remember to feed the elephant tonight.

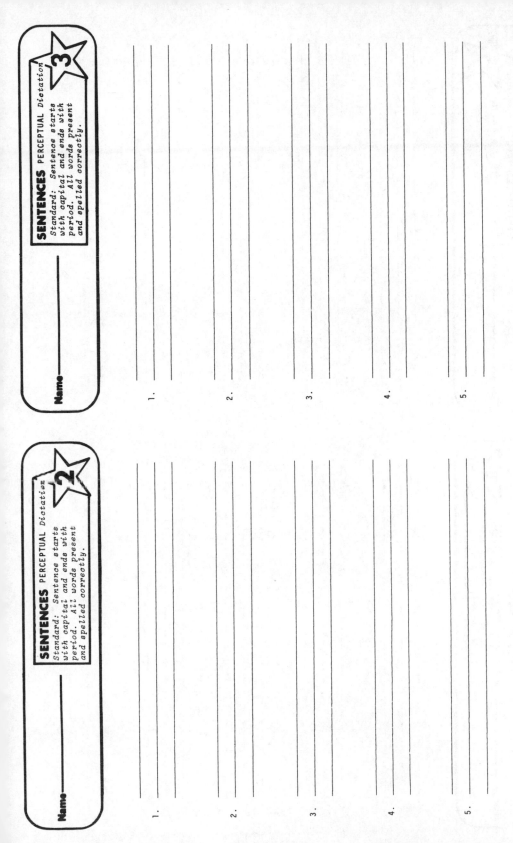

SENTENCES PERCEPTUAL *Dictation*

Name ____

Standard: Sentence starts
with capital and ends with
period. All words present
and spelled correctly.

2

1. ____

2. ____

3. ____

4. ____

5. ____

SENTENCES PERCEPTUAL *Dictation*

Name ____

Standard: Sentence starts
with capital and ends with
period. All words present
and spelled correctly.

3

1. ____

2. ____

3. ____

4. ____

5. ____

185

SENTENCES PERCEPTUAL *Dictation*

⭐5

Standard: Sentence starts with capital and ends with period. All words present and spelled correctly.

Name _____

1. _____

2. _____

3. _____

4. _____

5. _____

SENTENCES PERCEPTUAL *Dictation*

⭐4

Standard: Sentence starts with capital and ends with period. All words present and spelled correctly.

Name _____

1. _____

2. _____

3. _____

4. _____

5. _____

SENTENCES ⭐1

GRAMMATICAL *Capitalization*
(initial words; names; personal pronouns)

Circle each letter that should be a capital in the sentences below.

1. dick saw a dog.

2. mrs. jones is my teacher.

3. jane and i are friends.

4. do you know mr. brown?

5. where is your new book?

6. the best runner is tom.

7. dan, john, and i play ball.

8. who is your doctor?

9. i go to dr. james.

10. did dad drive you to school?

SENTENCES PERCEPTUAL *Dictation* ⭐6

Standard: Sentence starts with capital and ends with period. All words present and spelled correctly.

1. _____

2. _____

3. _____

4. _____

5. _____

SENTENCES — 3

GRAMMATICAL Capitalization
(titles, names and initials)

Name _____

Circle every letter that should be a capital.

1. Mary k white is our principal.

2. The newspaper reporters met with general eisenhower.

3. The church was dedicated by father george.

4. At the picnic we talked with mayor smith.

5. Everyone gathered to hear the speech by the mayor.

6. Mr. and mrs. lewis came to hear the speech.

7. "I will do my best, your majesty."

8. J. a. johnson, president of the club, resigned yesterday.

9. His father died at the age of 83.

10. We had a party to celebrate uncle ed's birthday.

SENTENCES — 2

GRAMMATICAL Capitalization
(place names)

Name _____

Circle every letter that should be a capital.

1. Our teacher is from london, england.

2. The city of chicago is often windy.

3. The southern part of the city is older.

4. Last summer we traveled to the west.

5. I have never seen new york city.

6. Our french teacher is not from france.

7. This ship travels on lakes michigan and huron.

8. I always fall asleep in geography class.

9. In english class we can read stories.

10. The california desert is hot and dry.

SENTENCES

GRAMMATICAL *Capitalization*
(buildings; addresses; organizations)

Name _____

Circle every letter that should be a capital.

1. I would be afraid to go to the top of the empire state building.

2. In six months we will move to 454 garden drive.

3. I am going to the library to return a book.

4. We attended a meeting of the greenville board of education.

5. The republican party is having a fund drive.

6. The university of michigan is near here.

7. Tom is a member of the boy scouts.

8. The dallas symphony is giving a concert today.

9. The building is on the southside highway.

10. I buy my food at the nu-way grocery mart.

SENTENCES

GRAMMATICAL *Capitalization*
(time related names)

Name _____

Circle every letter that should be a capital.

1. I can hardly wait until christmas.

2. Valentine's day is on friday this year.

3. My favorite month is july.

4. The program is on at 8 p.m. eastern standard time.

5. School begins three days after labor day.

6. We are studying about the middle ages in history class.

7. My dog was born last spring.

8. We will help the voters on election day.

9. This bulletin board tells about national book week.

10. Atomic energy was first developed in the twentieth century.

189

Circle every letter that should be a capital.

1. It is exciting to follow the progress of project apollo.

2. We flew to california on a boeing 707.

3. This play is about life on a steamboat.

4. The ss united states is a huge ship.

5. Our garden is full of virginia creeper.

6. My favorite flower is black-eyed susan.

7. Mr. Knowles trains king charles spaniels.

8. My favorite dog is the irish setter.

9. My sister wants to buy a miniature poodle.

10. This year we planted golden bantam corn.

Circle every letter that should be a capital.

1. In church we read from the bible.

2. Jack was raised as a roman catholic.

3. Tom, on the other hand, is baptist.

4. They each worship god in their own way.

5. I have been reading a book about buddhism.

6. She was baptized at an evening worship service.

7. Members of different churches say the apostle's creed.

8. The story of David is found in the old testament.

9. A jewish church is called a synagogue.

10. The baseball game is between st. mary's and first presbyterian.

Name _____

SENTENCES

GRAMMATICAL *Capitalization*
(trade names; astronomical terms)

Circle every letter that should be a capital.

1. Mother usually buys gold metal flour.

2. My favorite soft drink is gingerale.

3. My older brother likes coca cola better.

4. Do you need another box of kleenex?

5. When I get a headache I take an aspirin.

6. On a clear night we can see the milky way.

7. In columbus' time, sailors used the north star to tell their
   position.

8. The rocket was speeding past the moon toward the sun.

9. The spaceship will reach venus in two years.

10. Then it will return to earth.

Name _____

SENTENCES

GRAMMATICAL *Capitalization*
(direct quotations)

Circle every letter that should be a capital.

1. "where is your dog?" asked joe.

2. he called, "don't forget your umbrella."

3. "please help me," jane asked, "with this package."

4. we sang america the beautiful.

5. "my music lesson is tomorrow," he explained.

6. next month," she said, "we will go to the city."

7. "no," said the farmer. "we didn't plant corn."

8. the sign said no smoking.

9. "who wants to go" asked the teacher.

10. have you read the adventures of sherlock holmes?

191

Make each one below.

1.   Period

2.   Comma

3.   Question Mark

4.   Quotation Marks

5.   Exclamation Point

6.   Colon

7.   Semicolon

Circle every letter that would be a capital.

1.   Last week I read nancy drew solves a mystery.

2.   Our newspaper is called centerville city free press.

3.   My favorite poem is the charge of the light brigade.

4.   Last year we learned paul revere's ride.

5.   Learning to spell is our spelling book.

6.   Have you read the owl and the pussycat yet?

7.   I looked up the word in the american college dictionary.

8.   He is waiting for the next issue of dynamite magazine.

9.   My mother used to watch "the mickey mouse club" on television.

10. View of toledo is a painting by El Greco.

192

After each sentence place a period or a question mark.

1. What is your favorite animal

2. My mother works every day

3. I wondered if you could swim

4. When is the report due

5. Where is your new sweater

6. When Mom calls I have to go home

7. The teacher asked us to bring our books

8. Can you come to my party tomorrow afternoon

9. I do not like mashed potatoes

10. Do you like mashed potatoes

11. Write a sentence that needs a question mark.

_____

_____

SENTENCES

GRAMMATICAL *Punctuation*

(period)

Name _____

Place periods in the proper places in the sentences below.

1. I must go to school

2. I don't want to be late today

3. Today we will see a movie

4. Mrs Jones is a good teacher

5. School runs from Sept to June

6. After school I will see Dr Smith

7. My Uncle Joe plays football.

8. William the Conquerer landed in 1066 A D

9. School begins at 8:30 A M this year

10. King William had two sons

11. Write a sentence that needs a period.

_____

_____

193

SENTENCES

GRAMMATICAL *Punctuation*

(quotation marks)

Name _____

Place quotation marks in the following sentences.

1. Dad called, Don't forget your books.

2. Where is my shoe? asked Henry.

3. I didn't know the answer, said Jack.

4. I hope, Mother said, you like your new teacher.

5. I have just read Romeo and Juliet.

6. Don't fall! shouted Mother. The cliff is steep.

7. The Star Spangled Banner is our national anthem.

8. Ouch! called Jane, that cocoa is hot!

9. Were you late, Jane asked, for the movie?

10. Yes, replied Jack, I will bring cookies.

SENTENCES

GRAMMATICAL *Punctuation*

(periods; question mark; exclamation point)

Name _____

After each sentence place a period, question mark, or exclamation point.

1. What an awful mess

2. What is your favorite color

3. Look out

4. There were four horses in the barn

5. How terrible for you

6. I don't know how to spell

7. You were very rude to your teacher

8. Did the children finish their dinner

9. What a lovely surprise

10. Don't ever do that again

11. Write a sentence that needs an exclamation point.

_____

_____

In the following sentences, place commas, periods, question marks, exclamation points, and quotation marks in the correct places.

1. My favorite color is blue said Mary

2. Would you like asked Mother some more chocolate cake

3. Look out shouted Dan That car is coming fast

4. What a terrible thing to happen cried Joan

5. She has gone to the store John explained

6. I can't wait exclaimed Tom

7. The sign said Don't Feed the Tigers

8. He told me not to wait

9. Jack asked Can I go swimming

10. Jack asked if he could go swimming.

11. Write a sentence that needs quotation marks.

⎯⎯⎯⎯⎯⎯⎯⎯⎯⎯⎯⎯⎯⎯⎯⎯⎯⎯⎯

⎯⎯⎯⎯⎯⎯⎯⎯⎯⎯⎯⎯⎯⎯⎯⎯⎯⎯⎯

Place commas in the proper places.

1. Jack said "I like white cake."

2. "My friend s Jane " said Mary.

3. "Where is my shirt?" asked Dad.

4. Mom shouted "Don't fall!"

5. "What a wonderful surprise!" she exclaimed.

6. "Tell me " Dad said "about the party."

7. "I hope you learned " he added "to swim."

8. "What are you doing " Mom asked "with the book?"

9. "Oh no!" he called "my bat is broken."

10. "I like to play ball " he explained "in the back yard."

SENTENCES

GRAMMATICAL Punctuation
(comma: series, coordinate adjectives)

Name _____

Place commas in the proper places. Commas are not needed in every sentence.

1. My favorite months are March June and December.

2. Jane Mary and Ann came to the party.

3. I don't like cake cookies or candy for lunch.

4. The teacher the principal and my mother met in the office.

5. I ordered steak and French fries.

6. It is going to be a long hot summer.

7. I have a dark blue jacket.

8. I have one fancy frilly white dress.

9. The old man sat in a high-backed wooden rocking chair.

10. We picked apples peaches plums and pears.

SENTENCES

GRAMMATICAL Punctuation
(comma: compound sentences)

Name _____

Place commas in the proper places. Commas are not needed in every sentence.

1. I tried to run but my feet would not move.

2. The band began to play and Jack stood up to sing his solo.

3. Can you bring cookies to the party or would you rather bring cake?

4. I go up Mother made my breakfast and then I left for school.

5. The little black dog and the big white dog ran up the driveway.

6. Mary loves cats and is planning to get one.

7. He wanted to hit a home run so he swung as hard as he could.

8. I hurried to catch up with the group but they were going much too fast.

9. I want to go to camp this summer and I hope to learn to swim.

10. First we drew the pictures then we painted them and then we hung them in the hall.

★ 10

SENTENCES

GRAMMATICAL Punctuation
(comma; interjections,
transitionals)

Name _____

Place commas in the proper places. Commas are not needed in every sentence.

1. Well I thought you had gone home.

2. Yes I think I will like this movie.

3. After all you are my mother.

4. Oh no you didn't forget your homework!

5. However we took the test later.

6. You after all are my favorite uncle.

7. We left after all the other guests had gone.

8. Perhaps Joe will become a doctor.

9. Joe perhaps will become a doctor.

10. We will try therefore to find the lost book.

Place commas in the proper places. Commas are not needed in every sentence.

1. Next summer we will visit the capital Washington D.C.

2. I want to find Miss Drew the third grade teacher.

3. Baby cats or kittens are fun to play with.

4. I stayed up late to read my book a mystery story.

5. The sign "Keep off the Grass" is often found in parks.

6. My best friend Jane is going to stay overnight.

7. He gave the answer "No" to every question.

8. The President of the United States President Johnson was from Texas.

9. On the wall was a picture of President Johnson.

10. The tree in our yard an elm is dying.

Name _____

SENTENCES
GRAMMATICAL *Punctuation*
(commas: antithetical elements)

13 ★

SENTENCES
GRAMMATICAL *Punctuation*
(commas: dates, places, titles)

Worksheet 12

Place commas in the proper places. Commas are not necessary in every sentence.

1. The most interesting and also hardest class is math.

2. He can and probably will hit a home run.

3. John often called "Jack" is my best friend.

4. Joan not Mary is the best reader in the class.

5. The more I read this book the less I like it.

6. The sooner the better.

7. Whatever you say I will do the opposite.

8. This road leads away from rather than toward home.

9. The roses not the marigolds need water.

10. The fastest runner and winner of the meet was Sally.

Worksheet 13

Place commas in the proper places. Commas are not needed in every sentence.

1. I was born on May 22 1972.

2. We moved to 542 Oak Street Central City Mississippi.

3. Abraham Lincoln President of the United States was assassinated.

4. She is from Detroit Michigan.

5. This is Mrs. Brown leader of our Brownie Troop.

6. William of Orange became King of England.

7. We plan to visit Denver Colorado next summer.

8. My pen pal is Maria Gonzalez of Brazil.

9. The meeting was held in April 1974.

10. Our teacher invited Mr. Tompkins Chief of Police to speak to our class.

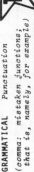

Name _____

SENTENCES 15

GRAMMATICAL   Punctuation
*(comma: mistaken junctions;
that is, namely, for example)*

Place commas in the proper places. Commas are not needed in every
sentence.

1. He asked all his friends namely John, Jack, and Ted.

2. We had delicious desserts at camp--for example chocolate
   cake and apple pie.

3. Poodles, schnauzers and dachshunds are examples of dogs who do
   not shed.

4. Members from several European countries (that is France, England,
   and Germany) attended the meeting.

5. Some dogs (for example poodles, schnauzers and dachshunds)
   do not shed.

6. To Susy Blake was always a hero.

7. Soon after the bell rang and we left.

8. My family (that is my sisters and brothers) go to bed at 9:00 p.m.

9. Standing next to Jean wearing a blue jacket is Ken.

10. Before he went to the store for bread.

Place commas in the proper places. Commas are not needed in every
sentence.

1. Jane will be it appears fifteen minutes late.

2. Dogs it is generally believed shed their hair.

3. Schnauzers I have found do not shed hair.

4. The teacher was to say the least upset.

5. I had to swim (luckily I am a good swimmer) clear across the lake.

6. Old Mrs. Winston I remember had a lovely black cat.

7. Ted Smith--he has a 300 batting average--is up at bat.

8. My trumpet teacher told me to practice thirty minutes every day--
   I never have.

9. Mother wants me to get 100% on my test so she says.

10. On my birthday I will have a party I hope.

199

SENTENCES

☆16

GRAMMATICAL   *Punctuation*
(comma: introductory phrases
and clauses)

Name _____

Place commas in the proper places. Commas are not needed in every sentence.

1. Having just finished running home he was very tired.

2. Tired from pulling weeds she took a nap.

3. Pulling the loaded cart was a black and white horse.

4. After reading the letter Henry was excited.

5. After lunch we will take a walk.

6. If you are late we will wait for you.

7. Next Wednesday school begins.

8. Running home from school is my favorite exercise.

9. When you have finished come home for lunch.

10. Giggling and screaming the girls ran down the hall.

SENTENCES

☆17

GRAMMATICAL   *Punctuation*
(comma: nonrestrictive phrases
and clauses)

Name _____

Place commas in the proper places. Commas are not needed in every sentence.

1. Paul agreed to go although he didn't want to.

2. Paul agreed to go if I would go too.

3. Paul would not go when he heard how cold it would be.

4. Paul could not go because the bus was late.

5. The chocolate cake that we had for dinner is my favorite.

6. We had chocolate cake which is my favorite for dinner.

7. The little girl living in that house is named Mary Ann.

8. Mary Ann living in that house for ten years wanted to leave.

9. Mary Ann Smith who lives in that house is my best friend.

10. I found out when the newspaper came that Mr. Brown had died.

SENTENCES

Name _____

GRAMMATICAL *Punctuation*
(semicolon: series)

19

Place commas and semicolons in the proper places.

1. I put in my suitcase all these things: sweaters pants underwear and my jacket.

2. The orchestra played: Symphony No. 1, by Beethoven Slavonic Dance No. 6, by Dvorak and the St. Lawrence Overture, by Washburn.

3. People from each city attended the meeting: Detroit, three members Chicago, four members Atlanta, one member and New York, five members.

4. I found that some of my crayons were missing: red black orange and pink.

5. You should cut down on sugar because (1) it causes heart ailments (2) it makes you fat and (3) it is not necessary in your diet.

6. James told the teacher that (1) he forgot his lunch (2) he has no money with him and (3) he would like to borrow twenty-five cents, if she has it.

7. I read three books last month: Huckleberry Finn, which is my favorite Tom Sawyer, which is boring and Treasure Island which is all right.

8. The score of the card game was: Jim, 10 Ken, 8 Fred, 3 and Tom, 0.

9. Last night we played: Rummy Old Maid Fish and Canasta.

10. For example: Ann is a poor student Judy is a good student Ann and Judy are good friends.

SENTENCES

Name _____

GRAMMATICAL *Punctuation*
(semicolon: sentence break)

18

Place commas or semicolons in each of the following sentences.

1. We picked ten apples then we made apple pie.

2. Marion, who had studied piano for ten years, was asked to attend a special camp but she got sick and couldn't go.

3. It took us three hours to climb to the top and then we climbed down again.

4. James was a good hitter however this time he struck out.

5. Fred likes all comics but Superman is his favorite.

6. I got a good report card therefore Dad gave me a dollar.

7. Frogs like wet places yet there are many in my back yard.

8. George was sick and so I went on to school alone.

9. We were very noisy this morning thus we cannot go out for recess.

10. Please bring your money tomorrow or else you may not go on the trip.

201

Place commas and colon in the proper places.

1. You know the rule No talking.

2. We visited three states namely Ohio, Wisconsin, and Michigan.

3. The members of the club are Jane, Ann, Mary, Joan, and Sally.

4. We have lived in three states New York, California, and Tennessee.

5. To make chocolate milk (1) pour one cup of milk, (2) measure 1 spoonful of chocolate, and (3) stir briskly.

6. We discovered two reasons for his headaches he was allergic to peanuts, and he was allergic to milk.

7. Speeches usually begin in the same way Ladies and Gentlemen...

8. I remember his words "You'll never regret this action."

9. He said "You'll never regret this action."

10. He likes most classical music for example the music of Beethoven, Brahms, and Mozart.

Place punctuation in the sentences below.

1. Don't move he shouted until I can tie this rope.

2. The bully said Come here kid we ran in the other direction

3. We start school in Sept but Karen starts in August

4. We always shop at Brown and Co

5. We had to sing The Star Spangled Banner

6. Where is my dog asked Henry

7. Write a sentence that needs a semicolon and a period.
   _____
   _____

8. Write a sentence that needs a colon, a comma, and a period.
   _____
   _____

Rewrite each of these sentences, making it plural.

1. I am going home.

2. That woman is wearing slacks.

3. The number is hard to read.

4. He walks to school.

5. My foot is cold.

6. The boy always asks questions.

7. A tree is falling.

8. This dog was lost.

Rewrite each of these sentences, making it singular.

1. We are going home.

2. They read this book.

3. Dogs ran after the cat.

4. We do our work.

5. The children like to play.

6. They have a new pet.

7. Those men run in the street.

8. These colors are bright.

Rewrite each of these sentences, using a pronoun for the underlined words.

1. <u>Jack and Bob</u> went downtown.

2. Give those books to <u>the girls</u>.

3. We forgot <u>our books</u>.

4. <u>The trees</u> are dead.

5. I got these cookies for <u>Mary</u>.

6. <u>Ken</u> is late for school.

7. The teacher gave <u>Ken</u> a pencil.

8. <u>Mrs. Brown</u> drives a car.

9. <u>The pencil</u> is on the floor.

10. Mom gave <u>the box</u> to me.

Rewrite each of these sentences, making it negative.

1. You are my friend.

2. I live in this town.

3. I took my lunch to school.

4. I will sing this song.

5. They have seen this before.

6. He is doing the test.

7. We have been trying to find it.

8. They will have been here three weeks.

SENTENCES
GRAMMATICAL *Transformations*
(present tense)

Rewrite each of these sentences, changing it to present tense.

1. Jack found his shoe.

2. She will swim in the lake.

3. We went to school.

4. It was time for lunch.

5. The dog was afraid of me.

6. He had spoken to my mother.

7. I will not take this cake.

8. He washed his hands.

SENTENCES
GRAMMATICAL *Transformations*
(pronouns)

Rewrite each of these sentences, using a pronoun (or a different pronoun) for the underlined words.

1. Jack and <u>myself</u> came to the party.

2. These books are for <u>ourselves</u>.

3. I saw <u>Tom's</u> new dog.

4. <u>Jane's</u> sweater is blue.

5. The <u>car's</u> horn is broken.

6. We went to the <u>children's</u> school.

7. I bought those books for <u>myself</u>.

8. <u>Jack's</u> dog chased <u>Tom and Fred</u>.

Rewrite each of these sentences, changing them to past tense.

1. I have three dogs.

2. We will bake a cake.

3. He has to bring the book.

4. The firemen will put out the fire.

5. They are fishing for perch.

6. She is holding the baby.

7. He runs to school.

8. I do not like chocolate.

SENTENCES
GRAMMATICAL *Transformations*
(future tense)

Name _____

8

Rewrite each of these sentences, changing it to future tense.

1. The boys went out the door.

2. I am digging a deep hole.

3. I do not sing that song.

4. He lives in the big house.

5. The sun shone brightly.

6. The car turned the corner.

7. I am twelve years old.

8. They cut down the trees.

SENTENCES

GRAMMATICAL *Transformations*
(*auxiliaries: have*)

10

SENTENCES

GRAMMATICAL *Transformations*
(*auxiliaries: be*)

Name _____

Rewrite each of these sentences, using the word in parentheses.

1. We go to school. (Use have.)

2. You looked for the dog. (Use had.)

3. She drew a picture. (Use has.)

4. We will try to climb the tree. (Use will have.)

5. That dog barks at me. (Use has.)

6. They did the job. (Use have.)

7. I could not see the parade. (Use have.)

8. You cut your thumb. (Use have.)

Name _____

Rewrite each of these sentences, using the word in parentheses.

1. I bring the newspaper. (Use am.)

2. You won the race. (Use are.)

3. He watched a flying saucer. (Use was.)

4. They caught a lot of fish. (Use were.)

5. You gave me a dollar. (Use will be.)

6. I took piano lessons. (Use will be.)

7. I went to camp. (Use am.)

8. The moon shines brightly. (Use is.)

207

Rewrite each of these sentences, making it passive.

1. The dog chased the cat.

2. We have seen that movie.

3. Jack brought the cookies.

4. They sang The Star Spangled Banner.

5. Mary drew the map of our school.

6. My little brother lost the bat.

7. I did not bring that cake.

8. We did not break the dish.

Rewrite each of these sentences, using the words in parentheses.

1. I drank the milk. (Use <u>have been</u>.)

2. She does her homework. (Use <u>has been</u>.)

3. The wheat grew very tall. (Use <u>has been</u>.)

4. They stood in the rain. (Use <u>will have been</u>.)

5. We tried to call you. (Use <u>have been</u>.)

6. The girls play baseball here. (Use <u>have been</u>.)

7. I was sick for a week. (Use <u>will have been</u>.)

8. We are having lunch. (Use <u>have been</u>.)

SENTENCES
GRAMMATICAL *Transformations*
(links)

Name

Make two sentences of each sentence below. Keep the meaning the same. Change the words where necessary.

1. Joe brushed his teeth and then he combed his hair.

2. I have to hurry or I will be late.

3. We tried to climb that tree, but it was too high.

4. We played cards while it was raining.

5. He ran away when he saw me coming.

6. I am happy today because it is my birthday.

7. Mary can't go to school, since she is only four.

8. She didn't finish her homework, so she can't watch television.

SENTENCES
GRAMMATICAL *Transformations*
(links)

Name

Make one sentence of each two sentences below. Keep the meaning the same. Change words where necessary.

1. You may have some ice cream. First you must eat your dinner.

2. Mary brought cookies. Jane brought cake.

3. This tree grew very tall. The reason is that the soil is good.

4. I have to go to bed. Otherwise, I will be tired tomorrow.

5. It is hot today. I think I will go swimming.

6. The music was playing. I was sleeping all that time.

7. I ate too much turkey. Therefore I feel awful.

8. I did well on the test. That's why I am happy.

Make one sentence of each two sentences below. Keep the meaning the same.
Change words where necessary.

1. Jim is the tallest boy in the class. He is only twelve.

2. I like this food best. It is chocolate.

3. You must brush your teeth. Otherwise, you will get cavities.

4. You can use my crayons. However, you must put them away afterwards.

5. This horse is a palamino. It was the fastest runner in the race.

6. I want to watch this program. It is my favorite.

7. You will miss the bus. However, this is true only if you don't hurry.

8. This flower is blooming. It is a rose.

Make two sentences of each sentence below. Keep the meaning the same.
Change the words where necessary.

1. Jane, who is my best friend, moved away.

2. The bike that I got for my birthday is blue.

3. We are having liver, which I hate.

4. The book that I read last week is exciting.

5. I will give this blouse, which is too big, to Mary.

6. If I finish my homework, then I can watch television.

7. My dad, who is forty-six, runs a mile every day.

8. Either it rains today, or this corn will die.

SENTENCES
GRAMMATICAL *Transformations*
(word order)

A sentence can be said in several different ways.
For example: We will go for a walk in the evening.
In the evening we will go for a walk.
Walking in the evening is our plan.

All three sentences mean the same thing.

Rewrite the sentences below, starting with the words on the line.
You may have to use some different words, but keep the meaning the same.

1. Uncle Joe gave me this birthday present.

   This birthday present _____

2. This sunny day is the day of our picnic.

   Our picnic _____

3. Jane is washing the dog.

   Washing _____

4. My favorite sandwich is peanut butter and jelly.

   I like _____

5. Jim is shorter than Tom.

   Tom _____

6. Sally received a glass of water from Mom.

   Mom _____

7. I beat Mary in the race.

   In the race _____

   Mary _____

SENTENCES
REFERENTIAL
Directions

1. Circle the number........A Y 4 L

2. Underline the animal.....red dog big car

3. Cross out the color......cat little boy green

4. Circle the word after cat.   The cat ran up the tree.

5. Underline the number before 8.   4 6 8 9 2 1

6. Cross out the word above red.

   green
   blue
   yellow
   red
   brown
   black

7. Circle the word below cow.

   cat
   dog
   horse
   cow
   duck
   pig

8. Underline the number above 3.

   6 8 9
   5 3 2
   1 0 7

9. Circle the name below Jane.

   Mary Sally Jill
   Jane Kim Polly
   Ann Joan Pam

SENTENCES
REFERENTIAL
Directions

Name _____

1. Put an X next to the color.   ( ) bike ( ) baby ( ) blue

2. Draw a line under the Letter.   8 A 7 5 3

3. Draw an arrow toward the <u>T</u>.   T

4. Draw an arrow away from the <u>G</u>.   G

5. Draw a line through the animal.   pig big page dig peg

6. Draw a line between the words that are the same.

	the
just	said
her	went
two	just

7. Put an X under the tree.   oak wagon walk boy girl

8. Put an X over the boy's name.   Mary Tom Jane Sally

9. Draw a line from the Y to the M.   A M / Y P / U S

10. Make an X above the word after <u>grass</u>.   tree plant grass flower

SENTENCES
REFERENTIAL
Questions (who)

Name _____

Write a "Who" question that is answered by each of the sentences below.

1. Jack won the race.

2. Mom packed a lunch for Joe.

3. The prize was won by Tom.

4. This book belongs to me.

5. It is time for the boy to wash the dog.

6. We all looked for Sally's shoe.

7. It is Jane's birthday.

8. My Dad is six feet tall.

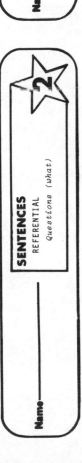

Name ____________

SENTENCES

REFERENTIAL

Questions (what)

2

Write a "What" question that is answered by each of the sentences.

1. Jack won a prize.

2. Mom packed a lunch for Joe.

3. The book was lost yesterday.

4. This dog lost its collar.

5. Jane wrote her name.

6. He is swimming across the lake.

7. She likes to climb trees.

8. We wash our dog every month.

9. Jim can't drive yet.

Name ____________

SENTENCES

REFERENTIAL

Questions (where)

3

Write a "Where" question that is answered by each of these sentences.

1. I am going to school tomorrow.

2. I found Sally's shoe under the bed.

3. I live in a big red house.

4. Julie dropped her clothes on the floor and went to bed.

5 I have to practice my drums in the basement.

6. I like to go shopping in the city.

7. The boys are playing ball in the park.

8. The dining room was buzzing with the voices of children.

SENTENCES

5

REFERENTIAL
Questions (why)

Name _____

Write a "Why" question that is answered by each of these sentences.

1. He soaked his feet to get them clean.

2. Everyone was looking for the lost shoe.

3. Since I am the tallest, I have to sit in the back.

4. Jim was sad because he lost the race.

5. Mom was very angry when I told her I lost the book.

6. The bus was late, so I was late for school.

7. He was afraid that the lion would get out of the cage.

8. We won't be home tonight, as we are going to the circus.

SENTENCES

4

REFERENTIAL
Questions (when)

Name _____

Write a "When" question that is answered by each of these sentences.

1. We will eat lunch at 12:00.

2. The book was lost yesterday.

3. We wash our dog every month.

4. Jim will be able to drive after he is sixteen.

5. I am going to school tomorrow.

6. I was born in 1946.

7. The morning sun shines brightest.

8. I love to see the colored leaves in the Fall.

214

Left worksheet

Write a "How" question that is answered by each of these sentences.

1. Mom was angry when I told her I lost the book.

2. Jim was sad because he lost the race.

3. He soaked his feet to get them clean.

4. We talked very quietly so we wouldn't wake the baby.

5. Jack did his work faster than anyone.

6. Mrs. Brown told me that Betty was sick.

7. Grandmother sent me this money for my birthday.

8. I burned my hand on the stove.

Right worksheet

Make an (X) beside the sentence that best describes the picture.

1. ( ) "Look at my foot."
   ( ) "Look at my doll."
   ( ) "I fell down and hurt myself."

2. ( ) "I found my truck."
   ( ) "I hurt my hand."
   ( ) "I have no toys."

3. ( ) "I wish I could reach the cookies."
   ( ) "I am too tired to eat."
   ( ) "I dropped my cookie."

4. ( ) He lost his shoe.
   ( ) She does the dishes.
   ( ) She wears a hat.

5. ( ) "Good bye, Kitty."
   ( ) "Come in, Kitty."
   ( ) "Kitty has a bone."

215

Read the paragraph. Then decide where the sentence should go, at the beginning, in the middle, or at the end.

1.   (BEGINNING) Along with food and clothing, it is one of man's most basic needs. Man must be protected from wind and rain, from heat and cold, from wild animals, and from other dangers. (MIDDLE) Man could not live long without shelter, except in a mild climate. (END)

Sentence: Shelter is a place for protection.
Position: ( ) BEGINNING   ( ) MIDDLE   ( ) END

2.   (BEGINNING) Jane entered the room timidly. She didn't recognize anyone there. No one stopped talking and walked over to greet her. (MIDDLE) No one offered her a sandwich or a soda. No one asked her to sit down and join the conversation. (END)

Sentence: So she stood there for five minutes, feeling miserable.
Position: ( ) BEGINNING   ( ) MIDDLE   ( ) END

3.   (BEGINNING) People build their homes of materials that are found nearby. If forests grow in an area, people build wooden houses. (MIDDLE) If there is no clay or forest, they build stone houses. (END)

Sentence: Where there is clay, they make bricks for their homes.
Position: ( ) BEGINNING   ( ) MIDDLE   ( ) END

Make an (X) beside any sentence that doesn't make sense.

( ) 1. Joe went out to climb the water.

( ) 2. The fence sang beautifully.

( ) 3. My dog barks at strangers.

( ) 4. My father shaves her whiskers every morning.

( ) 5. We always have supper at 6:00.

( ) 6. The teacher told us to do our homework.

( ) 7. My dog has brown heads.

( ) 8. The bush smiled at me.

( ) 9. The puppy wagged his tooth when he saw me.

( ) 10. I ride to school on a bus.

Make an (X) by the sentence that means the same as the first sentence.

1. The teacher told us to shape up.

    ( ) The teacher told us to cut out the picture.

    ( ) The teacher told us to do better.

2. This knife made a hash of my finger.

    ( ) This knife cut my finger badly.

    ( ) I used this knife to make the hash.

3. The rain put a monkey wrench into our plans for today.

    ( ) The rain ruined our plans for today.

    ( ) Today we tried to fix it in the rain.

4. Traffic was moving at a snail's pace.

    ( ) There was a lot of traffic.

    ( ) Traffic was moving very slowly.

5. It's time to hit the road.

    ( ) It's time to fix the highway.

    ( ) It's time to get started on our trip.

6. First I will give you a rundown.

    ( ) First I will tell you what will happen.

    ( ) First I will take you where you want to go.

7. Mrs. Smith passed away yesterday.

    ( ) Mrs. Smith went on a trip yesterday.

    ( ) Mrs. Smith died yesterday.

8. That girl is off her rocker.

    ( ) That girl is mistaken.

    ( ) That girl is crazy.

9. Just take a whiff of this!

    ( ) Just smell this!

    ( ) Just cut a little off!

10. He put on his new threads.

    ( ) He started to sew.

    ( ) He put on his new clothes.

Make an (X) by the sentence that means the same as the first sentence.

1. We sat around the fire, spinning yarns.

    ( ) We sat around the fire telling stories.

    ( ) We sat around the fire, knitting.

2. The party went like clockwork.

    ( ) The party was on time.

    ( ) The party went smoothly.

3. Susy hates hand-me-downs.

    ( ) Susy hates to be lifted up by the hands.

    ( ) Susy hates second-hand clothing.

4. If we can weather the storm, things will be easier.

    ( ) If we can forecast the weather, things will be easier.

    ( ) If we can stick it out, things will be easier.

5. Joe has always been a stick-in-the-mud.

    ( ) Joe has always disliked new things.

    ( ) Joe has always been mean to people.

6. He was cool as a cucumber.

    ( ) He was calm.

    ( ) He was shivering.

7. It is coming down in torrents.

    ( ) It is sliding down the hill.

    ( ) It is raining hard.

8. Well, this is a pretty pickle!

    ( ) What a lovely picture!

    ( ) What a mess!

9. It's time to take a breather.

    ( ) It's time to breathe deeply.

    ( ) It's time to rest for awhile.

10. I came off with flying colors.

    ( ) I did well.

    ( ) I did it fast.

Make an (X) next to the sentence that means the same as the first sentence.

1. This place is off the beaten track.

  ( ) This place is not in the most popular area.

  ( ) This place is next to the race track.

2. Now it lies in Davy Jones' locker.

  ( ) Now it lies at the bottom of the sea.

  ( ) Now it lies in the hold of the ship.

3. Bob certainly has a thick skin.

  ( ) Bob certainly has a deep sun tan.

  ( ) It is certainly hard to insult Bob.

4. We all made a beeline for the bus.

  ( ) We lined up to get on the bus.

  ( ) We hurried straight to the bus.

5. She has a stitch in her side.

  ( ) She has a cramp.

  ( ) She had an operation.

6. Joan always had a thin skin.

  ( ) Joan was easily hurt by people's remarks.

  ( ) Joan was sensitive to the sun.

7. He left under a cloud.

  ( ) It was raining as he left.

  ( ) People were suspicious of him when he left.

8. We saw the handwriting on the wall, and left.

  ( ) We heeded the warning, and left.

  ( ) We left after we had posted the bulletin.

9. He just couldn't cut the mustard.

  ( ) He just couldn't try again.

  ( ) He just couldn't succeed.

10. I think you are barking up the wrong tree.

  ( ) I think you are wrong.

  ( ) I think you are angry.

Writers often use figurative language to describe things. The following sentences describe one of the items listed in capital letters. Decide which item the sentence refers to, and write in the blank. You will use some items more than once.

Items: CLOUDS   DEW   MOUNTAINS   OCEAN   THUNDER

1. "The only birds that never sleep..." _____

2. "Bare steeps where desolation stalks..." _____

3. "The always wind-obeying deep..." _____

4. "Earth's undying monuments..." _____

5. "Heaven's artillery..." _____

6. "The wavy waste..." _____

Items: DEATH   HISTORY   MAN   MUSIC   POETRY   PAINTING

7. "The aristocrat among animals..." _____

8. "Painting with the gift of speech..." _____

9. "The unrolled scroll of prophesy..." _____

10. "Silent poetry..." _____

11. "The harmonious voice of creation..." _____

12. "That dreamless sleep." _____

13. "A cyclic poem, written by time, upon the memories of man..." _____

Directions: Put an (X) above the correct paragraph form.

1.
    A ( )   B ( )

The sun comes up.   The sun comes up. The birds
The birds are singing.   are singing. It is morning and
It is morning and I must   I must hurry to school.
hurry to school.

* * * * * * * *

2.
    A ( )   B ( )

A raccoon washes his   A raccoon washes his food
                        before he eats it. Sometimes
food before he eats it.   there is no water near his lunch.
Sometimes there is no water So, he washes it in the air.
near his lunch. So, he

washes it in the air.

* * * * * * * *

3.
    A ( )   B ( )

Bread is made from   Bread is made from
flour and water or milk.   flour and water or milk.
Sometimes other good   Sometimes other good things
things are added. Bread   are added. Bread is good
is good to eat.   to eat.

* * * * * * * *

4.
    A ( )   B ( )

July is my favorite   July is my favorite
month. There is no school, month. There is no
so I can play all day. I   school, so I can play
like the warm, sunny days. all day. I like the
                        warm, sunny days.

* * * * * * * *

5.
    A ( )   B ( )

My cat climbed a tree this   My cat climbed a tree
morning. When he got to   this morning. When he got
the top, he could not get   to the top, he could not get
down. Dad rescued him with down. Dad rescued him with
a ladder.   a ladder.

* * * * * * * *

219

PARAGRAPHS

FORMAT   *Form Convention*

Standard: Sentences are written con-
secutively. First word of paragraph
is indented. Left margin is even.

Name

⭐ 2

Copy the sentences below to make a paragraph. Use the correct paragraph form.

My dog knows a new trick.

He can stand on his back legs.

He learned it when I held up
a bone.

Now he does it when I hold
anything above his head.

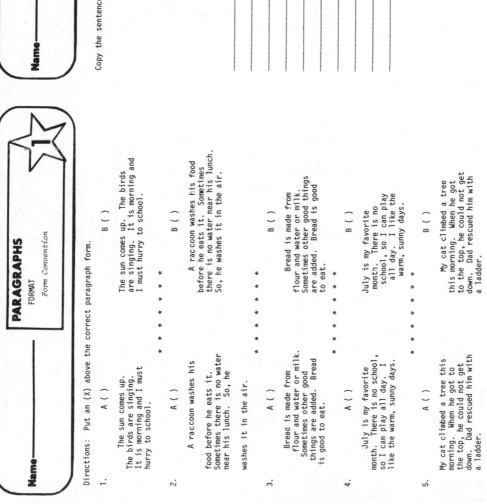

Complete each paragraph by choosing the sentence that **is** parallel in pattern to others in the paragraph.

1. There are several steps in cleaning your room. First, make your bed. Second, pick up all toys. Third, pick up all dirty clothes.

( ) Fourth, sweep the floor.
( ) Fourth, the floor needs to be swept.
( ) Then be sure to sweep the floor.

2. The Chinook salmon looks the way a fish should look. It has grace and strength. Its silver body glistens and shimmers. Its back and fins are black spotted.

( ) A firm and rounded body is typical.
( ) It is typical for the fish to have a rounded body.
( ) Its body is rounded and firm.

3. The spotted sandpiper is found in the United States and southern Canada. The Bartramian sandpiper is found on the dry uplands of the United States and Canada.

( ) Along the Atlantic and Gulf coast is found the willet sandpiper.
( ) The willet sandpiper is found along the Atlantic and Gulf coasts.
( ) The willet is the type of sandpiper that lives along the coasts.

4. Before the white man came, Eskimos relied upon the seal for many of their needs. The meat was used for food. The oil was used for cooking, lighting and heating. The sinews were used for sewing.

( ) Skins were used for clothes.
( ) Eskimos used skins for clothes.
( ) Clothes were made out of skins.

5. Finish the following paragraph with a parallel sentence.

Jane sat down to do her homework. First she did her math. Then she finished her spelling.....

_____

Read each paragraph and decide whether it has parallel grammatical structure that is, whether the sentences are constructed in the same way.

1. Joe hurried home. Tom was hurrying to baseball practice. I had piano lessons, so I hurried too.

( ) PARALLEL STRUCTURES   ( ) NOT PARALLEL STRUCTURES

2. In different parts of the world, different animals are used for milk. Cows provide milk in the United States and Canada. Goats supply milk in Norway, Switzerland, and Latin America. Sheep give milk in Spain, Italy and the Netherlands.

( ) PARALLEL STRUCTURES   ( ) NOT PARALLEL STRUCTURES

3. In different parts of the world, different animals are used for milk. Camel milk is popular in the deserts of Arabia and Central Asia. People drink llama milk in some areas of South America. In India and the Philippines, the water buffalo supplies milk.

( ) PARALLEL STRUCTURES   ( ) NOT PARALLEL STRUCTURES

4. Milk fat contains vitamins A, D, E, and K. One quart of milk contains 34 to 44 grams of fat. One drop of milk contains about 100,000,000 fat globules.

( ) PARALLEL STRUCTURES   ( ) NOT PARALLEL STRUCTURES

5. There are four types of stringed instrument. In the first type, the string is bowed. In the second type, it is hammered. In the third type, it is plucked. In the fourth type, the strings vibrate in the wind.

( ) PARALLEL STRUCTURES   ( ) NOT PARALLEL STRUCTURES

6. You can learn to appreciate music in several ways. You should listen to lots of music on the radio, on the television, and on records. You should learn to concentrate your attention on listening. You should try to play an instrument or to sing.

( ) PARALLEL STRUCTURES   ( ) NOT PARALLEL STRUCTURES

PARAGRAPHS

FORMAT
Grammatical Patterns
(consistent number)

Name _____

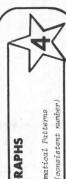

It is usually better to write a paragraph using singular or plural exclusively. Read each paragraph below and decide whether it is singular, plural, or mixed.

1. A person becomes seasick because of a disturbance in his inner ear. They can become ill by swaying in a hammock, or by travelling in a car, boat, or airplane. A person can reduce the problem by eating simple meals before travelling. He can also take certain drugs, which may help.

   ( ) singular   ( ) plural   ( ) mixed

2. A silhouette can be made by drawing an outline around a person's shadow. He should sit between a lighted candle and a piece of paper on a wall. Or, he can stand in front of a window and be photographed.

   ( ) singular   ( ) plural   ( ) mixed

3. The Indians of South America eat only corn, beans, potatoes, and a little meat. They use many kinds of peppers to season their food. They often lack fresh fruits and vegetables.

   ( ) singular   ( ) plural   ( ) mixed

4. Spiders eat many harmful insects and are very helpful to men. He usually does not bite unless he is disturbed. They all carry poison in their fangs, but it is such a small amount that it is usually harmless to man. Their bite is usually no worse than a mosquito bite.

   ( ) singular   ( ) plural   ( ) mixed

5. A man on a submarine is not going on a pleasure cruise. He has small living quarters and practically no room for exercise. When they must conserve oxygen, they must lie on their beds, moving as little as possible. But a man does get extra pay, much time off, and good food.

   ( ) singular   ( ) plural   ( ) mixed

PARAGRAPHS

FORMAT
Grammatical Patterns
(consistent tense)

Name _____

It is usually better to write a paragraph in one tense exclusively. Read each paragraph below and decide whether the tense is present, past, future, or mixed.

1. I walk into the store and tell the man that I need peanut butter. He says that they are out just now. I say that I can't wait. So I leave.

   ( ) PRESENT   ( ) PAST   ( ) FUTURE   ( ) MIXED

2. I will pack for camp. I'll need some white blouses, and I will have to buy some blue shorts. We wear tennis shoes and white socks.

   ( ) PRESENT   ( ) PAST   ( ) FUTURE   ( ) MIXED

3. Dad used to go fishing often. He always caught a lot of fish. His favorite bait was earthworms. He likes to catch perch and bass. Once he caught a pike.

   ( ) PRESENT   ( ) PAST   ( ) FUTURE   ( ) MIXED

4. I like to eat cookies for dessert. My favorite is peanut butter. However, I do like chocolate chip and oatmeal also. I did not care for plain vanilla cookies. They are so bland!

   ( ) PRESENT   ( ) PAST   ( ) FUTURE   ( ) MIXED

5. In Scotland, only one-fifth of the people live in farm areas. The rest are crowded into the industrial areas. They work in shipyards, steel mills, and other industrial plants. While most of the people are Scottish, about seven percent are Irish or English.

   ( ) PRESENT   ( ) PAST   ( ) FUTURE   ( ) MIXED

6. Scotland was settled by a tribe of Celts from Ireland. These people were Christian and converted the Picts who lived there. In 844, Scotland was united by Kenneth MacAlpin. For the next three centuries, the Scottish protected themselves from the English and Norsemen who raided their shores.

   ( ) PRESENT   ( ) PAST   ( ) FUTURE   ( ) MIXED

Read each paragraph below and decide whether or not it shows rhyme.

1. I'm going to cut the grass today.
   Its much too long, you know.
   I'll also trim the hedge a bit
   To let the sunshine in.

   ( ) rhyme
   ( ) no rhyme

2. I never saw a purple cow,
   I never hope to see one.
   But I can tell you, anyhow,
   I'd rather see than be one.

   ( ) rhyme
   ( ) no rhyme

3. All sorts of things and weather
   Must be taken in together.
   To make a year
   And a sphere.

   ( ) rhyme
   ( ) no rhyme

4. It was the time when lilies blow,
   And clouds are highest up in air,
   Lord Ronald brought a lily-white doe
   To give to his cousin, Lady Clare.

   ( ) rhyme
   ( ) no rhyme

5. Winds blow south, or winds blow north,
   Day come white, or night come black
   Home, or rivers, and mountains from home,
   Singing all time, minding no time,
   While we two keep together.

   ( ) rhyme
   ( ) no rhyme

6. This be the verse you grave for me:
   Here he lies where he longed to be,
   Home is the sailor, home from the sea,
   And the hunter home from the hill.

   ( ) rhyme
   ( ) no rhyme

Two words rhyme when they end with the same sound. When two words begin with the same sound we call it "alliteration." Read each paragraph below and decide whether it shows alliteration.

1. The wily wicked warrior
   With battle-axe in hand,
   Approached the frightened farmers,
   Demanding all their land.

   ( ) alliteration
   ( ) no alliteration

2. Under a spreading chestnut tree
   The village blacksmith stands;
   The smith, a powerful man is he,
   With large and sinewy hands.

   ( ) alliteration
   ( ) no alliteration

3. All the world's a stage
   And men and women merely players:
   They have their exits and their entrances;
   And one man in his time plays many parts,
   His acts being seven ages.

   ( ) alliteration
   ( ) no alliteration

4. The gray-green grass,
   The bright blue sky,
   The ripe, red rose
   Met my startled eyes.

   ( ) alliteration
   ( ) no alliteration

5. Solitary the thrush,
   The hermit withdrawn to himself, avoiding the settlements,
   Warbles by himself a song.

   ( ) alliteration   ( ) no alliteration

6. Once upon a midnight weary, while I pondered weak and weary,
   Over many a quaint and curious volume of forgotten lore,--
   While I nodded, nearly napping, suddenly there came a tapping,
   As of someone gently rapping, rapping at my chamber door.

   ( ) alliteration   ( ) no alliteration

PARAGRAPHS

FORMAT

Phonological Patterns
(rhythm)

★ 3

Read each paragraph below and decide whether or not it shows a regular pattern of rhythm.

1. By the shores of Gitche Gumee,
    By the shining Big Sea-Water,
    Stood the wigwam of Nokomis.
    Daughter of the Moon, Nokomis.

    ( ) rhythm
    ( ) no rhythm

2. The Indian walked
    Into the forest to find
    Some deer for
    Dinner. He hoped he would be lucky.

    ( ) rhythm
    ( ) no rhythm

3. There dwelt a miller, hale and bold,
    Beside the River Dee;
    He worked and sang from morn till night,
    No lark more blithe than he.

    ( ) rhythm
    ( ) no rhythm

4. Theirs not to make reply,
    Theirs not to reason why,
    Theirs but to do or die.

    ( ) rhythm
    ( ) no rhythm

5. I watch the flowers for hours.
    They wave in the wind.
    Their gay colors delight my friend.

    ( ) rhythm
    ( ) no rhythm

6. He left the village.
    He mounted the steep steps
    The village lay tranquil beneath him.

    ( ) rhythm
    ( ) no rhythm

7. One day I caught a giant fish.
    He fought a hero's fight.
    I almost let him go again
    To fight another day.

    ( ) rhythm
    ( ) no rhythm

PARAGRAPHS

FORMAT

Phonological Patterns
(rhyme, rhythm, alliteration)

★ 4

A poet may use the techniques of rhythm, rhyme, or alliteration. Or, he may use none of them. Read the poems below, and decide which of the techniques have been used. More than one may be used in a poem, or none may be used.

1. On Friday morn when I awake,
    It's back to school for me.
    I'll grab my books and catch the bus,
    No more fun and games!

    ( ) rhyme
    ( ) alliteration
    ( ) rhythm
    ( ) none

2. The day is gray.
    It wouldn't be so bad but I feel sad today.
    Instead, I'll go to bed.

    ( ) rhyme
    ( ) alliteration
    ( ) rhythm   ( ) none

3. Lilacs in dooryards
    Holding quiet conversations with an early moon:
    Lilacs watching a deserted house
    Settling partways into the grass of an old road;

    ( ) rhyme
    ( ) alliteration
    ( ) rhythm
    ( ) none

4. When lilacs then in the dooryard bloomed,
    And the great star early drooped in the western sky in the night,
    I mourned, and yet shall mourn with ever-returning spring.

    ( ) rhyme   ( ) alliteration   ( ) rhythm   ( ) none

5. The wind was a torrent of darkness among the gusty trees,
    The moon was a ghostly galleon tossed upon cloudy seas,
    The road was a ribbon of moonlight over the purple moor,
    And the highwayman came riding--riding--riding--
    The highwayman came riding, up to the old inn door.

    ( ) rhyme   ( ) alliteration   ( ) rhythm   ( ) none

6. Deep into that darkness peering, long I stood there wondering, fearing,
    Doubting, dreaming dreams no mortal ever dared to dream before;
    But the silence was unbroken, and the stillness gave no token,
    And the only word there spoken was the whispered word, "Lenore."

    ( ) rhyme   ( ) alliteration   ( ) rhythm   ( ) none

We use special words to talk about certain subjects. Each paragraph below is special subject writing. What kind of special subject writing is seen in each paragraph?

1. In the fifth inning, Wilson hit a long one into the left field stands. The crowd cheered as two runners scored.

   Kind of writing:　　chemistry　　baseball　　army
   　　　　　　　　　　*　　*　　*　　*

2. Sift one cup of flour with the salt and baking soda. Blend in the butter and eggs.

   Kind of writing:　　crime　　television　　cooking
   　　　　　　　　　　*　　*　　*　　*

3. John is going to play a solo in the concert. The piece is written in the key of C.

   Kind of writing:　　music　　boy scouts　　politics
   　　　　　　　　　　*　　*　　*　　*

4. Seeds may be started in flats indoors. Transplant to sunny spot when all danger of frost is past.

   Kind of writing:　　football　　gardening　　automobiles
   　　　　　　　　　　*　　*　　*　　*

5. Martin's Soup is made with chunks of delicious beef and garden fresh vegetables. You'll wish you had made it yourself.

   Kind of writing:　　advertising　　fishing　　art
   　　　　　　　　　　*　　*　　*　　*

6. A cold front is expected to move through the region tomorrow, bringing cooler temperatures and scattered showers. Wednesday will be partly cloudy.

   Kind of writing:　　farming　　business　　weather
   　　　　　　　　　　*　　*　　*　　*

1. Write two lines, using RHYME.

   _____
   _____
   _____

2. Write two lines, using RHYTHM.

   _____
   _____
   _____

3. Write two lines, using ALLITERATION.

   _____
   _____
   _____

4. Write two lines, using RHYME, RHYTHM, and ALLITERATION.

   _____
   _____
   _____

224

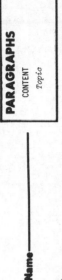

PARAGRAPHS

Name _____

CONTENT

Topic

TEACHER'S SCRIPT

Listen as I read some sentences. Listen to find out what the sentences are about. We call that the topic. Say topic. When I finish reading, circle the picture that names the topic of the sentences.

1. John collects keys. He has 10 door keys and 5 car keys. His mother gave him the key to her jewelry box. His little sister gave him a skate key.

2. Marianne has a new pet. Her father brought her a baby kitten. It is black and white, and likes milk. Marianne's dad found the kitten sitting by a flower.

3. The letter A is very important. It is found in many words, like ant, apple, and, ape. It is the first letter of the alphabet. Capital A is shaped like a triangle.

4. When I want to write, I use a pencil. Crayons are too thick, and pens are too messy. I like pencils with big erasers, because I often make mistakes.

5. The clown had three balloons. He gave a red one to a little boy in a blue cap. He gave a yellow one to a little girl with red hair. The last balloon was blue, and he gave it to me.

PARAGRAPHS

Name _____

CONTENT

Universe of Discourse

Each paragraph below is a different kind of writing. Decide whether each paragraph is one of the following:

SCIENCE   POETRY   NARRATIVE (A Story)   ESSAY (A Discussion)

1.
    They searched about, and soon found the troll's stony boots going away through the trees. They followed the tracks up the hill, until hidden by bushes they came on a big door of stone leading to a cave. But they could not open it, not though they all pushed while Gandalf tried various incantations.

SCIENCE   POETRY   NARRATIVE   ESSAY
* * * * * * *

2.
Far over misty mountains cold
To dungeons deep and caverns old
We must away ere break of day
To seek the pale enchanted gold.

SCIENCE   POETRY   NARRATIVE   ESSAY
* * * * * * *

3.
    Another term for cartilage is gristle. This elastic material, found in the skeleton of man and animals with backbones, is a translucent, bluish-white tissue. It supports and connects other tissues of the body.

SCIENCE   POETRY   NARRATIVE   ESSAY
* * * * * * *

4.
    I would like to identify six problem areas which must be solved to spur both the world development and world economy. These are tasks which require the cooperation of the United States and all other countries.

SCIENCE   POETRY   NARRATIVE   ESSAY
* * * * * * *

225

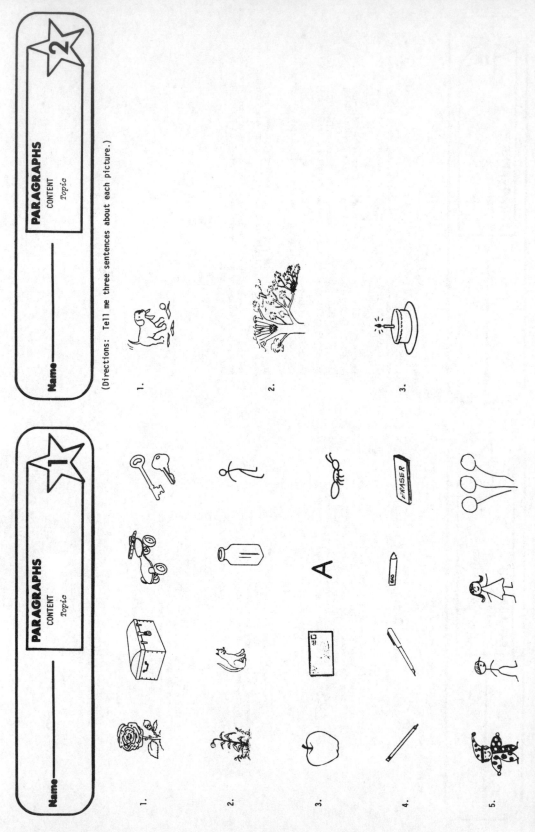

PARAGRAPHS
CONTENT
Topic

Name

(Directions: Tell me three sentences about each picture.)

1.

2.

3.

PARAGRAPHS
CONTENT
Topic

Name

1.

2.

3.

4.

5.

226

Circle the topic of each paragraph.

1. A ball is round. We play games with balls. Some balls are made of rubber.

   TOPIC: ( ) games   ( ) balls   ( ) rubber
   * * * * * * *

2. Today is my birthday. I am six years old. I will have a party. Mom made a cake for me.

   TOPIC: ( ) birthday   ( ) six   ( ) days
   * * * * * * *

3. Trees are big plants. They have green leaves. Children like to climb trees. Some fruits come from trees.

   TOPIC: ( ) children   ( ) plants   ( ) trees
   * * * * * * *

4. Joe's mother called him. He ran home. Good food was on the table. It was lunch time.

   TOPIC: ( ) food   ( ) lunch time   ( ) Joe's mother
   * * * * * * *

5. A teacher is sitting at her desk. The children are working. Soon the bell will ring. It will be time to go outside and play.

   TOPIC: ( ) home   ( ) school   ( ) streets
   * * * * * * * * * * *

Put an (X) by the sentences that belong with the topic sentence.

1. A bus carries people.
   ( ) Children go to school on a bus.
   ( ) Many people take a bus to work.
   ( ) My dad works in a big building.
   ( ) Buses stop for people waiting at a bus stop.
   ( ) I am in the fourth grade at school.

2. Joe lost his mittens.
   ( ) He looked for them in school.
   ( ) Joe's lunch is in a brown bag.
   ( ) Perhaps the mittens are on the bus.
   ( ) He likes to swing at recess.
   ( ) Joe will have cold hands if he can't find them.

3. Lions are big wild animals.
   ( ) A father lion has a mane.
   ( ) The mother lion takes care of the cubs.
   ( ) Monkeys live in trees.
   ( ) Mother lions are fierce hunters.
   ( ) There is a small lake in the jungle.

4. The race had begun.
   ( ) John is often late for school.
   ( ) Tom was off to a fast start.
   ( ) Ted is a good reader.
   ( ) Jim fell behind after a few yards.
   ( ) It looked like Mike would be the winner.

PARAGRAPHS

CONTENT *Plot*

*(A is similar to B;
A is different from B)*

Name _____

There are several kinds of paragraphs. One kind of paragraph tells how something is different from another thing. One kind of paragraph tells how something is similar to another thing. Read each paragraph below and decide which kind of paragraph it is:

SIMILAR   DIFFERENT

1. The baby ostriches, like Easter chicks, are kept in brooding boxes. During the day they are turned out to feed on green alfalfa. They must have moist food or plenty of water to drink.

    SIMILAR   DIFFERENT

    * * * * * * *

2. The ostriches' long neck, it's spreading two-toed foot, it's humped back, and its desert ways remind Arabians of a camel. Like the camel, the ostrich never becomes friendly with people. It is not surprising that they sometimes call the ostrich the "camel bird."

    SIMILAR   DIFFERENT

    * * * * * * *

3. The ostrich is the largest of all living birds. But it cannot fly like other birds. Its wings are too small. It uses its wings for a different purpose—to get up speed in running.

    SIMILAR   DIFFERENT

    * * * * * * *

4. A hen is very patient when sitting on her eggs. However, the ostrich is not so patient. If the eggs have been stuck in the sand unevenly, they may be uncomfortable to sit on. So the ostrich will kick out the eggs that annoy her.

    SIMILAR   DIFFERENT

    * * * * * * *

5. The male ostrich has beautiful feathers. His body is black, and his wings and tail are fringed with white. But the female ostrich is not so pretty. Her plumes are gray-brown or pale gray.

    SIMILAR   DIFFERENT

    * * * * * * *

PARAGRAPHS

CONTENT *Topic*

Name _____

Identify the topic of each paragraph.

1. A shrew is a small animal, about the size of a mouse. It has a long, slender snout, which it can move about quite easily. It has tiny eyes and ears. Its home is in the forest leaf carpets.

    TOPIC: _____

2. The Singing Tower is located at Mountain Lake, Florida. The park is a bird refuge, and contains many trees and lovely pools. The tower is 250 feet high and contains one of the biggest sets of bell chimes in the world.

    TOPIC: _____

3. Most dogs have a heavy coat of hair. However, the Mexican hairless dog is bare except for a tuft of hair on its forehead, and some fuzz along its tail. The dog originated in China, and was imported to Mexico by sailors in the Fourteenth Century.

    TOPIC: _____

4. Dad felt a tug on his fishing line. He reeled it in and discovered a big bass. It was 17 inches long and weighed three pounds. We ate it for dinner, and it was delicious.

    TOPIC: _____

5. The plates used to print money are made by skillful engravers. On each denomination is a portrait of a famous American. To the right or left is a seal. The color of the seal depends upon the type of money it is.

    TOPIC: _____

6. Suddenly Jane noticed that her bike was bumping along on the rim. The tire was as flat as a pancake. She got off and wheeled it to the gas station. It would do no good to put in some more air. There was a gash about an inch long, with a jagged piece of glass sticking out.

    TOPIC: _____

228

PARAGRAPHS 2

Name _____

CONTENT

Plot

(similar, different)

1. Add a sentence or two to the sentence below to make a paragraph that shows how something is SIMILAR to another thing. _____

   Jack's coat is very much like mine.

   _____
   _____

   * * * * * * * * *

2. Add a sentence or two to the sentence below to make a paragraph that shows how something is DIFFERENT from another thing. _____

   It is easy to tell dogs from cats.

   _____
   _____

   * * * * * * * * *

3. Write a short paragraph (two or three sentences). Make it either a SIMILAR type or a DIFFERENT type.

   _____
   _____
   _____
   _____
   _____

Which type of paragraph did you write?   SIMILAR   DIFFERENT

PARAGRAPHS 3

Name _____

CONTENT   *Plot*

(A is an example of B;
A is a reason for B)

There are several kinds of paragraphs. One kind of paragraph shows that something is a reason for another thing. One kind of paragraph gives examples. Read each paragraph below and decide which kind of paragraph it is: EXAMPLE   REASON

1. The beaver has special tools for his work. One tool is his sharp, strong teeth. They are like a good chisel with a hard steel edge. His tail is also useful. It helps him balance, and can sound a loud warning.

   EXAMPLE   REASON

   * * * * * * * *

2. The beaver does not sleep during the winter. Therefore, he must have a safe, warm home. He usually builds it from mud and sticks in the waters of a pond.

   EXAMPLE   REASON

   * * * * * * * *

3. Beavers have beautiful, valuable fur. They have been hunted for their fur since the white man came to America. Now beavers are protected by law in many states.

   EXAMPLE   REASON

   * * * * * * * *

4. The beaver keeps his kitchen well stocked. For instance, he spends the autumn gathering juicy sticks and twigs to last through the winter. Even after the pond has frozen, he finds branches and plants under the ice of his pond.

   EXAMPLE   REASON

   * * * * * * * *

5. There are many different kinds of rodents in America. Beavers are the largest, and live in or near the water. Squirrels are smaller, and live in trees. Rats and mice are also rodents.

   EXAMPLE   REASON

   * * * * * * * *

PARAGRAPHS

CONTENT   *Plot*

(A and B exist in spatial array;
A and B exist in temporal sequence)

There are several kinds of paragraphs. One kind of paragraph describes the appearance of something, or where things are located. One kind of paragraph tells when something happened, or the order of events. Read each paragraph below and decide which kind of paragraph it is: WHERE   WHEN

1. Only about one fourth of the land in Germany can be used for farming. More than half of this land is in East Germany. In the north, farming is possible only if the soil is heavily fertilized. The narrow valley of the Rhine and its branches provides the best land for raising crops.

WHERE   WHEN

* * * * * * * *

2. To make white ginger, wash the roots carefully and scrape them. Then they may be dried. To preserve the ginger, boil it and dip it in sirup every 24 hours for a week.

WHERE   WHEN

* * * * * * * *

3. Grandma arrived wearing her usual outlandish costume. A long black skirt flowed from beneath a heavy, tattered red sweater. Perched on her head was a tiny straw hat, covered with velvet daisies.

WHERE   WHEN

* * * * * * * *

4. The Girl Scouts began in England after Lord Baden-Powell introduced the Boy Scouts there. In 1909, the organization was officially recognized. Later, the movement spread and became popular.

WHERE   WHEN

* * * * * * * *

5. Mary looked around frantically. Over in the corner three boys were whispering. The tall girl with freckles was at the window, looking out. The teacher was sitting at her desk. But Joan had disappeared!

WHERE   WHEN

* * * * * * * *

PARAGRAPHS

CONTENT

Plot

(example, reason)

1. Add a sentence or two to the sentence below to make a paragraph that gives an EXAMPLE.

Some fruits come from a tree. _____

_____

_____

* * * * * * * * *

2. Add a sentence or two to the sentence below to make a paragraph that tells a REASON.

I was late for school this morning. _____

_____

_____

* * * * * * * * *

3. Write a short paragraph (two or three sentences). Make it either an EXAMPLE type or a REASON type.

_____

_____

_____

_____

Which type of paragraph did you write?   EXAMPLE   REASON

PARAGRAPHS

CONTENT *Plot*

*(A is a restatement of B;
A is a cause of B)*

★ 7

There are several kinds of paragraphs. One kind of paragraph shows that something is a cause of something else. One kind of paragraph says something and then repeats it again in other words. Read each paragraph below and decide which kind it is:

CAUSE   REPEAT

1. Joe eats twice as much as his dad. He spends all his money on candy. No wonder he is so fat!

    CAUSE   REPEAT

    * * * * * * * *

2. Ducks are aquatic birds. That is, ducks spend much of their time in the water.

    CAUSE   REPEAT

    * * * * * * * *

3. I like Jane. I think she is a nice person.

    CAUSE   REPEAT

    * * * * * * * *

4. The duck saw a minnow that was just the right size for dinner. Quick as a wink he dove.

    CAUSE   REPEAT

    * * * * * * * *

5. Joe has a big appetite. He eats a lot. He is always hungry.

    CAUSE   REPEAT

    * * * * * * * *

6. I don't like Mary. She hits me and calls names at me.

    CAUSE   REPEAT

    * * * * * * * *

PARAGRAPHS

CONTENT

Plot

(space, time)

★ 6

1. Add a sentence or two to the sentence below to make a paragraph that tells WHERE. _____

    Our class went on a field trip yesterday. _____

    _____

    _____

    _____

    * * * * * * * *

2. Add a sentence or two to the sentence below to make a paragraph that tells WHEN. _____

    Pat's dog has had puppies twice. _____

    _____

    _____

    _____

    * * * * * * * * *

3. Write a short paragraph (two or three sentences). Make it either a WHERE type or a WHEN type.

    _____

    _____

    _____

    _____

    _____

Which type of paragraph did you write?   WHERE   WHEN

231

PARAGRAPHS

CONTENT

Referential Links

The sentences in a paragraph are connected by linking words. One kind of link is shown below:

The <u>boy</u> was sad. <u>He</u> cried.

<u>He</u> in the second sentence refers to the <u>boy</u> in the first sentence. In the short paragraphs below, a word in the first sentence is underlined. Find the linking word in the second sentence. Draw a line under it.

....

1. <u>Mom</u> lost her purse. She is looking for it.

2. Mom lost her <u>purse</u>. She is looking for it.

3. The teacher asked me a <u>question</u>. I answered it.

4. The teacher asked <u>me</u> a question. I answered it.

5. Where is <u>Dad</u>? I want him to help me.

6. <u>Joe</u> has a new bike. It is his first two wheeler.

7. Here are two <u>books</u>. Which one do you want?

8. In the paragraph below, find 4 links that refer to <u>monkeys</u>.

   There are so many <u>monkeys</u> in this zoo. In all, there are five hundred kinds. Some are tiny and others are big. They all like to climb trees.

9. In the paragraph below, find 4 links that refer to <u>dogs</u>.

   Most dogs do not see very well. Some can see better than others. To them, all colors look like different shades of black, white, and gray. Their sense of smell, however, is very good.

PARAGRAPHS

CONTENT

Plot

(restatement, cause)

1. Add a sentence or two to the sentence below to make a paragraph that tells a CAUSE.

   Mother is not feeling well today. _____

   _____

   _____

   * * * * * * * *

2. Add a sentence or two to the sentence below to make a paragraph that REPEATS a statement in other words.

   Mother is not feeling well today. _____

   _____

   _____

   * * * * * * * * *

3. Write a short paragraph (two or three sentences). Make it either a CAUSE type or a REPEAT type.

   _____

   _____

   _____

   _____

Which type of paragraph did you write?   CAUSE   REPEAT

PARAGRAPHS
CONTENT
Relational Links

★ 1

Choose the word or phrase that could replace the underlined word with the same meaning.

1. Joe was hungry. <u>So</u> he ate the whole pie.
   therefore   but   nevertheless

2. We cut the paper. <u>Then</u> we pasted it to make a chain.
   but   therefore   next

3. I like apples. <u>And</u> I like peaches.
   so   also   but

4. I got home late. <u>Therefore</u> I missed my favorite program.
   for that reason   all together   in spite of that

5. Joe is tall. <u>But</u> I am taller.
   however   then   therefore

6. Tom was leaving. <u>At the same time</u>, his father was coming home.
   next   then   meanwhile

7. I won the prize. <u>Certainly</u> I tried harder than anyone else.
   so   without doubt   all together

8. Ann is the fastest runner. <u>Of course</u> she won the race.
   meanwhile   naturally   however

9. We counted the cookies. <u>All together</u> there were fifteen.
   of course   in all   for that reason

10. We went inside. <u>At once</u> everyone shouted "Surprise."
    immediately   therefore   also

PARAGRAPHS
CONTENT
Referential Links

★ 2

If you repeat the same words in every sentence, it can be boring to read. So, we often use different links to make a paragraph sound better. Read the paragraph below, with no referring links.

The grasshopper is an interesting insect.
The grasshopper has a big head, long wings, and
long hind legs. The grasshopper's eyes stick out
on all sides, so that the grasshopper can see in
all directions. An enemy can't sneak up on a
grasshopper.

Now, change the paragraph by putting in <u>referring links</u>.

The grasshopper is an interesting insect.
_____ has a big head, long wings, and
long hind legs. _____ eyes stick out
on all sides, so that _____ can see in
all directions. An enemy can't sneak up on
_____.

* * * * * * * *

Write a two sentence paragraph about a car. Use a referring link in the second sentence. Draw a line under it, and draw an arrow to the word it refers to.

_____
_____
_____
_____

* * * * * * * *

233

Name _____

PARAGRAPHS
CONTENT
Relational Links

The sentences in a paragraph are connected by linking words. Some links are shown below.

The boys hurried home. And they were just in time for lunch.

We have no chicken. But we do have beef.

These links show how two statements are related. In each paragraph below, draw a line under the relating link.

1. We have no bananas today. However, the strawberries are good.
2. Tom can't swim. He must therefore wear a life preserver.
3. We ran home from school. And there on the porch was a puppy.
4. They worked hard all morning. But in the afternoon they rested.
5. Mary looked for her shoes. She did not find them, however.
6. Dad never catches any fish. Still, he likes to try.
7. Mom made pancakes. We naturally ate them all up.
8. I failed my spelling test. Nevertheless, Dad let me go to the show.
9. We finished work early. So we came home.
10. I dropped my marbles. I can find them all, hopefully.
11. Tom won the contest. Thus, he is going to New York.

Sometimes, a group of words can be a relating link. In the paragraphs below, circle the two-word group or three-word group that is a link.

12. John broke his arm yesterday. Of course, he can't play today.
13. Jean is so smart. Without doubt, she will get an A.
14. It is raining. For that reason I brought my umbrella.
15. We asked fifteen people to the party. In all, twelve came.

Name _____

PARAGRAPHS
CONTENT
Relational Links

Choose the word or phrase that could replace the underlined word without changing the meaning.

1. The men ran to the dock. Previously, they had seen the boat enter the harbor.
   consequently   before that   in summary

2. Tom, Dick and Harry have the mumps. Jill, Jane and Judy have the measles. In short, everyone is sick.
   meanwhile   in summary   in addition

3. Mother used the flour. Ann used all the sugar. Thus, I can't bake a cake.
   therefore   however   ideally

4. Everyone on our block voted for Mr. Brown. In spite of that, he lost.
   hopefully   therefore   nevertheless

5. This cup is made of plastic. Ideally, it should be made of glass or china.
   moreover   thus   preferably

6. Joe came in first in the race. Accordingly, he was awarded the prize.
   consequently   preferably   previously

7. I turned in my homework. I did well on the test. Regarding that, my teacher is pleased.
   before that   concerning that   in summary

8. I have fun in the summer. I like to swim and play ball. Still, I prefer winter.
   nevertheless   therefore   without doubt

9. Dogs are intelligent and loyal. They will protect their owners. Besides, they are easy to care for.
   in spite of that   in addition   for that reason

10. My dad is a gastronome. That is, he likes good food.
    nevertheless   in addition   in other words

PARAGRAPHS CONTENT
Relational Links
Standard: Links changed appropriately
Pronouns changed where necessary

Rewrite Sentences (1) and (2) in each item in a different order.
Do not change the meaning. Change the words as necessary.

1. I mowed the lawn. Before that I fixed the lawn mower.
   (1)   (2)

   _____
   (2)

   _____
   (1)

2. Joe likes baseball. Also, he likes football.
   (1)   (2)

   _____
   (2)

   _____
   (1)

3. My first class is English. Then I have Social Studies.
   (1)   (2)

   _____
   (2)

   _____
   (1)

4. Ann Didn't want to come. However, she came to the party.
   (1)   (2)

   _____
   (2)

   _____
   (1)

5. I have two dogs. And I have a fluffy cat.
   (1)   (2)

   _____
   (2)

   _____
   (1)

PARAGRAPHS CONTENT
Relational Links

The sentences in a paragraph are connected by linking words.
One kind of link is shown below.

> Mary picked up the blocks.
> <u>Next</u> she put her dolls away.
> <u>Then</u> she rested.

These links (<u>Next</u>, <u>Then</u>) tell the order of things that happened.
In each paragraph below, draw a line under an <u>order</u> link.

1. Draw a circle. Then make an X in the center.

2. We ate a big dinner. It was fun playing games afterwards.

3. A butterfly begins life as a caterpillar. He grows beautiful wings later.

4. Beforehand everybody was nervous. They did well anyway.

5. Codfish used to be salted and dried. Now more are sold frozen.

6. Baby salmon are kept alive by food from the eggs which
   are attached to their bodies. The young fish, called "fry",
   then begin to swim and look for food.

7. Find 4 order links in the paragraph below.

   Late in the summer, tadpoles begin to swim
   to the surface of the water. They take a gulp
   of air and then go under again. Now they are
   beginning to have lungs. Afterwards they may
   live either on land or on water.

Read the paragraph below and answer the questions.

    Jane had a new dress. It was red and white. Jane liked it very much. She wore it to school Thursday. The teacher liked it. The children liked it. Even the bus driver said, "What a pretty dress!" Jane was very happy.

* * * * * * * *

Circle every correct answer. There may be more than one.

1. Who had a new dress?   Jane   teacher   children   bus driver

2. Who liked the dress?   Joan   teacher   children   bus driver

3. What did Jane have?   bus   school   dress   children

4. What colors was it?   blue   red   pink   white   green

5. Where did Jane wear it?   school   vacation   library

6. When did Jane wear it?   Monday   Friday   Thursday

7. How did Jane feel?   afraid   happy   sad   cold

The sentences in a paragraph are connected by linking words. Some links are RELATING links, like: but, however, therefore, so, of course, nevertheless, and many more.

Some links are ORDER links, like: first, then, next, later, and many more.

The paragraph below does not have the relating links and order links that it needs. Put in at least 4 links, by writing them in the blanks. YOU DO NOT NEED TO FILL IN EVERY BLANK. PUT IN AT LEAST 4 LINKS.

    My dog never learned to beg. _____ I did try to teach him. _____ I got a dog cookie from the kitchen. _____ I showed it to my dog. I know he was hungry. _____ he didn't know what to do. I told him to sit up. _____ he just looked at me. _____ he walked away.

* * * * * * * *

Put in links that make sense.

1. My alarm clock did not go off. _____ I was late.

2. _____ I drank my milk. Then I ate my toast.

3. It was raining. _____ I got wet.

4. I had a sandwich for lunch. It was peanut butter _____.

5. I usually like apples. _____ this one is sour.

6. I played my records. _____ I put them away.

236

Read the paragraphs below and answer the questions.

The baby bees are called larvae. They are very hungry. They are fed nectar, pollen, and honey. One of the baby bees will grow up to be the new queen.

1. What are baby bees called?   nectar   larvae   pollen
2. What do baby bees eat?   pollen   honey   nectar   larvae
3. Who will be a new queen?   a nurse bee   a baby bee   a drone
4. When will the bee become queen?   when it is hungry   when it is grown up
5. Why do the baby bees eat?   They are hungry.   They are larvae.

* * * * * * * *

The bee is looking for nectar. She sees some flowers that hold nectar. She hurries back to the hive. The other bees watch as she dances, wiggles her feelers and wings. She is telling the bees where to find the nectar.

6. Who is looking?   fly   bee   bird
7. What is she looking for?   wings   hive   nectar
8. What holds nectar?   bee   flower   hive
9. What does she see?   hive   wings   flowers
10. Where does she go after she finds nectar?   flower   hive   tree
11. Who watches her dance?   bees   flowers   birds
12. Why does she dance?   She feels happy.
      She wants to show them a new dance.
      She wants to tell them about the flowers.

Read the paragraph below and answer the questions.

After school, Joe and Tom went home. On the way they saw a dog. The dog barked. Joe was afraid, but Tom was not. Tom talked to the dog. Soon the dog stopped barking. He began to wag his tail.

* * * * * * * *

Circle every correct answer. There may be more than one.

1. Who went home?   Tom   Joe   dog
2. Who was afraid?   Tom   Joe   dog
3. Who was not afraid?   Tom   Joe   dog
4. Who barked?   Tom   Joe   dog
5. Who wagged his tail?   Tom   Joe   dog
6. Who talked to the dog?   Tom   Joe   dog
7. What did Tom and Joe see?   tree   dog   house
8. What did the dog wag?   tail   ear   bark
9. What did the dog do first?   play   cry   bark
10. What did the dog do later?   bark   wag   run
11. Where were Tom and Joe going?   school   home   store
12. When did they see a dog?   after lunch   after school   morning
13. Why was Joe afraid?   The dog was wagging.   The dog was barking.
14. Why did the dog stop barking?   Tom was afraid.   Tom talked to it.

237

Read each paragraph below and answer the questions. There may be more than one answer to a question.

Modern computers can do routine jobs faster than people can. They can do millions of calculations in one second. But computers do not think in the same way that men do.

1. What does jobs faster than people?

   machines   computers   animals

2. How many calculations can they do in a second?

   ten   hundreds   thousands   millions

3. What kind of job does a computer do?

   digging   cooking   reading   calculating

4. How do computers think?

   different from men   same as men

* * * * * * * * *

Computers are made up of tiny electric switches. Each one can turn off or on. These switches are called relays, and can turn off or on hundreds of millions of times each second.

5. What is a computer made from?

   switches   cells   lights   turns

6. What is a computer switch called?

   second   electric   relay   computer

7. What do the switches do?

   turn on lights   make sounds   turn on and off

8. How fast can the switches operate?

   very fast   very slowly   at a medium rate

238

Read each paragraph. Then make up questions about it.

Patterns of on-off signals form a kind of code. Information is translated into this code and put on cards. The cards are then fed into the computer. The computer can store the information in its memory.

1. A <u>what</u> question: _____

2. A <u>where</u> question: _____

3. A <u>where</u> question: _____

4. A <u>where</u> question or
   a <u>what</u> question: _____

* * * * * * * * *

A computer must be told what to do at every step. Such instructions are called a program. Men who prepare the program are called programmers. The program tells the computer how to use the information stored in its memory.

5. A <u>what</u> question: _____

6. A <u>who</u> question: _____

7. A <u>what</u> question: _____

8. A <u>what</u> question or
   a <u>where</u> question: _____

PARAGRAPHS

CONTENT

Information

7

Read each paragraph below. Then make up questions about the paragraph.

On top of the nest, the pack rat places any junk he can find. He will use newspapers, tin cans, sticks and stones. But his favorite material is cactus, because it is full of thorns. That makes it hard for another animal to dig away the junk and get to the nest below.

1. A <u>what</u> question: _____

2. A <u>what</u> question: _____

3. A <u>why</u> question: _____

4. A <u>what</u> question <u>or</u>
   a <u>why</u> question: _____

* * * * * * * * *

During the summer, the days are long and hot in the desert. The mound aoove the nest helps to keep it cool during the hottest part of the day. The pack rat has adapted nicely to his life in the desert.

5. A <u>when</u> question: _____

6. A <u>what</u> question: _____

7. A <u>who</u> question: _____

PARAGRAPHS

CONTENT

Information

6

Read each paragraph below and answer the questions. There may be more than one correct answer to a question.

The white-throated wood rat is also called a pack rat or desert rat. It may be seen in the desert country of the Southwestern United States. Its home is made of piles of sticks, stones, and cactus.

1. What is another name for the white-throated wood rat?
   southwestern rat   cactus rat   desert rat   pack rat

2. Where is the white-throated wood rat seen?
   Southwest   Northeast   Southeast   Northwest

3. What does he use to make his home?
   sticks   bricks   stones   sand   cactus

4. In what kind of country does the white-throated wood rat live?
   forest   swamp   farmland   desert   mountains

* * * * * * * * *

A pack rat's nest is not just a pile of junk. He carefully chooses a small hollow in the ground and weaves pieces of bark or grass to make a nest. He then gathers softer material to line the nest.

5. Where does a pack rat build his nest?
   in a hollow   in a tree   on a hill   in the water

6. What does the rat use to weave the nest?
   branches   bark   grass   straw   cactus

7. What kind of material lines the nest?
   hard   rough   soft   cool   warm

8. When does he gather material to line the nest?
   before he starts to build   after he weaves the nest

239

Read the paragraph below. Answer each question. There may be more than one correct answer to each question.

A Country Mouse invited a City Sister of hers to a dinner, where she spared nothing that the place afforded-- as mouldy crusts, cheese-parings, musty oatmeal, rusty bacon, and the like. The City Dame was too well bred to find fault with her entertainment; but yet represented that such a life was unworthy of a merit like hers; and letting her know how splendidly she lived, invited her to accompany her to town.

1. Who invited the City Mouse?
   her mother   the Country Mouse   the City Dame

2. Why did she invite her:
   for a party   for a vacation   for a meal

3. What did they eat?
   mouldy crusts   cheese pie   oatmeal   bacon

4. Why didn't the City Mouse complain?
   She didn't care.   She was too polite.   She liked the meal.

5. What did the City Mouse do after dinner?
   invited Country Mouse to her home   hurried home to entertain

6. What did City Mouse think of Country Mouse's home?
   It was beautiful.   It was unworthy of her.   It was too cold.

7. Why did City Mouse invite Country Mouse to town?
   to show off her home   to get help with decorating her home

240

Read the paragraph below. Then make up questions about it.

The Country Mouse consented, and away they trudged together, and about midnight got to their journey's end. The City Mouse showed her friend the larder, the pantry, the kitchen, and other places where she stored her supplies. After this, she took her friend to the parlour, where they found, there upon the table, the relics of a mighty entertainment of that very night. The City Mouse offered to her companion those things she herself liked best. They fell to eating upon a velvet couch.

1. A who question: _____

2. A when question: _____

3. A what question: _____

4. A where question: _____

5. A what question: _____

6. A what question or
   a where question: _____

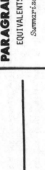
Make an (X) in the box next to the sentence that summarizes each paragraph.

1. Mary brought a cake.
Jane brought hot dogs.

( ) The girls brought food.
( ) Mary likes to eat cake.

2. Jack has measles. Tom
has mumps. Bob has a cold.

( ) The boys have to go to school.
( ) The boys are sick.

3. I have a collie.
I also have a poodle.

( ) I like collies best.
( ) I have two dogs.

4. The boy was not afraid of
lions. He was not afraid of tigers.

( ) The boy was brave.
( ) The boy was afraid of elephants.

5. Ann sharpened her pencil.
A few minutes later it broke.
She sharpened it again.

( ) Ann broke her pencil twice.
( ) Ann sharpened her pencil twice.

6. Horns blasted. Trucks
rumbled by. Brakes screeched.

( ) It was noisy.
( ) The truck was stopping.

7. The wheel came off Tommy's
truck. The fender was dented.
The window was cracked.

( ) Tommy's truck was broken.
( ) Tommy fixed his truck.

8. The farmer picked the beans.
He cut the wheat. He dug up the
carrots.

( ) The farmer fixed his dinner.
( ) The farmer harvested his crops.

Name

PARAGRAPHS
EQUIVALENTS
Summarization

2

Make an (X) in the box next to the sentence that summarizes each paragraph.

1. One pumpkin was large, round, and bright orange.
Another was long, shaped like a banana, and yellowish green.
A tiny oval shaped pumpkin was still green, since it had not
yet ripened. The funniest looking one was lop-sided, pale
orange, and about as big as a football.

( ) The largest pumpkin was orange.
( ) The pumpkins were different sizes, shapes and colors.
( ) The small oval shaped pumpkin was not ripe yet.

2. Mary and Jack gathered the dirty clothes and sorted them
into piles. All the white things went in one pile. All the
dark things went in another pile. Colored clothes were put in
a third pile. Then mother put the clothes into the washer and
added some soap. When the clothes were ready, they all hung
them out to dry.

( ) The clothes were dirty and needed to be washed.
( ) Dirty clothes must be sorted before they are washed.
( ) The children helped their mother with the laundry.

3. After an hour, I finally got a bite. I jerked on my line,
but I must have pulled too hard. The hook came flying out of
the water—quite empty. A little later my luck improved, but
not much. A tiny perch took my bait. But it was too small to
keep. I was ready to go in when I felt something big on my line.
I reeled it in to discover a large mass of seaweed.

( ) I had bad luck while fishing.
( ) Don't pull too hard when you get a bite.
( ) Perch are too small to keep.

241

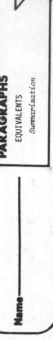
Sometimes a summarizing sentence is found in a paragraph. Find the summary statement in each paragraph. Draw a line under it.

1. It was a beautiful scene. The flowers were blooming. The grass was bright green. Only a few fluffy white clouds could be seen in the brilliant blue sky. A doe and her fawn stood under a tree.

2. I like to plant flowers and vegetables. It's exciting to see the tiny plants peek from beneath the rich, black soil. I even enjoy pulling weeds and hoeing between plants. Gardening is my favorite hobby.

3. The children had a meeting. They decided to help with the lawn work. Joe would cut the grass. Dick would trim around the trees and sidewalk. Jack would rake up leaves and grass clippings. Jim would plant some bushes and flowers.

4. Before the white men came, Indians had explored almost all the land in North America and discovered important natural resources. They had found the best trails over mountains and across rivers. They had found mineral springs, copper, turquoise, gold, silver, and other minerals. They gathered rubber and grew tobacco.

5. Farmers grow chickens, pigs, and cattle in order to send meat to the cities. They grow wheat and other grains for flour and cereal. They grow vegetables and fruits also. It can be said that farmers feed the world.

Find the summary statement in each paragraph. Draw a line under it.

1. A "fixed star" always seems to be in the same place, although it does move. The distance between stars is so great that one may move along at great speed, and still seem to be hardly moving when seen from the earth. After a long time has gone by, however, we can see that a fixed star has changed position.

2. Broccoli and cauliflowers are undeveloped groups of flowers. The blossoms of dandelions and elderberries are used to make wine. The flavoring, cloves, is the pickled blossom of the clove tree. Another pickled flower is the caper, used as a relish. Violet blossoms are candied. Many flowers serve as foods or flavorings.

3. One of America's favorite sports is football. On fall weekends, millions of spectators fill the stadiums to watch college or professional teams battle to victory. More than 100,000 spectators can watch a single important game. Millions more will watch on television or listen to radio.

4. The Great Lakes carry much trade. The most common boat seen is the ore carrier. It is especially designed for lake traffic. It is an awkward-looking ship, since it lies low in the water when fully loaded. From a special dock, ore can be poured into the open hatches. Giant electric shovels will unload it at its destination.

PARAGRAPHS

EQUIVALENTS
Summarization

Name _____

Finish the summary statement for each paragraph.

1. Your feet should be washed as often as necessary. A deodorant powder will keep them smelling nice. If they itch, soak them in warm water. Cut and clean your toenails.

   You should _____

2. A missile may be guided by a command system. In that case, it is controlled by radar after it is launched. A homing system does not need to be guided by men. It uses built-in radar to steer the missile to its target. A pre-set missile has a path built in to the control system before it is launched.

   Missiles are guided _____

3. Benjamin Franklin was the only man to sign all four of the key documents in United States history. He signed for the Declaration of Independence, the Treaty of Alliance with France, the Treaty of Peace with Great Britain, and the Constitution of the United States. He served as minister to France, and was considered one of the best diplomats in our history. He was an inventor, a writer, a scientist, and public benefactor.

   Benjamin Franklin _____

PARAGRAPHS

EQUIVALENTS
Induction (Inference)

Name _____

Put an (X) by the statement that is <u>probably</u> true.

1. I dropped a cup. Mom will be mad at me.
   - ( ) The cup is broken.
   - ( ) The cup is red.
   - ( ) Mom does not like cups.

2. My dog will not bark at you. He knows you.
   - ( ) My dog barks at everyone.
   - ( ) My dog barks at friends.
   - ( ) My dog barks at strangers.

3. Tom ran after me. He threw a rock. He tried to hit me.
   - ( ) Tom is my best friend.
   - ( ) Tom cannot run fast.
   - ( ) Tom is mad at me.

4. I have ten pennies. I am going to the candy store. Do you want to come with me?
   - ( ) I lost my pennies.
   - ( ) I will buy candy.
   - ( ) I can't buy anything.

5. Pat was wearing a dress. It was a sunny day.
   - ( ) Pat is a girl.
   - ( ) Pat is a boy.
   - ( ) Pat is going to play.

6. Pat wants to be like Dad. They both wore red coats.
   - ( ) Pat is a girl.
   - ( ) Pat is a boy.
   - ( ) Pat does not like red.

PARAGRAPHS 2

Name _____

EQUIVALENTS
Induction (Inference)

Put an (X) by the statement that is probably true.

1. Dinner was brought to the King. He drank his soup in one gulp. He gobbled his meat and potatoes. He stuffed the cake in his mouth.

   ( ) The King likes ice cream.
   ( ) The King was hungry.
   ( ) The King was tired.

2. A huge shark swam in the waters around the island. It was known to have attacked several swimmers. The brave men of the village got their food from the sea. But for two weeks no one had gone fishing.

   ( ) The shark ate all the fish.
   ( ) The men liked to see sharks nearby.
   ( ) The men were afraid of the shark.

3. The old man took his potatoes to market. Many people stopped to look at them. "Those potatoes are blue!" they exclaimed. "Why are those potatoes blue?" they asked. Everyone was interested in the potatoes. But no one bought them.

   ( ) People did not like the old man.
   ( ) People do not like blue potatoes.
   ( ) The potatoes tasted like carrots.

4. Dad was going to take us to school. I finished breakfast a little late. Bob could not find his books. By the time we were ready, Dad had gone without us.

   ( ) Dad does not like to wait.
   ( ) Dad does not know the way to school.
   ( ) Bob ate breakfast early.

PARAGRAPHS 3

Name _____

EQUIVALENTS
Induction (Inference)

Answer the questions about the paragraphs.

1. Suddenly the sky got dark. A big, black cloud filled the sky. I could hear thunder in the distance. Lightening flashed.

   What kind of weather is expected? _____

2. The Tigers were the worst team in the neighborhood. They were happy to welcome a new player. During the first game, the new boy caught four passes, made two touchdowns, and blocked the other team's field goal. The Tigers won their first game this season.

   What kind of player is the new boy? _____

3. The kitten jumped onto the kitchen counter. But he misjudged the distance and slipped noisily into the sink, which was filled with water. He scrambled out, and spent the next fifteen minutes snaking the water from his paws. A more unhappy kitten was never seen.

   Why was the kitten unhappy? _____

4. The fire engine raced down Main Street, screeching its warning. I stopped reading and ran outside. This was no false alarm. I followed on foot, hoping the engine would not turn a corner. It didn't.

   Where was I going? _____

5. I woke up to find that the alarm clock had not gone off. I pulled on my clothes. No time for breakfast. I grabbed my books, hoping I wouldn't be late. The teacher had been very angry last week when this happened.

   Where was I going? _____
   What happens to make the teacher angry? _____

244

Answer the questions after each paragraph.

1. At the castle, a general cleaning and polishing was taking place. Servants rushed to and fro, frequently colliding with a dreadful clamor of falling pots and pans. The floors were washed and waxed. The walls were white-washed. All furniture shone with its new coat of beeswax. By nightfall it would look glorious.

    Think of two reasons why they might have been cleaning the castle.

    1. _____

    2. _____

2. For Christmas, George used his new chemistry set to make presents for everyone. For his mother he concocted a beautiful perfume from lemon juice, spices, and other mysterious ingredients. Mom seemed to love the gift, but several months later George found the full bottle at the back of the medicine chest. None apparently had been used.

    Think of two reasons why Mom might not have used the perfume.

    1. _____

    2. _____

3. Brain operations were performed to relieve mental illness in the past. The surgeon would destroy a small part of the brain in the hopes that it would change the behavior of the patient. Nowadays, doctors rarely recommend such surgery.

    Think of two reasons why doctors no longer recommend it.

    1. _____

    2. _____

Put an (X) by the correct statement after each paragraph.

1. The Pacific Islands are the home of several peoples. The Polynesians are the tallest, and have light brown hair. The Melanesian tends to be stocky, and has protruding features and frizzy hair. The hair of the Micronesian is black, and may be either straight or curly.

    ( ) The Polynesians, Melanesians and Micronesians are similar.
    ( ) The Polynesians, Melanesians and Micronesians are different.

2. Poison ivy is the name for several harmful shrubs. Contact with these plants cause many people to have an itchy rash. The plants are related to sumac, and are sometimes called "poison sumac." Poison oak is another name for poison ivy, but is sometimes applied only to the bushy forms.

    ( ) Poison ivy, poison sumac and poison oak are similar.
    ( ) Poison ivy, poison sumac and poison oak are different.

3. Poker is a card game for two or more people. People often make bets on the hands they hold. In draw poker, each person is dealt five cards. He may discard as many as three cards, and replace them by drawing from the deck. In stud poker, each person receives one card face down and one card face up. After bets are laid, three more cards are dealt face up.

    ( ) Draw poker and stud poker are similar.
    ( ) Draw poker and stud poker are different.

4. Aspen and cottonwood are varieties of poplar. The leaves of these trees are pointed, and have toothed edges. They grow best in moist places. Although they are fast growing, they do not live long. The wood is soft, and is used for making boxes, excelsior, and paper pulp.

    ( ) Aspen and cottonwood are similar.
    ( ) Aspen and cottonwood are different.

One statement after each paragraph is true. You can be sure it is true because of what the paragraph tells you. Circle the true statement.

1. Ducks have feathers. Wilbur is a duck.
( ) Wilbur is three years old.
( ) Wilbur has feathers.
( ) Feathers are white or green.

2. My favorite dessert is cake. We are having my favorite dessert tonight.
( ) We are having cake tonight.
( ) Tomorrow we will have cake.
( ) Cake is better with ice cream.

3. Dirty clothes should be washed. My pants are dirty.
( ) All my clothes are dirty.
( ) I am washing my pants right now.
( ) My pants should be washed.

4. We finish school at 3:00. It is now 3:30.
( ) School begins at 9:00.
( ) We have finished school today.
( ) I get home at 3:30.

5. You can only get mumps once. I had mumps when I was five.
( ) I cannot get mumps now.
( ) I have mumps again.
( ) I had mumps five times.

6. The foot prints led to the river. Now I had a clue to where the robber had gone.
( ) The robber had stolen my money.
( ) The robber wore boots.
( ) The robber went to the river.

7. Only female cats can have kittens. I didn't know whether my cat was male or female. Then my cat had kittens.
( ) My cat is a male.
( ) I still don't know.
( ) My cat is a female.

Answer the questions about the paragraphs.

1. Marian heated the fudge sauce. When it was hot, she poured it over the mountain of ice-cream. As she watched, gullies formed along the sides and the brown liquid collected into a lake at the bottom of the dish. Before long, the mountain and the lake had disappeared.

Why did they disappear? _____

2. George woke up to a beautiful, sunny day. He had just finished a long, hot shower when the phone rang. He picked it up. He listened for a long time. When he hung up he turned to his brother and said, "What a rotten day!"

Why did George change his mind? _____

3. JoAnn found a tiny bird that had fallen from a nest. She waited, but no mother bird appeared. Finally she took it home. She fed it from a medicine dropper every two hours. Soon it grew stronger and could eat by itself. One day the little bird flapped his wings and flew away. JoAnn cried. When her mother asked her why she was crying, she said, "Because I am happy and I am sad."

Why was JoAnn happy? _____

Why was she sad? _____

4. Sheep are rather stupid. They are easily frightened by thunder and lightening. They wander blindly in rain or snow. Since they follow one another so closely, one after another will bump into a wall, or fall off a cliff. When a storm threatens, a sheepherder will take his animals to a sheltered valley.

Why does he take them there? _____

Circle the answer that is certainly true, based on the paragraph.

1. Curtains should be fireproof and washable. Cotton is easily washed but catches fire promptly. Fiber glass, however, is fireproof, and it can be washed in a home washing machine.

   ( ) Fiber glass is a good fabric for curtains.
   ( ) Cotton should always be used for curtains.
   ( ) Fireproof fabric is not recommended for curtains.

2. Joe always reads the latest books. Just last week he read these six books. Unfortunately, I don't read that fast. I would like to know which of the six books is easiest to read.

   ( ) I can read six books this week.
   ( ) I can ask Joe which book is easiest.
   ( ) Joe only reads the easiest books.

3. The pollen of some weeds is easily carried through the air. This pollen causes many people to have hay fever. The pollen of goldenrod is often believed to cause hay fever. However, goldenrod pollen is heavy and sticky and does not float easily through the air.

   ( ) Goldenrod causes many people to have hay fever.
   ( ) Sticky pollen is often carried in the air.
   ( ) Goldenrod pollen does not cause hay fever.

4. More than one fourth of the people in Greece have not gone to school. They cannot read or write. This is strange, since Greeks have always honored learning. There are many schools, and a law requires all boys and girls between the ages of 6 and 14 to go to school.

   ( ) The law is not always enforced.
   ( ) Boys and girls go to different schools.
   ( ) Reading is more important than writing in Greece.

Finish the sentence below each paragraph with a true statement, based on the paragraph.

1. Unlike most other insects, flies have only two wings. Other insects have four wings. Flies also have a pair of balancers located just behind the wings. They vary greatly in size.

   In order to tell a fly from another type of insect, look at _____

2. Sometimes Ann's mother was not home when Ann got home from school. In that case, she always left a note and some cookies and milk. When Ann got home on Tuesday, no one was home. As usual she went to the kitchen. She read the note. Mom would be home in an hour. Then she looked around. Nothing on the table, nothing under the table. Nothing at all!

   Ann was looking for _____.

3. During a heavy rain, soil is washed away. This washing away is called erosion. In a forest, trees act as an umbrella to break the force of rainfall. In that way, soil is not washed away. Instead, rain drips slowly into the earth and is absorbed. It then drains away slowly.

   In order to prevent erosion, you might _____

4. Flotsam and jetsam are goods voluntarily thrown overboard, usually in an emergency to lighten the load. Flotsam is that material which floats. Jetsam is material which sinks. The owners of this material do not give up their rights to it. According to the law, it remains their property. The finder of such material may receive a reward, but cannot claim it.

   If I found a piece of flotsam, I could not expect _____

A paragraph might describe a setting, an action, a time, etc. But often one of these factors will be emphasized. We might say that the focus of the paragraph is on the setting, or on the action, or on any of the other factors. In the paragraphs below, decide which factor is the focus.

1. Today was the day of the class picnic. The sun was warm. Fleecy clouds raced across the sky. A small breeze ruffled the leaves. Jack could hardly wait.

   FOCUS: ( ) setting   ( ) reason   ( ) time

2. A shrew is a tiny animal, about the size of a mouse. It has a long slender snout, and tiny eyes and ears. It makes its home in the forest.

   FOCUS: ( ) setting   ( ) topic description   ( ) time

3. I looked at the clock. Only a half hour until the bell will ring. I must not be late again. Five minutes to dress, three minutes to eat breakfast, ten minutes to do my spelling homework, twelve minutes to walk to school. Could I do it?

   FOCUS: ( ) setting   ( ) topic description   ( ) time

4. At the sound of the gun, the race started. Ann was off to a good start. She ran steadily, not worrying that some of the runners passed her. She knew she would keep this pace until the finish line.

   FOCUS: ( ) time   ( ) action   ( ) topic description

5. Gigantic pines surrounded a small clearing. The forest floor was covered with pine needles, with an occasional shrub. A tiny rabbit scampered out of sight.

   FOCUS: ( ) reason   ( ) setting   ( ) action

Sometimes sentences in a paragraph describe the time in which an action takes place. In the paragraphs below, underline the sentences that describe time.

1. In 1898 we fought the Spanish-American War. The ground forces were led by General Shafter. Commodore Schley commanded the American naval vessels.

2. Julie put the cake in the oven. After an anxious half hour, she opened the door. The cake was beautiful! She took it out and called her friends.

3. People faced many dangers during the Middle Ages. Robbers and other criminals roamed the countryside. There were frequent wars. Wooden houses were built close together, and a fire could destroy a whole town.

Sometimes sentences in a paragraph describe the reasons or motives behind the topic. In the paragraphs below, underline the sentences that tell about motives or reasons.

4. During the Middle Ages, towns grew up around castles. These castles were usually located on the top of a hill, and often were surrounded by a moat. In this way they could be easily defended in case of attack.

5. Joe grabbed his ball and bat. He put on his cap and hurried out the door. It was cold but he had no time to find his jacket. He didn't want to be late for baseball practice.

6. I hurried down to the kitchen when I smelled the smoke. It was so thick that at first I couldn't see what might be causing the trouble. Then I remembered that I had left a pot full of potatoes simmering on the stove when the phone rang.

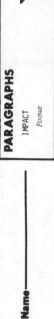
Often there are sentences in a paragraph that tell what the topic looks like, or what it is made from. These sentences describe the topic. In each paragraph below, underline the sentences that describe the topic.

1. The Singing Tower is located at Mountain Lake, Florida. It is 250 feet high, and contains one of the largest sets of bell chimes in the world. Someday I would like to see it.

2. A shrew is a small animal, about the size of a mouse. It has a long, slender snout and tiny eyes and ears. It makes its home in the forest leaf carpet.

3. Dad caught a big fish. It was 17 inches long and weighed three pounds. Its mouth was so big that I could put my fist inside. Dad was really proud.

4. Mom made a chocolate cake. It had two layers, with butter cream frosting between. The top and sides were frosted with chocolate, and Mom had decorated it with cherries. I hope we have some for dinner.

5. Each piece of paper money has a portrait of a famous American on it. To the left or right is a seal. On different types of money, the seal is a different color. The plates used to print the money are made by skillful engravers.

6. Mexican hairless dogs originated in China in the Fourteenth Century. They were imported into Mexico by sailors. Their skin is bare except for a tuft of hair on the forehead and some fuzz along the tail.

7. The may apple belongs to the barberry family. It grows in wooded areas in the eastern part of the United States. It has large leaves with five to seven lobes.

Often a paragraph contains sentences describing the "setting," that is, describing the place where the topic of the paragraph is located, or where the action takes place. In each paragraph below, underline the sentences that describe the setting.

1. The lake was clear blue. The sky was cloudless. Jim was hoping to catch a big fish.

2. Mom was making a cake. When she finished, the kitchen was a mess. Flour and egg shells were strewn around the counter. There was a puddle of milk on the floor.

3. Suddenly Jane noticed that her bike was bumping along on its rim. It must be a flat tire. By now it was raining hard. What awful luck!

4. A shrew is a small animal, about the size of a mouse. It has a long slender snout, and tiny eyes and ears. It makes its home in the forest leaf-carpet.

5. The chief battles of the Spanish-American War were fought near San Juan and Santiago de Cuba. General Shafter led our ground forces. Commodore Schley commanded the American naval vessels.

6. The Singing Tower is located at Mountain Lake, Florida. The park is a bird refuge, and contains many trees and lovely pools. Someday I would like to see it.

7. Mark sat down angrily. He didn't notice the new picture on the wall. Nor did he realize that Mom had made his bed and swept the floor. He was too angry. All he could think of was his bad luck in losing his best mitt.

PARAGRAPHS
IMPACT
Focus

Often sentences in a paragraph describe some action that is taking place, or will take place, or took place in the past, or is desired to take place. It could be one action; sometimes more than one action is described in a paragraph. In the paragraphs below, underline the sentences that describe action.

1. The lake was clear. The sky was blue. Jim was reeling in the sixth fish he had caught that day.

2. Dad caught a big fish. It was seventeen inches long and weighed three pounds. Its mouth was so big that I could put my fist inside. In a few minutes Dad will have to clean it.

3. Mexican hairless dogs have bare skin, except for a tuft of hair on the forehead and some fuzz along the tail. Their skin is warm to the touch. They were imported into Mexico many centuries ago by sailors.

4. As Jane was riding her bike, she suddenly noticed that it was bumping along on the rim. It must be a flat tire. By now it was raining hard. What awful luck!

5. Mark sat down angrily. He didn't notice the new picture on the wall, nor the clean floor and newly made bed. He felt awful.

6. The kitchen was a mess. Flour and egg shells covered the counter. There was a puddle of milk on the floor. Splatters of batter decorated the wall. Julie was making a cake.

7. Mary, Queen of Scots, became Queen of Scotland at the age of one week. At 16 she married the prince of France. Eventually she was beheaded by Elizabeth I of England.

PARAGRAPHS
IMPACT
Point of View

Read each paragraph. Decide whose point of view it represents. The characters in this event are: Mrs. Brown, Jack, Tom, Newspaper Writer.

1. Jack threw the ball over the fence. I tried to catch it, but it was too high. The next thing I knew it had gone through Mrs. Brown's window. She came out screaming at me. I don't know why she was so mad. It was just an accident. And I didn't throw it.

Who is telling the story?
( ) Mrs. Brown   ( ) Jack   ( ) Tom   ( ) Newspaper Writer

2. I was worried when I heard those kids playing ball so close to the house. I closed the window to shut out the noise. I had just sat down to lunch when a ball crashed through the window and landed in my soup. Is it any wonder I was angry? I told those boys to be more careful.

Who is telling the story?
( ) Mrs. Brown   ( ) Jack   ( ) Tom   ( ) Newspaper Writer

3. I wanted to improve my throwing skill so I was practicing in the yard with Tom. Just as I let the ball go, Mrs. Brown slammed her window shut, distracting my attention. I threw the ball too high. Tom couldn't catch it. If only Mrs. Brown had left the window open, it wouldn't have broken.

Who is telling the story?
( ) Mrs. Brown   ( ) Jack   ( ) Tom   ( ) Newspaper Writer

4. An accident occurred at 944 West Oak Street this afternoon. Two boys were playing ball next door to the home of Mrs. Brown. A bad throw resulted in a broken window and a spilled cup of soup. No injuries were reported. The boys have agreed to pay for damage to the window.

Who is telling the story?
( ) Mrs. Brown   ( ) Jack   ( ) Tom   ( ) Newspaper Writer

PARAGRAPHS

IMPACT   Point of View
Standard: At least 2 sentences.
Accurate point of view.

Name _____

Suppose that the following events took place:

Mary is walking to school.
She walks by Joe's house.
Joe's dog bites her.

1. Write this story as though Mary is telling it.

_____
_____
_____

2. Write the story as though the dog is telling it.

_____
_____
_____

3. Read this paragraph:

Bob was late for school again this morning. He is becoming very careless. As his teacher, I feel I must help him to develop good habits. I will keep him after school today so that he will be less likely to be late again.

Rewrite this paragraph as though Bob is telling the story:

_____
_____
_____
_____
_____

Read each paragraph below. Decide on the point of view of the author.

1. Spinach is a low-growing annual plant which produces a cluster of succulent, deep green leaves. It is an excellent source of vitamins A and C, and also contains a fair amount of vitamin B. Its delightful, full-bodied flavor has made it a special dish in Europe for many years.

   Is the author for or against spinach?   ( ) for   ( ) against

2. High school sports place too much emphasis on winning. As a result, only those students with natural ability are allowed to compete. Those who might profit more from the activity must sit on the sidelines. The students who do participate are subject to an unhealthy amount of pressure from coach and classmates, and rather than developing sportsmanship, are likely to feel bitter and ashamed of any failure.

   Is the author for or against school sports?   ( ) for   ( ) against

3. Frequent use of slang marks a person as a member of a particular group, and may hinder his acceptance by other groups. In addition, studies have shown that heavy use of slang limits one's use of standard English, and may prevent one from learning to use English most effectively.

   Is the author for or against slang?   ( ) for   ( ) against

4. High school sports, such as football, baseball, basketball and track, provide opportunities for numerous students to increase their physical skills. Aside from encouraging good physical health, participants learn sportsmanship in healthy competition with other students. Sports events provide a focus for feelings of pride and loyalty for the school, and encourage school spirit.

   Is the author for or against school sports?   ( ) for   ( ) against

5. Spinach, when cooked, is an unappetizing off-green color. While it used to be thought that spinach was a good source of iron in the diet, scientists now recognize that its iron is not in a form that can be easily utilized in the body. Its slightly bitter, acrid taste has limited its popularity in the United States.

   Is the author for or against spinach?   ( ) for   ( ) against

Read each paragraph below. Decide if it is sad or happy.

1. I woke up eagerly this morning, knowing that it was my birthday, wondering what surprises lay in store for me. Little did I know! My alarm had failed to go off, so everyone had finished breakfast and left the house. There was no indication that anyone remembered the importance of the day. At school I failed my math test and made ten mistakes while reading aloud. My best friend played with other kids at recess. I fell off my bike on my way home and skinned both knees. I also tore up the homework paper that was almost done.

   ( ) sad   ( ) happy

2. When I opened the door, bleeding and almost in tears, the room was dark. As I stepped into the room, the lights when on and all my friends shouted, "Surprise!" They had all gathered for a surprise birthday party. A beautiful cake stood on the table, surrounded by gaily wrapped gifts. We played games. We ate dinner, and had a generally great time.

   ( ) sad   ( ) happy

3. Mary I of England burned more than 300 persons at the stake in her attempt to bring Catholicism back to her country. She married Philip II of Spain, who persuaded her to join Spain in a war against France. It was a disaster, and Philip left her. She lived her last days alone, knowing that most of her actions had been in vain. She knew that when Elizabeth came to the throne after her, Protestantism would be restored.

   ( ) sad   ( ) happy

4. In great anticipation, the boys dug up the treasure chest. The lock was rusty, and they finally broke it with a hammer. They lifted the lid. Diamonds, rubies, saphires, gold coins, and bars of silver met their eyes.

   ( ) sad   ( ) happy

PARAGRAPHS

Name _____

IMPACT   Point of View
Standard: At least 2 sentences.
           At least one reason given.

4

1. Write a paragraph in favor of watching television.

   _____
   _____
   _____
   _____

2. Write a paragraph against watching television.

   _____
   _____
   _____
   _____

3. Suppose you were going on a long trip. You must decide whether to drive, fly, or take a train. Write a paragraph in favor of one of these choices.

   _____
   _____
   _____
   _____

The paragraphs below are exciting in different ways. Read each one. Then decide if it is mysterious or adventurous.

1. I lay there listening to the sounds of a house at night. Suddenly a sound was different. Footsteps were approaching my door. As I watched, the doorknob turned and the door began to swing open.

( ) mysterious ( ) adventurous

2. Joe was about half way across the railroad trestle when he heard a train. There was not enough time to reach either end of the bridge. The river below was a hundred foot drop. The train came closer. What could he do?

( ) mysterious ( ) adventurous

3. It was a lovely day for canoeing. Mary was appreciating the trees and the birds, and not paying close enough attention to the river. Suddenly she felt a jolt. The canoe tipped and the next thing she knew, Mary was in the water. She was being pulled rapidly downstream. She remembered that there were a series of dangerous rapids around the bend. But she could not seem to make progress toward the shore.

( ) mysterious ( ) adventurous

4. The night was hot and still. As Don looked out the window, he saw a faint glimmer in the direction of the cemetery. Thinking it might be vandals, he hurried out to chase them away. But there were no vandals, and the glimmer seemed to grow brighter as he walked toward it. He suddenly felt very cold.

( ) mysterious ( ) adventurous

5. The old house was a source of fascination for all the boys in the neighborhood. Strange lights and weird noises were said to occur on the 12th of each month. Only Bob had ever gone inside, and he claimed that an invisible barrier had kept him from going upstairs.

( ) mysterious ( ) adventurous

253

Read each paragraph below. Decide if it is humorous or serious.

1. Polly hurries back into the kitchen to finish dinner. First she checks the potatoes. Are they supposed to turn black? Never mind. Now the meat. It looks lovely on the outside, but the fork won't go in more than an inch. It must be frozen in the middle. The broccoli has been cooking for an hour and a half. She wonders why it is a mass of greenish mush. It will be a meal fit for a ....king?

( ) humorous ( ) serious

2. Polly hurries back to the kitchen to finish dinner. The potatoes have been cooking almost an hour. The meat is nearly done. It is time to start the broccoli and set the table. She decides to make a Hollandaise sauce for the broccoli if there is time. It should be a meal fit for a king!

( ) humorous ( ) serious

3. I hurried to Jack's house to pick up the baseball bat he had left in the garage. I wasn't worried about his big German shepherd because Jack had assured me that he never bites. As I approached the building I heard a low growl. I talked nicely to the dog, assuring him that I had Jack's permission to be there, but at every step the growl grew louder. I tried to explain about the forgotten bat, but the dog didn't take my explanation seriously. I know that barking dogs don't bite, but what about growling dogs?

( ) humorous ( ) serious

4. The job of a sheep dog is to keep the flock together and turn back any wandering sheep. He also protects the flock from wolves and other animals. He is loyal to the shepherd, and makes an excellent companion for the long lonely days and nights. He must be intelligent to carry out such responsibilities.

( ) humorous ( ) serious

PARAGRAPHS

IMPACT *Oral Reading*
Standard: No more than 3 words
mispronounced. Paragraphs read with
appropriate intonation.

★ 2

Name _____

1. As I watched, a little red bird landed on the branch. It looked like a cardinal. It sat there quietly for a minute, hardly moving. Then, suddenly, he cocked his head and looked in my direction. I must have moved, for he spread his wings and flew away.

2. Mother looked around as she walked into the playroom. Immediately she noticed the crayon marks on the wall. "Who was drawing on the wall?" she demanded. "Whoever did it had better get a bucket and soap and a rag. If that wall is not clean in thirty minutes, there will be no ice cream tonight."

3. Steve is my best friend. He moved in next door three years ago. At first we didn't like each other at all. But slowly we got to know one another. We found that we had many things in common. We both like baseball and hate football. He collects stamps and I collect coins. And we both detest spinach.

PARAGRAPHS

IMPACT *Oral Reading*
Standard: No more than 3 words
mispronounced. Paragraphs read with
appropriate intonation.

★ 1

Name _____

1. Ann went to the zoo with Dick. She liked to see the lions. She wanted to give them some peanuts. She also liked to see the elephants. She wanted to ride on one. She liked the tigers best of all. She wanted to play with them!

2. Where is my dog? I called and called. But he did not come. I looked behind the trees. I looked at Jim's house. But he was not there. I have not seen him for three hours. Now it is time for dinner. I will make some dinner for my dog, too.

3. Oh, Mom! Don't make me get up now. I am too tired. I went to bed very late. I was having nice dreams. I don't want to get up. I want to sleep some more. I will get up in an hour.

Name _____

PARAGRAPHS

IMPACT Oral Reading
Standard: No more than 3 words
mispronounced. Paragraphs read with
appropriate intonation.

1. As Ted approached the dog, he held his hand out, palm up. It was an old trick he had learned from a friend who trained dogs. "When you want to make friends with a strange dog," he had said, "never raise your hand above his head. He might think you are going to strike him. Instead, hold your hand palm up and slide it slowly under his chin."

2. The boy threw himself onto the wild pony's back, grabbing the hair loop around its neck. The pony whinnied in rebellion, broke loose from the herd, and galloped out into the open. It bucked, reared, turned, twisted, omitted no tricks it knew in its attempt to dislodge its rider. But the boy clung to its mane, tightening the hair loop when necessary. He yelled and pounded his heels against the sides of the wild horse. He felt elated and triumphant. He would ride this horse.

3. Old Mr. Brown had lived a colorful life. He was famous for his kindness to runaway slaves. His home was a stop on the famous "underground railroad." He had been arrested several times for helping slaves to escape, and had been fined so heavily that he was left without a cent. He was criticized strongly for his activities, but through it all he kept his sense of humor.

Name _____

PARAGRAPHS

IMPACT Oral Reading
Standard: No more than 3 words
mispronounced. Poem read with
appropriate intonation.

1. Swiftly walk o'er the western wave,
   Spirit of Night!
   Out of the misty eastern cave,
   Where, all the long and lone daylight,
   Thou wovest dreams of joy and fear,
   Which make me terrible and dear--
   Swift be thy flight.

   From To Night by Percy Shelley

2. The wind was a torrent of darkness
   among the gusty trees,
   The moon was a ghostly galleon
   tossed upon cloudy seas,
   The road was a ribbon of moonlight
   over the purple moor,
   And the highwayman came riding--
   Riding--riding--
   The highwayman came riding,
   up to the old inn-door.

   From The Highwayman by Alfred Noyes

3. In the swamp in secluded recesses,
   A shy and hidden bird is warbling a song.

   Solitary the thrush,
   The hermit withdrawn to himself, avoiding the settlements,
   Sings by himself a song.

   Song of the bleeding throat,
   Death's outlet song of life, (For well dear brother I know,
   If thou wast not granted to sing thou would'st surely die.)

   From When Lilacs Last in the Dooryard
   Bloomed by Walt Whitman

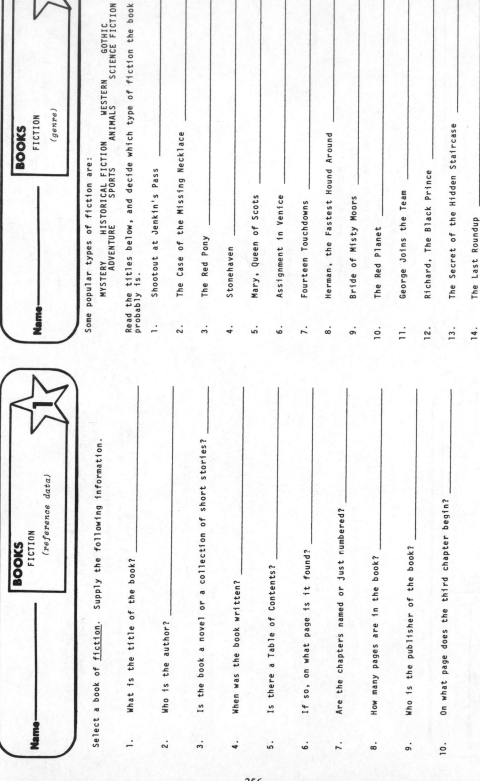

Name _____

BOOKS
FICTION
(reference data)

Select a book of fiction. Supply the following information.

1. What is the title of the book? _____

2. Who is the author? _____

3. Is the book a novel or a collection of short stories? _____

4. When was the book written? _____

5. Is there a Table of Contents? _____

6. If so, on what page is it found? _____

7. Are the chapters named or just numbered? _____

8. How many pages are in the book? _____

9. Who is the publisher of the book? _____

10. On what page does the third chapter begin? _____

Name _____

BOOKS
FICTION
(genre)

Some popular types of fiction are:

MYSTERY   HISTORICAL FICTION   ANIMALS   WESTERN   GOTHIC
ADVENTURE   SPORTS   SCIENCE FICTION

Read the titles below, and decide which type of fiction the book probably is.

1. Shootout at Jenkin's Pass _____

2. The Case of the Missing Necklace _____

3. The Red Pony _____

4. Stonehaven _____

5. Mary, Queen of Scots _____

6. Assignment in Venice _____

7. Fourteen Touchdowns _____

8. Herman, the Fastest Hound Around _____

9. Bride of Misty Moors _____

10. The Red Planet _____

11. George Joins the Team _____

12. Richard, The Black Prince _____

13. The Secret of the Hidden Staircase _____

14. The Last Roundup _____

15. A Path to Glory _____

BOOKS
FICTION
(book reports)

★ 3

Name _____

Read a book of fiction, and fill out the following Book Report Form.

BOOK REPORT FORM

Describe 2 of the major characters. _____
_____
_____

Describe the setting of the story (when and where it takes place)
_____
_____

Circle the type of story: Adventure...Animals...Gothic...Mystery...
Historical Fiction...Humor...Sports...Western...Other _____

Who should read this book? _____
_____

Why should someone read it? _____
_____
_____
_____

BOOKS
FICTION
(writing stories-character)

★ 4

Name _____

Read the following setting:

It was a hot summer day. The long
green grass was alive with grasshoppers.
A few fleecy clouds decorated the bright
blue sky. Robins chirped in the trees.

Write the next paragraph of the story, introducing a character.

_____
_____
_____
_____
_____
_____
_____
_____
_____
_____
_____
_____
_____

257

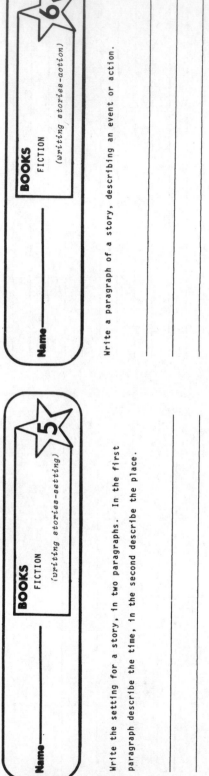

BOOKS

FICTION

(writing stories—setting)

5

Name —————

Write the setting for a story, in two paragraphs. In the first paragraph describe the time, in the second describe the place.

BOOKS

FICTION

(writing stories—action)

6

Name —————

Write a paragraph of a story, describing an event or action.

258

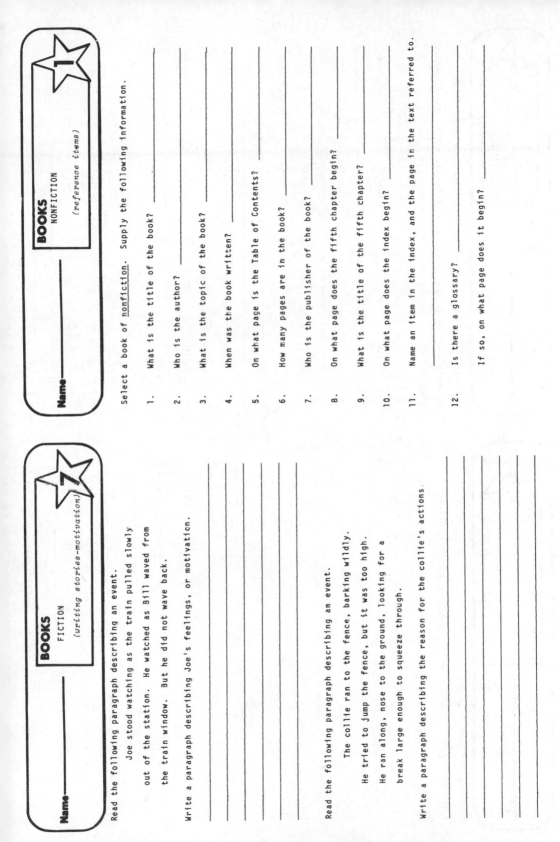

BOOKS

FICTION

(writing stories—motivation)

Read the following paragraph describing an event.

Joe stood watching as the train pulled slowly

out of the station. He watched as Bill waved from

the train window. But he did not wave back.

Write a paragraph describing Joe's feelings, or motivation.

_____

_____

_____

Read the following paragraph describing an event.

The collie ran to the fence, barking wildly.

He tried to jump the fence, but it was too high.

He ran along, nose to the ground, looking for a

break large enough to squeeze through.

Write a paragraph describing the reason for the collie's actions.

_____

_____

_____

_____

BOOKS

NONFICTION

(reference items)

Select a book of nonfiction. Supply the following information.

1. What is the title of the book? _____

2. Who is the author? _____

3. What is the topic of the book? _____

4. When was the book written? _____

5. On what page is the Table of Contents? _____

6. How many pages are in the book? _____

7. Who is the publisher of the book? _____

8. On what page does the fifth chapter begin? _____

9. What is the title of the fifth chapter? _____

10. On what page does the index begin? _____

11. Name an item in the index, and the page in the text referred to.

_____

12. Is there a glossary? _____

If so, on what page does it begin? _____

Some types of nonfiction are:

BIOGRAPHY   HUMOR   PLAYS   POETRY   HOBBIES   HISTORY   SCIENCE

Read the titles below. Then decide which type of nonfiction it is.

1. A Child's Garden of Verses ——————————

2. American Coin Collectors Guide ——————————

3. A Study of Pond Life ——————————

4. World War I ——————————

5. Ann of Cleves ——————————

6. A Treasury of Shakespeare ——————————

7. Weaving Your Own Designs ——————————

8. Famous British Poems ——————————

9. The Favorite Jokes of Bennet Cerf ——————————

10. The United States: 1776-1850 ——————————

11. Astronomy for the Layman ——————————

12. The Life of Abraham Lincoln ——————————

13. Modern Swedish Drama ——————————

14. The Funniest Man Alive ——————————

15. Louis Pasteur, Man of Science ——————————

Go to the library and select three nonfiction books which you might use
to write a report on the following subjects. Do not use encyclopedias.
Write the title, author, and catalog numbers.

1. The life of Queen Elizabeth I

    TITLE   AUTHOR   CATALOG NO.

    —————————— —————————— ——————————

2. The Civil War

    TITLE   AUTHOR   CATALOG NO.

    —————————— —————————— ——————————

3. Dinosaurs

    TITLE   AUTHOR   CATALOG NO.

    —————————— —————————— ——————————

4. Stamp Collecting

    TITLE   AUTHOR   CATALOG NO.

    —————————— —————————— ——————————

BOOKS — NONFICTION *(research)* — 4

Name _____

The topics for Test 3 were: The life of Queen Elizabeth

The Civil War

Dinosaurs

Stamp collecting

These topics are too large for a short report.
Think of two topics connected with each of these large topics that would be better for a short (1 page) report.

1. The life of Queen Elizabeth

   1. _____

   2. _____

2. The Civil War

   1. _____

   2. _____

3. Dinosaurs

   1. _____

   2. _____

4. Stamp collecting

   1. _____

   2. _____

BOOKS — NONFICTION *(research)* — 5

Name _____

On Test 3, you selected three source books for each of four topics.

On Test 4, you suggested 2 subtopics for each large topic.

On this Test, you must select one of those sub-topics and write a one page report. Use at least two of the source books. List your sources at the bottom of the page.

TITLE: _____

_____

_____

_____

_____

_____

_____

_____

SOURCES (Title, Author, Year)

_____

_____

Teacher's Script:

For this test, use a book with pictures. Place the book on the desk or table in front of the child. Read the following script.

1. ( ) Open the book.

2. ( ) Turn to the beginning of the book.

3. ( ) Turn to the end of the book.

4. ( ) Turn to a page in the middle.

5. ( ) Turn three pages, as if you were reading.

6. ( ) Point to the page number.

7. ( ) Find a picture.

8. ( ) Look through the book at the pictures. Then tell me what this story might be about.

Use your textbook for social studies or for science. Find the following information.

What is the title? _____

Who is the author(s)? _____

What is the year of the last copyright? _____

On what page is the Table of Contents? _____

On what page does the third chapter begin? _____

Does the third chapter have a name, or just a number?

If it has a name, what is it? _____

On what page does the index begin? _____

Name an item in the index, and the page on which it is found.

_____

Does the textbook have a glossary? _____

If so, what does it contain? _____

If so, on what page does it begin? _____

BOOKS

TEXTBOOKS

(skimming)

Name _____

Select a textbook (such as for social studies or science). Select a chapter that you have **not** read, and which is at least ten pages long. Ask someone to time you, or use a stop watch. Skim the chapter in two minutes, then answer the following questions about your chapter, without looking back at the text.

1. What is the general topic of the chapter? _____

2. Are there any pictures? _____

3. Are there any charts or graphs? _____

4. Are the paragraph headings in bold print or italics? _____

5. Name at least 2 headings (if there are headings): _____

6. Write two true statements, based on the information given in the text. _____
_____

7. Is there an introduction, or overview? _____

8. Are there study questions after the chapter? _____

BOOKS

TEXTBOOKS

(reference data)

Name _____

The following items may be found in a textbook. Decide which item would help to answer the questions below, which you might ask about a textbook.
TITLE...AUTHOR...COPYRIGHT...TABLE OF CONTENTS...INDEX...GLOSSARY

1. How old is this book? _____

2. Who wrote this book? _____

3. What does this word mean? _____

4. Where will I find something about John Adams? _____

5. What is this book about? _____

6. Where will I find this book in the library? _____

7. On what page does Chapter 5 begin? _____

8. Does this book tell about the Civil War? _____

9. How many people wrote this book? _____

10. How many chapters are in this book? _____

Select a textbook (such as for social studies or science). Select a chapter that you have <u>not</u> read, and which is at least ten pages long. Skim the chapter in two minutes............

Now read the chapter more slowly, and as you go, formulate ten study questions from the chapter. (If there are study questions at the end of the chapter, do not use these, although you should skim them while you are skimming the chapter.) These questions should be those that you expect might be on a test on the chapter.

1. _____

2. _____

3. _____

4. _____

5. _____

6. _____

7. _____

8. _____

9. _____

10. _____

Select a textbook (such as for social studies or science). Skim and formulate ten questions on a chapter. (You may use the questions you prepared for Test 4.) Prepare answers to these questions. First, go through the questions and answer all those that you can remember without looking at the text. Then go back to the text to prepare the other answers. Finally, check your answers with the text. You may need more paper.

_____

_____

_____

_____

_____

_____

_____

_____

_____

_____

_____

_____

264

BOOKS

REFERENCE WORKS
(dictionary)

You will need a dictionary for this test.

1. What is the name of your dictionary? ⎯⎯⎯⎯⎯⎯

2. When was your dictionary published? ⎯⎯⎯⎯⎯⎯

3. Find the pronunciation key at the bottom of any page (usually). It tells you how to pronounce the sounds of vowels and some consonants. What key word is given for:

ä ⎯⎯⎯⎯⎯

ē ⎯⎯⎯⎯⎯

th ⎯⎯⎯⎯⎯

zh ⎯⎯⎯⎯⎯

Look up the following words, and answer the questions about them.

4. debut
   What page is it on? ⎯⎯⎯⎯⎯
   What index words appear at the top of the page? ⎯⎯⎯⎯⎯
   What part of speech is it? ( ) adverb ( ) noun ( ) verb ( ) adjective
   How many definitions are given? ⎯⎯⎯⎯⎯
   From what language is the word derived? ⎯⎯⎯⎯⎯

5. forsake
   What are the index words? ⎯⎯⎯⎯⎯
   What part of speech? ( ) adverb ( ) noun ( ) verb ( ) adjective
   How many definitions? ⎯⎯⎯⎯⎯
   Write out one definition ⎯⎯⎯⎯⎯
   What is a synonym for forsake? ⎯⎯⎯⎯⎯

6. short
   What page is it on? ⎯⎯⎯⎯⎯
   What part of speech? ( ) adverb ( ) noun ( ) verb ( ) adjective
   How many definitions? ⎯⎯⎯⎯⎯
   Write out one definition. ⎯⎯⎯⎯⎯
   What is a synonym for short? ⎯⎯⎯⎯⎯

BOOKS

TEXTBOOKS
(defining technical terms)

Select a textbook (such as for social studies or science). Select a chapter which you have not read. Skim the chapter. Then go through the chapter again, listing five technical terms. If you do not find five, skim the next chapter, and do the same. Write a definition for each technical term, in your own words. Then write a sentence, using the term correctly.

1. Term: ⎯⎯⎯⎯ Definition: ⎯⎯⎯⎯⎯

   Sentence: ⎯⎯⎯⎯⎯

2. Term: ⎯⎯⎯⎯ Definition: ⎯⎯⎯⎯⎯

   Sentence: ⎯⎯⎯⎯⎯

3. Term: ⎯⎯⎯⎯ Definition: ⎯⎯⎯⎯⎯

   Sentence: ⎯⎯⎯⎯⎯

4. Term: ⎯⎯⎯⎯ Definition: ⎯⎯⎯⎯⎯

   Sentence: ⎯⎯⎯⎯⎯

5. Term: ⎯⎯⎯⎯ Definition: ⎯⎯⎯⎯⎯

   Sentence: ⎯⎯⎯⎯⎯

BOOKS

REFERENCE WORKS

(encyclopedia)

Name _____

You will need to use an encyclopedia for this test.

1. What is the name of your encyclopedia? _____

2. When was the encyclopedia published? _____

3. How many volumes are in the encyclopedia? _____

4. Find Bird in your encyclopedia. What are the index words on the
   page? _____ On what page is it? _____
   List three headings (usually in dark print) in the article about birds.
   _____

5. Find Samuel Morse in your encyclopedia. Answer these questions.
   What did he invent? _____
   When was he born? _____ Where was he born? _____

6. Find Whale in your encyclopedia. Answer these questions.
   Name 4 kinds of whales. _____

   Name two products made from whales. _____

7. Does your encyclopedia have a Reading and Study Guide? _____
   If so, study it. Why would you use a guide of this sort?
   _____

BOOKS

REFERENCE WORKS

(dictionary)

Name _____

You will need a dictionary for this test.

1. Write the correct word divisions for these words:

   routine _____   necessary _____
   superior _____   warden _____
   general _____   centimeter _____

2. Find the correct spellings for these words (some may be correct):
   (Please descuss this with your friend.)
   descuss _____
   compliment _____   (She paid her a compliment.)
   wether _____   (Find out wether you can go.)
   turmite _____   (That bug is a turmite.)
   precipitation _____   (The forecast is light precipitation.)
   higiene _____   (This course is about mental higiene.)
   recieve _____   (Did you recieve my letter?)
   menagery _____   (There are 45 animals in this menagery.)
   peace _____   (I want a peace of pie.)
   sent _____   (These flowers have a beautiful sent.)
   periodic _____   (We have periodic tests.)
   precedent _____   (He was elected precedent of the club.)

3. Underline the syllable that is accented. (The first one is done for you.)

   sub **scrip** tion   por   tion
   brach i o pod   ga ze bo
   ac cel er a tor   eb o ny
   ga rage   to bac co
   tran quil   pul sar

4. Most dictionaries have special sections, or Appendices, at the end of the book.
   List the kind of sections found in the back of your dictionary.
   _____

If you were writing a report on a topic, you would want to look it up in the encyclopedia. Sometimes you will not find the first entry that you think of. Sometimes you will want to look at several topics.

For each topic below, think of two entry words that might contain information about the topic.

1. Precious metals: _____

2. Robins: _____

3. King George V (of England): _____

4. Beef: _____

5. Roses: _____

Name three entry words that might contain information about these topics.

6. Money: _____

7. Religion: _____

8. Lumber: _____

9. Niagara Falls: _____

10. Bones: _____

When writing a report, it is helpful to look up related topics in the encyclopedia. You must not, however, copy your report directly from the encyclopedia article. Read the article below, which is from the 1957 Edition of the World Book Encyclopedia. Rewrite the article.

Baum, Lyman Frank (1856-1919), an American writer, wrote children's books about the mythical country of Oz. The Wonderful Wizard of Oz (1900), his most popular Oz book, became a musical comedy in 1901 and a motion picture in 1939. His Oz series of 14 stories was perhaps the first attempt to construct a fairyland out of American materials. Baum was born in Chitenango, New York. (by Frederick J. Hoffman)

Rewrite the paragraph, retaining all important information.

_____

_____

_____

_____

_____

_____

_____

_____

_____

_____

_____

BOOKS — REFERENCE WORKS (thesaurus) — ★ 6

Name _____

A thesaurus is used when it is necessary to find alternative words for the same idea. Read the sentences below, and use a thesaurus to find two alternative words for the underlined word in the sentence.

1. He read the poem aloud.
   Alternatives: _____

2. We listened to the musician play his violin.
   Alternatives: _____

3. After the play, everyone clapped.
   Alternatives: _____

4. He is a student in this school.
   Alternatives: _____

5. This is a good pie.
   Alternatives: _____

6. That is not true.
   Alternatives: _____

7. There are ghosts in that house.
   Alternatives: _____

8. Just give me a small piece.
   Alternatives: _____

9. What is the title and date of your thesaurus? _____

BOOKS — REFERENCE WORKS (almanacs) — ★ 7

Name _____

Use an almanac to answer the following questions for the most recent date included.

1. What is the name of the almanac you are using? _____

2. In what year was it published? _____

3. What is the population of South Carolina? _____

4. How many farms are there in Maine? _____

5. How many marriages were there in the U.S.? _____

6. How many forest fires were there in the U.S.? _____

7. What is the highest mountain in the United States (except Alaska)?
   _____ What is the elevation? _____

8. What is the lowest point in the United States?
   What is the elevation? _____

9. How many drug addicts are there in the U.S.? _____

10. Which religion is the largest in the U.S.?
    ( ) Baptist
    ( ) Lutheran
    ( ) Roman Catholic
    ( ) Jewish
    ( ) Presbyterian

BOOKS
REFERENCE WORKS
(library)

⑧

Draw a map of your library--either your school library or the public library.

Include the following:

Librarian's desk	Children's Books
Card Catalog	Fiction Books
Book Check Out	Nonfiction Books
Reference Books (Encyclopedias, Almanacs, etc.)	Dictionary

BOOKS
REFERENCE WORKS
(library)

⑨

In the library, under what letter would you find these fiction books filed?

1. The Green Man Mystery, by Andrew Carver

   ( ) G   ( ) T   ( ) A   ( ) M   ( ) C   ( ) B

2. Shadows on the Stairs, by Emma Harris

   ( ) F   ( ) S   ( ) H   ( ) E   ( ) B   ( ) T

3. Doctor Nathan's Last Case, by William Upton

   ( ) D   ( ) U   ( ) N   ( ) D   ( ) L   ( ) C

4. Landing on Planet X, by Jean Shaw

   ( ) X   ( ) L   ( ) S   ( ) P   ( ) J   ( ) B

5. The Will of Jenny Moore, by Horace Paxton

   ( ) W   ( ) P   ( ) M   ( ) H   ( ) J   ( ) O

Find books on the following topics (nonfiction), and write their titles and call numbers.

	TITLE	CALL NO.
6. A play:	_____	_____
7. A biography:	_____	_____
8. A history book:	_____	_____
9. A hobby book:	_____	_____
10. A science book:	_____	_____

Make a one page newspaper of your own. Include these features: a news article, a coming events article, human interest story, weather, comics, a want ad, and any other items you wish.

You will need a daily newspaper for this test.

1. What is the name of the newspaper: _____

2. What is its date? _____

3. What is the headline? _____

4. Find the index of the features in the newspaper. On what page is it? _____

5. What was the high temperature reported in the weather column? _____

6. On what page are the comics? _____

7. What pages carry the want-ads? _____

8. Find an article on sports. What is its heading? _____

9. Find an article on world events. What is the heading? _____

10. Find an article on local events. What is its heading? _____

11. What is the topic of the editorial? _____

12. Make an (X) by each of the columns below that appears in your paper.

( ) Advice on   ( ) Money,   ( ) Health   ( ) Humor   ( ) Ettiquette
    personal   Economics
    problems

In your library, find magazines that you would like to read if:

1. You like sports: _____

2. You want to cook something new: _____

3. You want to know what is
   happening in the world: _____

4. You want to find out which
   product to buy: _____

5. You like to read stories: _____

6. You like hunting: _____

7. You like auto racing: _____

8. You like gardening: _____

9. You want to find a magazine
   for your mother: _____

10. You want to find a magazine for
    your little sister: _____

Read the letter below. Then answer the questions.

423 Green Street
Circle City, Indiana   36712
January 9, 1978

Dear Sally,

I hope you had a nice Christmas. Did you get the gift I sent?
I mailed it late and was afraid it would not reach you by Christmas.
Santa gave me a baby elephant. It is something I've always
wanted. The only problem is finding a place to keep him. The
neighbors are beginning to complain. Unfortunately, I was late
feeding him the other day and he ate all Mrs. Smith's roses. Yesterday he got loose and ate all the branches from Mr. Jones' birch tree.
Do you have any suggestions?

I am looking forward to your visit next week. Write soon to
tell me when you will arrive.

Love,

Mary

1. What is the complimentary close? _____

2. What is the heading? _____

3. What is the salutation? _____

4. How many lines are in the body? _____

5. What is the signature? _____

BOOKS
LETTERS

Name _____

Read the letter below, then answer the questions.

132 Oak Street
Greenville, Montana
December 12, 1977

John A. Smith, President
Ace Shoe Co.
Liston, Kentucky

Dear Sir:

I am writing to inquire whether you manufacture shoes of size 14AA (men's). My neighbor has recommended the quality of your shoes. If you have my size, please send me a catalog, or other information. Send it to: Tom Brown, 132 Oak St., Greenville, Montana, 76118.

Sincerely,

Tom Brown

1. What is the heading of this letter? _____

2. What is the complimentary close of the letter? _____

3. What is the first word of the body? _____

4. What is the signature? _____

5. What is the date? _____

6. What is the inside address? _____

7. What is the salutation? _____

BOOKS
LETTERS *(friendly letters)*
Standard: Correct heading, salutation, complimentary close; news given; question asked.

Name _____

Write a letter to a friend. Tell him/her some news. Ask some questions.

You may write to a real friend, or make one up.

BOOKS LETTERS (complaint)

Standard: Product identified, purchase date given, complaint voiced, action requested, correct heading, salutation, date, closing.

Name ―――――

You ordered a product by mail, and when it arrived you were not satisfied with it. Write a letter of complaint to the manufacturer.

(Make up whatever information you need.)

★5

BOOKS LETTERS (request)

Standard: Correct heading, salutation, date, closing; request politely made; return address included.

Name ―――――

Write a letter to a business or to a professional person making a request. You may request information of some kind, or you may order a product. (Make up any information you need.)

★4

BOOKS LETTERS *(survey reply)*

Standard: Correct heading,
salutation, closing; date in-
cluded; favorite program named;
reasons given.

The producer of children's television programs is making plans for

next year's programs. He has sent you a letter asking for your

opinion of the best television program (the one you like best), in

order to aid him in making his decision. Write a reply, explaining

the reason for your choice, and offering him any other help you can.

(Make up whatever information you need.)

STARS Progress Chart

In the chart below, all STARS tests are arranged by <u>approximate</u> grade level. The placement of a test at a particular grade level reflects (1) data obtained during the try-out of STARS, and conformity to the usual curriculum practices in the United States. There should be <u>no</u> implication that a given test cannot be mastered earlier if appropriate training is given.

Test Series	K	1	2	3	4	5	6
Letters 1 (Shapes)	1 2	3 4 5	6 7 8				
Letters 2 (Manuscript)	1	2 3 4 5 6 7 8 9 10 11 12	13 14				
Letters 3 (Cursive)				1 2 3 4 5 6	7 8 9 10 11		
Letters 4 (Names)		1 2 3	4 5 6 7 8				
Letters 5 (Equivalents)			1 2	3 4 5 6 7 8	9 10 11 12		
Letters 6 (Functions)	1	2 3	4		5	6	
Words 1 (Shapes)			1 2	3 4	5		
Words 2 (Phonology)	1	2 3 4 5	6 7 8 9	10 11 12 13 14 15 16 17	18		
Words 3 (Recognition)		1	2 3 4	5 6	7 8	9 10	11
Words 4 (Spelling)		1	2	3	4	5	
Words 5 (Syntactic)		1 2	3 4 5	6 7 8 9	10	11 12	13
Words 6 (Range)			1 2 3 4	5 6 7	8 9 10 11 12 13 14	15 16 17 18 19 20	
Words 7 (Semantic)			1 2 3	4 5 6	7 8	9	
Words 8 (Classification)			1 2	3	4 5 6	7 8 9 10 11 12	
Words 9 (Fluency)		1	2 3 4 5	6 7			
Sentences 1 (Oral)				1	2		3
Sentences 2 (Spaces)		1					
Sentences 3 (Memory)		1	2				
Sentences 4 (Dictation)		1	2	3	4	5 6	
Sentences 5 (Capitals)					1	2 3 4	5 6 7 8 9 10
Sentences 6 (Punctuation)				1	2 3 4	5 6 7	8 thru 21
Sentences 7 (Transformation)				1 2	3	4 5 6 7 8	9 thru 17
Sentences 8 (Directions)					1 2		
Sentences 9 (Questions)						1 2 3 4	5 6
Sentences 10 (Meaning)				1	2		3
Sentences 11 (Figurative)							1 2 3 4
Paragraphs 1 (Form)					1 2		
Paragraphs 2 (Grammatical)							1 2 3 4
Paragraphs 3 (Phonological)						1 2 3	4 5
Paragraphs 4 (Universe of)				1	2		
Paragraphs 5 (Topic)				1 2	3 4	5	
Paragraphs 6 (Plot)					1 2	3 4 5 6	7 8
Paragraphs 7 (Referential)							1 2
Paragraphs 8 (Relational)						1 2	3 4 5 6
Paragraphs 9 (Information)					1 2 3	4 5	6 7 8 9

(continued on next page)

Test Series	K	1	2	3	4	5	6
Paragraphs 10 (Summarization)						1	2 3 4 5
Paragraphs 11 (Induction)						1 2 3	4 5 6
Paragraphs 12 (Deduction)						1	2 3
Paragraphs 13 (Focus)						1 2	3 4 5
Paragraphs 14 (Point of View)						1 2 3 4	
Paragraphs 15 (Mood)						1	2 3
Paragraphs 16 (Oral)					1	2	3 4
Books 1 (Fiction)					1	2 3	4 5 6 7
Books 2 (Nonfiction)					1	2 3	4 5
Books 3 (Textbooks)	1		2			3	4 5 6 7
Books 4 (Reference)					1 2	3	4 5 6 7 8 9
Books 5 (Periodicals)					1	2 3 4 5	
Books 6 (Letters)						1 2	3 4 5 6

INDEX

A
B 7
C 8
D 9
E 0
F 1
G 2
H 3
I 4
J 5